D1557039

T

Troubled State

Civil War Journals of Franklin Archibald Dick

GARI CARTER

Truman State University Press

Cover art:

> *Camp Jackson MO.* Hand colored lithograph by Ch. Robyn and Co. after George G. Friedlein, 1st Lt., Topographical Engineers, 1861. Missouri Historical Society Photographs and Prints Collections. Photograph by David Schultz, 1997. NS 21862. Photograph and scan © 1997-2007, Missouri Historical Society.
> Portrait of Franklin Archibald Dick. Painting by D Frun[?], 1850[?]. Photo by Elizabeth Smith © 2007.
> Photo of Gari Carter by R. L. Geyer © 2007.

Section art, original photo: R. L. Geyer © 2007

Cover design: Teresa Wheeler
Type: Text is Adobe Caslon Pro. Heads are Tiepolo.
Printed by: Thomson-Shore, Dexter, Michigan USA

Library of Congress Cataloging-in-Publication Data (applied for)

Dick, F. A. (Franklin Archibald)
Troubled state : Civil War journals of Franklin Archibald Dick / Gari Carter.
    p. cm.
Includes bibliographical references.
ISBN 978-1-931112-74-1 (hardback : alk. paper)
1. Dick, F. A. (Franklin Archibald)—Diaries. 2. Soldiers—Missouri—Diaries. 3. United States. Army. Dept. of the Missouri—Officers—Diaries. 4. Missouri—History—Civil War, 1861–1865—Personal narratives. 5. Camp Jackson (Mo.)--History. 6. United States—History—Civil War, 1861–1865—Personal narratives. 7. Lawyers—Missouri—Saint Louis—Diaries. 8. Unionists (United States Civil War)—Missouri—Saint Louis—Diaries. 9. Saint Louis (Mo.)—History—Civil War, 1861–1865—Personal narratives.
I. Carter, Gari. II. Title.
  E470.4.D53 2008
  973.7'478—dc22

          2007043317

For Sully

For more reasons than can be listed here

Contents

Illustrations

Preface

Years ago in the 1960s, my mother said she had something special for me. She handed me a white cardboard gift box with gold scrolls up and down the top, in the middle of which was printed HBCO and Hutzlers...Baltimore. Strangely, it had no department store ribbon around it. My mother was known for wrapping presents in the funny papers and tying them up with paper ribbon with the ends carefully curled. I thought she was giving me a scarf, but the box felt heavier. Inside, wrapped in white tissue paper, were two old fragile books—one leather-bound and the other an old-fashioned school copybook with a cardboard cover. The box and the books gave off a sharp, musty smell. I gently opened the leather one and saw faded brown Spenserian script on yellowed pages. I asked whose it was. She said they were the Civil War journals of my great-great-grandfather, Franklin Archibald Dick, who had served as provost marshal in St. Louis, and she wanted to pass them on to me. My mother told me she had saved the journals from her grandfather's things. I remembered her grandfather, who pounded on the floor with his bamboo cane with an ivory handle. He made a terrifyingly loud noise with it in his fits of temper.

As an only child, I have been the caretaker of family things for my generation, which my mother says is both a gift and a burden. I was newly married and I thought of these journals as something interesting to keep for my future children. I leafed through the books, reading a few words here and there, but never sat down and read them. Over the years, I acquired more assorted possessions of ancestors. I have Franklin Dick's campaign chest, which held his clothes as he traveled around Missouri as provost marshal general. It is a tall, dark, wooden box, about the size of a small table, with iron bands around it. There are two hinged handles with square holes, which lift above its top. A post was inserted through these holes, and the chest was carried on the back of a mule. It is lined in silk and has about the same amount of room as an airline carry-on bag. My mother used it as an end table and I do the same, but I have now covered the top with glass for protection. My mother also gave me two swords, both looking to be Civil War era, but did not know whose they were. She remembered a photograph of Mira Alexander that used to hang in her grandfather's bedroom. On the back was a note that Mira's dress and carriage were used to spy during the Civil War. The photograph was lost in a later move.

Another cousin has Franklin Dick's youthful portrait. His eyes look seriously at the artist, the long straight Dick nose (which I see in my mother) is evident, and he has pink cheeks and a pleasant look. His wavy light brown hair is parted on the side and he is wearing a stylish black suit, pleated white shirt, and an elaborate black tie. His solid body is seated bolt upright on a red armchair and he holds a piece of paper in his right hand. A gold wall is behind him with a glimpse of nature to the side—sky, clouds, and trees. My mother thinks the portrait Franklin Dick mentions that was made of his son Otis may have been taken to Paris by his mother, Myra, when she moved there to be with her daughter; it has since disappeared.

I had heard many stories about my great-great-grandfather, but I knew almost nothing about the war he wrote about in these journals. When I had studied the Civil War at Randolph-Macon Women's College in Viriginia, we had focused on the East Coast battles. I knew little of Missouri, where Franklin Dick had lived. I was not especially interested in that war, which I had been taught had to do with money, Northern industry, and an attack on the Southern way of life with slaves and cotton. My mother said her grandmother had told her that conditions were really difficult for the family during the war in St. Louis and that several of their children had died. I was only able to find information about the death of their son Otis. My mother also heard that they had carried the childrens' coffins back to Philadelphia for burial, but she never saw the graves.

I kept the journals in the white Hutzler's Department Store gift box and, over the years, moved them with me all over Virginia, to Colorado, to Florida, and finally to North Carolina. After the publication of my first book, *Healing Myself,* the story of my ten-year reconstruction within and without after a devastating car accident, I thought about doing some detective work with the old journals. I went to the library and traced the family genealogy. I had a copy of an old family history my great-grandfather had commissioned, but it ended in 1940. In my research about Franklin Dick's life and his family, I discovered a hidden family scandal and was unable to track the descendants of one son. I discovered much more about my great-great-grandfather from books, papers, and the Internet. My cousin, Betty Garesché Torno, gave me information about St. Louis in the 1850s through 1870s and explained the local families' histories. I found letters written to my mother from a relative writing a book about the Alexanders—the family of Myra Dick—but found no record of the book ever being published. There were letters at Princeton University Library and the Library of Congress, which would be a second volume in themselves. There was more to this story than just the journals.

Stuck in the journals I found an old envelope addressed "The Hon. Frank P. Blair, Jr., M.C. [Member of Congress], Washington City, D. C." Where the stamp would be, the envelope was stamped "free." On the outside was a penciled note about a $2,000 stock certificate in the Bank of the Old Dominion owned by Mrs. Mira M. Alexander (the mother of Myra Dick), which must have been stored inside the envelope at some point. Inside the envelope, I found a letter written by Dick to his uncle Evans Rogers on June 12, 1857, about family financial dealings.

Slowly, I began transcribing Franklin Dick's writing from the journals onto the computer. I had to use a magnifying glass to decipher some difficult words, and tried different types of lights to see more clearly. At times, I still had trouble telling what he was writing. He mainly used pen, which was easier for me to decipher. Occasionally he ran out of ink or made a small blot, and on some pages the ink had faded. Sporadically he switched to pencil, which was lighter and smudged easily. Concerned about protecting the original journals, I took them out of the faithful Hutzler's box and put them in a waterproof, fireproof safe. After a while, I became accustomed to Dick's style and thinking, and could tell what a word should be if it were scribbled in faint ink. It felt as if I were his secretary, transcribing his dictation. When I finished, I had to make sure the transcription was accurate, so friends helped me go over it word by word, comparing the two versions.

I have endeavored to preserve the integrity of Franklin Dick's journals. His original text is transcribed as exactly as possible, retaining his frequent use of abbreviations and occasional variations in spelling and capitalization. Dick followed the nineteenth-century ubiquitous use of the dash for many forms of punctuation used by modern writers (commas, periods, colons, and semicolons). These have been retained and have been formatted as a long dash followed by a space. Dick occasionally underlined words of phrases lightly or heavily for emphasis; these underlines have been retained in the text.

Any editorial additions are placed within brackets: parentheses indicate text Dick himself placed within parentheses. He typically wrote without paragraph breaks; I have taken the liberty of introducing paragraphing along topical lines for easier reading. People, places, and many events mentioned in the journals are identified in brief annotations to the text. In addition, I have provided brief explanations or background of the events to which Dick refers in his journals.

My mother had rescued journals one and ten. The journals from the period of April 1862 through September 1864 have been lost. However, Dick wrote many letters to President Lincoln, his colleagues, and his relatives. A number of these are included in the section from that time period.

We are now several generations away from the Civil War. It is harder to understand how life was for people then without hearing it firsthand. Family stories usually last three generations. A man serves in a war and tells his child and his grandchild of his experiences, but the fourth generation will not hear it directly from him and the reality of the story is lost. It is incredibly important to preserve that quality before it disappears. Growing up, I was given the gift of family stories about ancestors who had lived in this country since the 1600s. Steeped in oral history, I gained a unique perspective as I listened to the tales of my ancestors who held offices under the king before the Revolution, and Tench Tilghman, who was George Washington's secretary, and Elisha Cullen Dick, who was one of Washington's doctors. Francis Scott Key, author of the national anthem, had passed down his grandfather clock and chair to my father.

It was exciting for me to read Franklin Dick's journals after hearing family stories about him. I now had a glimpse of what his life was like in his own words, with his thoughts, feelings, and observations of events as they evolved. My admiration and respect grew as I read his candid assessments of famous people, his concern about the South, and his feelings about his beloved Union. His perspective changed as the Civil War uprooted his carefully planned legal career on the frontier. Even though I knew what would happen, I felt compelled to keep reading to see how he reacted to events. It was a real page-turner. Franklin Dick, through his journals, provides us with an irreplaceable new perspective on the impact of history in our lives.

Acknowledgments
Gratitude

All of my family helped with research, information, and advice, especially Laura and Sully. In addition, Betsy photographed the portrait, Jean-Barry found obscure details, and Howard, Derek, and Nat critiqued and helped with the proofreading. Libraries in St. Louis, Black Mountain, and Sarasota, the University of Pennsylvania Archives, and the new College Library provided books, information, and contacts. Truman State University Press gave invaluable guidance from the beginning of this project. Special appreciation and thanks are due to the Writers of the Last Resort—Cinnamon, John, Nat, Kirsten, Rusty, and Dick.

Introduction

The Dick family was descended from William de Dick, who became the first magistrate of Edinburgh in 1296. The center of the family crest shows a sailing ship and the motto, "At spes infracta, via tuta virtus" meaning "But hope is unbroken, virtue is a safe path." Generations later, Archibald Dick, who was born in 1715 in Edinburgh, immigrated to America and bought an estate in Chichester, Chester County, Pennsylvania in 1771 for 456 pounds. He was a wealthy businessman who served in the Revolutionary War as a major. In his will, he freed all but one of his slaves, leaving each a legacy. "Cuff," who must have been elderly, was to be kept on the place and cared for the rest of his life. One of his sons, Elisha

Dick family crest. Photo by R. L. Geyer © 2007.

Cullen Dick, was a friend of George Washington's and the only doctor attending Washington's last illness who disagreed with the diagnosis and spoke against using leeches. The second son, Thomas Barnard Dick, a lawyer who also lived in Chester, drowned while fishing at age forty-five. His son, Archibald Thomas Dick, practiced law in Chester and served in the War of 1812. His only son was Franklin Archibald Dick (1823–85), the writer of these journals.

In the mid-nineteenth century, when Franklin Archibald Dick lived, the world was awash with ideas of independence, nationalism, and social reform. Spain and Portugal had lost control of their colonies in South America, Louis Napoleon was elected president of the French Republic, Italy was united under Sardinian king Victor Emmanuel II, Greece won its independence from Turkey, Belgium separated from the Netherlands, and the serfs were emancipated in Russia. Concertgoers enjoyed the music of Beethoven, Schubert, and Wagner; and Manet, Degas, and Corot were painting in Paris. The poetry of Edgar Allan Poe, Walt Whitman, and Alfred, Lord Tennyson was popular; Henry David Thoreau published *Walden*; and the novels of Charles Dickens were widely circulated, including his *American Notes*, in which he criticized the institution of slavery, which had been abolished in the British Empire in 1833. Louis Pasteur announced a germ theory of fermentation, the first horse-drawn trams appeared in London, and Samuel Morse patented the telegraph. In the United States, the Supreme Court ruled that a slave was not a citizen in the Dred Scott decision, the women's suffrage movement grew out of the anti-slavery movement, Frederick Douglass launched his abolitionist newspaper, and Harriet Tubman fled from Maryland to become a conductor on the Underground Railroad. Immigrants from Europe swelled the population and the new settlers, along with Americans from eastern states, flooded the new territories as the nation expanded westward.

Franklin Archibald Dick was born on May 2, 1834, in Philadelphia, the only son of Archibald Thomas Dick and Hannah Rogers. He had three sisters: Mary E., who married Peter Hill Engle; Phebe Ann, who married James H. Castle; and Emma L., who married Professor E. Otis Kendall. He mentions each sister in his journals. In 1839, sixteen-year-old Franklin Dick entered the University of Pennsylvania as a law student and became a member of the Philomathean Society. It had been founded in 1813 to create leaders in society and to emphasize rhetoric, oratory, and writing.[1] Franklin Dick graduated in 1842 and moved from Philadelphia to the frontier town of St. Louis, Missouri, where he set up a law practice in a building built by Montgomery Blair at Third and Chestnut streets. Blair had come to St. Louis to practice law with Senator Thomas Hart Benton, a friend of the family. He had been made U.S. attorney for Missouri and had recently been elected mayor of St. Louis. Blair's youngest brother, Frank, joined his law practice in 1843, and the three men became friends and close associates. Frank Blair and Franklin Dick later became law partners and political allies.

At the time, St. Louis was the largest city in the new state. Missouri had become a state in 1821, entering the Union as a slave state as a result of the Missouri Compromise of 1820, which allowed slavery in Missouri, but prohibited slavery from then on in territories north of Missouri's southern border. Although the compromise seemed to settle the issue of the spread of slavery to new territories, it also highlighted how divisive the issue of slavery had become. The debate over the spread of slavery came up again after the Mexican-American War (1846–48) when Congress attempted to exclude slavery from territories acquired as a result of that war. The proposal passed in the House, but was defeated in the Senate, causing bitterness on both sides of the issue.[2]

In Missouri, Governor Sterling Price, who was both pro-slavery and pro-Union, attempted to keep the peace, but the passage of the Kansas-Nebraska Act in 1854, authorizing residents of the Kansas and Nebraska Territories to determine the status of slavery within their territory, led to violence. Men with violently disparate views on slavery had settled along the border between the two states, and pro-slavery groups from Missouri clashed with anti-slavery emigrants from the North as each struggled for control of the territory. Reporters from Eastern newspapers wrote disparagingly of the Missourians as "Slavocrats" and "Border Ruffians" after one

---

[1]The Philomathean Society is still active today at the University of Pennsylvania as the oldest continually existing literary society. Their website says, "In two words, Philo is a breath mint." http://www.philomathean.org/About_Philo.

[2]For events in Missouri throughout the Civil War, see the Civil War St. Louis timeline found online at http://www.civilwarstlouis.com/timeline/index.htm.

of them punched the governor of the Kansas Territory in the face.[3] In the Kansas territorial elections, counted by voice, many pro-slavery Missouri men rode into Kansas and voted illegally. The pro-slavery candidates won and approved a constitution including slavery, angering the northern Free-Soilers. This laid the foundation for those men living along the border to mistrust each other and observe their own code of justice. Violence continued until 1862, when Kansas was admitted to the Union as a free state.

The Louisiana Purchase greatly expanded America's western frontier. St. Louis, situated at the confluence of the Mississippi and Missouri Rivers, was a gateway to the West. The western frontier was vast, wild, and sparsely settled. Missouri was a frontier state mostly populated by pioneers who moved from the South in the 1830s and 1840s. Some owned one or two slaves to work their small farms along the large rivers and lived a simple, conservative, typically rural Southern life. Others had large land holdings in the rich farm areas in central and western Missouri, and owned many slaves who worked vast plantations growing hemp, tobacco, or other agricultural products.[4] Settlers also came to Missouri from New England, Ohio, and Indiana, bringing their own cultural values, which included a strong anti-slavery sentiment. After 1816, waves of immigrants began flooding the new territories. Many were seeking refuge from the difficult economic and political times in Europe caused by changing weather patterns that resulted from the 1815 eruption of Mt. Tambora,[5] and later from the Irish potato famine. In 1850, almost half of the population of St. Louis had been born in Ireland or Germany. Of American-born residents of St. Louis at the time, 70 percent were from Kentucky, North Carolina, Tennessee, or Virginia.[6] Immigrants from Europe were generally strongly opposed to slavery. Most Germans arriving after 1850 were strongly abolitionist and nationalist, while many Irish immigrants were pro-slavery, seeing free blacks as competition for jobs.

When Franklin Dick arrived there in 1844, St. Louis was a rough frontier town; it was also a major center for overland and river trade from

[3]Meyer, *Heritage of Missouri*, 339.
[4]Freehling, *Road to Disunion*, 1:5–6; and Parrish, *History of Missouri*, 3:7.
[5]Fagan, *Little Ice Age*, 170–74.
[6]"Peopling St. Louis: The Immigration Experience." stlouis.missouri.org/government/heritage/history/immigrant.

the East coast to the South, West, and Southwest. St. Louis's main trade route had been southbound on the Missouri River to New Orleans. As railroads were built across Illinois, more freight went east to Chicago, turning St. Louis into a rugged boomtown, while the rest of Missouri was concentrated on farming and ranching. The Rock Island Railroad bridged the Mississippi River in 1856 near Davenport, Iowa, and, in 1858, the Hannibal and St. Joseph Railroad was completed across northern Missouri, opening new trade routes in the state.[7]

It was during this time of economic and population growth, and of conflict between pro-slavery and anti-slavery groups, between pro-Union and secessionist views, and between immigrants to Missouri from the South, the North, and Europe that Franklin Dick practiced law in St. Louis. He worked with his friend and colleague, Frank Blair, to help organize the Free Soil Party in Missouri, which, while not opposed to the idea of slavery, opposed the spread of slavery into territories, arguing that the new lands should be free of slaves.

On November 25, 1851, Franklin Dick married Myra Madison Alexander (January 12, 1832–December 22, 1919), the sister of Frank Blair's wife, Apolline. Myra was nineteen years old and Franklin was twenty-nine. The marriage catapulted Dick into the world of the Alexanders—another typical close-knit nineteenth-century family. In addition, by becoming Frank Blair's brother-in-law, Dick intensified his political, social, and emotional alliance with the extended Blair family, which included a number of prominent American men.

Frank Blair was the son of Francis Preston Blair Sr., who had been influential in national politics for years. The Blairs lived in Washington DC across Pennsylvania Avenue from the White House. Francis Blair Sr. became a good friend and advisor of President Andrew Jackson's, and hosted meetings of the "kitchen cabinet" in his house. Since Jackson's wife had died, Blair, his wife, and their four children (James, Montgomery, Frank Jr., and Elizabeth) became the president's new family. Frank Jr. was groomed to be a politician by his family and was introduced to those in power by his father. He studied at Yale, the University of North Carolina at Chapel Hill, and Princeton, from which he graduated in 1841; he

[7]Parrish, *History of Missouri*, 3:8.

moved to Missouri to practice law in 1843. In 1847, Frank Blair married Apolline Agatha Alexander, whose mother, Mira Madison Alexander, was the daughter of George Madison, governor of Kentucky. Mira's husband, Andrew Jonathan Alexander, had been killed in 1833 at an accident in his sawmill. Andrew and Mira had four surviving children—Apolline, George, Myra, and Andrew.[8] After Mira became totally blind in 1845, she spent part of her time at her Kentucky family home, Sherwood, and part of the year at the Blairs' house in St. Louis, where Myra Dick visited her. Blair served in the Missouri House of Representatives (1852–56) and in the U.S. Congress (1857–59, 1860, 1861–62). President Lincoln used him as an unofficial advisor on Missouri affairs during the Civil War.

Franklin Dick began keeping a journal in September 1861, stating his intention of "keeping a record of the rebellion." He begins by describing events he observed in January 1861 in St. Louis. Lincoln had been elected president in November 1860. The following month, South Carolina seceded from the Union. Mississippi, Florida, Alabama, Georgia, and Louisiana followed in January 1861, and Texas in February. They formed the Confederate States of America, with Jefferson Davis as president.

In Alabama, Florida, and Louisiana, state forces took control of federal arsenals in early January. In St. Louis, tensions mounted between pro-secessionist and pro-Union citizens. Early in January, federal troops arrived in St. Louis to guard the U.S. subtreasury and secure the federal arsenal. In response, pro-secession residents formed the Minute Men, a paramilitary organization that rivaled the Home Guard troops. The Minute Men used the Berthold Mansion as their headquarters, also the headquarters of the Democratic Party.

At the same time, a group of Unionists began meeting in secret and collecting arms and forces to defend the federal arsenal at St. Louis. With 60,000 assorted arms, more than 200 barrels of gunpowder, and other war equipment, this was the largest arsenal west of the Mississippi. On January 10, 1861, the group, which included Frank Blair and Nathaniel Lyon, met at Franklin Dick's law office on 5th Street near the Presbyterian Church to plan for a public meeting to be held the next day to formally set up the St.

---

[8]I was unable to discover why the mother's name was spelled Mira, and the daughter's, Myra. George appears later in the journals, when he went into the cartridge business with Franklin Dick.

Franklin Dick's campaign chest. Photo by R. L. Geyer © 2007.

Louis Committee on Safety. The committee met each night to assess actions by the Southern sympathizers. Mayor Oliver Filley, another member of the Committee on Safety, sent a large number of police to the public meeting to prevent disruption by the secessionists.[9]

Frank Blair began converting his Wide Awake clubs, which he had started in the German community for anti-slavery demonstrations, along with other like-minded men, into Home Guard troops.[10] Many old St. Louisans were uneasy that the "Damned Dutch" were on the streets in military groups, while the Germans were proud that they were serving their adopted country. On January 12, the Conditional Unionists, who wanted slavery but not secession, planned a public meeting in front of the courthouse. Franklin Dick, Frank Blair, and others initially told Republicans to stay away, but realized the need for unity in the Republican Party. The group called for a state convention to decide on Missouri's position in the national crisis.[11]

The state convention began meeting on February 28, first in Jefferson City, then moving to St. Louis on March 3. On March 4, Abraham Lincoln was sworn in as president. On that day, secessionists flew handmade Missouri "secessionist flags" from the front porch of the Berthold Mansion and from the courthouse. The flag above the courthouse was immediately removed, the one with the single star, crescent, and cross that remained flying from the Berthold Mansion drew a protesting crowd, which was met by armed Minute Men who surrounded the building.[12] The crowd could see the piles of bricks on the top veranda ready to be thrown. This division was reflected in the convention, where delegates debated the Crittenden Compromise, and in the state legislature, where secessionists and Unionists debated the fate of the state. Finally, on March 22, the state convention announced that it found no cause to leave the Union at that time.

Several weeks later, Confederate troops fired on federal forces at Fort Sumter in Charleston Harbor, forcing them to surrender in the first battle of the Civil War. In response, President Lincoln called for 75,000

[9]Gerteis, *Civil War St. Louis,* 80–81.
[10]Parrish, *History of Missouri,* 3:5.
[11]Gerteis, *Civil War St. Louis,* 80–83.
[12]Winter, *Civil War in St. Louis,* 31, 33; and Kirschten, *Catfish and Crystal,* 197.

volunteers to serve for three months to put down the rebellion. Governor Jackson, who was publicly supporting Lincoln while privately moving toward secession, refused the order to send 4,000 Missouri troops. Blair immediately offered his Home Guards, which were accepted into federal service. While Jackson met with secessionists planning to seize the federal arsenal and sent a message to the Confederate president Davis asking for weapons, Frank Blair and Nathaniel Lyon were working to raise volunteers for federal service. On April 20, state militia forces captured a small federal arsenal at Liberty, Missouri, and on April 22, Governor Jackson called for militia to muster at a site by the arsenal. On April 26, Lyon and Blair, concerned about the safety of the St. Louis Arsenal, sent a decoy of outdated weapons from the arsenal to the St. Louis levee, where they were seized by a mob.[13] Later that night, Lyon and Blair had Captain James H. Stokes remove 20,000 muskets and 100,000 cartridges onto a steamer at the arsenal wharf and sent them to safety in Alton, Illinois.[14]

In the East, Virginia, Arkansas, Tennessee, and North Carolina joined the Confederacy, and Richmond, Virginia, became the Confederate capital. Lincoln declared a blockade of Southern forts, and in May called more for more volunteers for three years of service. Behind the scenes, Blair had conservative General William S. Harney recalled to Washington, leaving Lyon temporarily in command of the troops in Missouri. As Blair and Lyon armed the Home Guards and put them into federal service, they occupied the buildings and area surrounding the arsenal, using Captain Totten's artillery for defense. With new orders, they mustered 10,000 more men to protect "the peaceable inhabitants of Missouri."[15] Meanwhile, Governor Jackson met with General Daniel Frost, called up the militia, ordered a special session of the legislature on May 2, and sent secret envoys requesting aid from the Confederate government in Montgomery and the seceded state of Virginia.

Jackson planned to group his militia on the heights south of the arsenal to capture the arms inside for the Confederacy. Lyon and Blair were able to occupy the area first. Jackson then sent General Frost with about 800 local men to assemble in Lindell Grove, about a half hour's

[13]McPherson, *Battle Cry of Freedom*, 291.
[14]Winter, *Civil War in St. Louis*, 40.
[15]Parrish, *History of Missouri*, 3:11–13.

march away from the arsenal.[16] Camp Jackson received boxes labeled "tamaroa marble" containing contraband Confederate arms that had been seized from the Baton Rouge arsenal by Jefferson Davis. Meanwhile, Lyon and Blair had four regiments of volunteers, commanded by Blair, Henry Boernstein, Franz Sigel, and Heinrich Schuettner,[17] ready to defend the arsenal.

At the time of the incident at Camp Jackson in 1861, events had moved with lightning speed instead of the normal slow pace. Due to the unrest, Franklin Dick had taken his family and Frank Blair's wife and children to Philadelphia for safety. Myra stayed with Dick's family and her sister Apo with the Biddle family who were Alexander relatives, and Dick returned to St. Louis.[18] When the confrontation finally came, Dick was there, serving as Nathaniel Lyon's adjutant general. On May 9, Lyon scouted Camp Jackson. Dick does not mention in his journal that Blair borrowed their mother-in-law's dress, veil, and hat for Lyon to use for a disguise, but several other accounts do. Lyon rode in Mira Alexander's carriage, with her coachman, into Camp Jackson to observe what General Frost and his troops were doing, taking advantage of the fact that Mrs. Alexander used to take a drive every afternoon. On Lyon's lap, was an egg basket with a gun concealed in it, which he did not have to use.[19]

The following day, General Lyon and his men marched on Camp Jackson and demanded the surrender of the forces camped there. General Frost was not prepared to defend the camp and so surrendered to Lyon. A crowd of civilians gathered to watch as Lyon's troops marched their prisoners out of the camp; some in the crowd hurled insults or threw stones at the federal troops and violence broke out, resulting in twenty-eight civilian deaths, the first casualties of the Civil War in Missouri.

Immediately after the seizing of Camp Jackson, James Yeatman, Hamilton Gamble, and a group of conservative Unionist citizens met with the mayor of St. Louis. Yeatman and Gamble were sent to Washington to

[16]Gerteis, *Civil War St. Louis*, 98–99.

[17]Gerteis, *Civil War St. Louis*, 94; Kirschten, *Catfish and Crystal*, 196–204; and Smith, *Francis Preston Blair*, 290–93.

[18]Parrish, *Frank Blair: Lincoln's Conservative*, 97.

[19]Gerteis, *Civil War St. Louis*, 100; Parrish, *History of Missouri*, 3:13; Parrish, *Frank Blair: Lincoln's Conservative*, 100; and family stories.

ask Edward Bates, Lincoln's attorney general, to help remove Lyon and promote Harney's conciliatory policies. Lyon and Blair considered the situation a major problem and wanted immediate measures taken against Southern sympathizers. General Harney returned to St. Louis on May 11 and issued a proclamation about preserving peace. Frank Blair, back in St. Louis, met directly with the general, and realized that Harney was trying to placate the Missouri rebels. Blair then sent his brother-in-law Franklin Dick to plead the case with the president. When Dick arrived in Washington, he went directly to find Montgomery Blair, now Lincoln's postmaster general. Together they walked across the street to the White House and met with President Lincoln, and Simon Cameron, Secretary of War. Dick explained the importance of rounding up rebels, and how essential it was for the continued Union control of the city and arsenal. He asked for Lyon's confirmation of his election as brigadier general and Harney's removal. Dick mentioned the influence of Harney's Southern background and his wife's connection with the secessionist Mullanphy family in St. Louis.[20] Lincoln later met with Yeatman and Gamble and decided to support Frank Blair by promoting Lyon to brigadier general, though for the moment publicly supporting General Harney's policies.[21] Lincoln sent Frank Blair a letter authorizing him to remove Harney at his discretion. After Harney met with General Sterling Price of the state militia to cooperate for peace over loyalty and issued the Harney-Price agreeeent, Frank Blair delivered Lincoln's orders on May 30, 1861, opening the way for Lyon to take control of troops in Missouri.[22]

A month after the Camp Jackson incident, pro-Unionists General Lyon and Colonel Blair met with secessionists Governor Price and General Jackson to discuss the situation. After four hours of debate, the meeting ended with Lyon asserting federal authority over the state and informing Price and Jackson that they would be escorted from the area. Lyon rapidly occupied Jefferson City and Boonville (north of St. Louis on the Missouri River) and sent troops under Franz Sigel on the railroad to Rolla and Carthage to the south. Lyon then controlled river traffic to

[20]Parrish, *Frank Blair: Lincoln's Conservative,* 94n39.
[21]Parrish, *Frank Blair: Lincoln's Conservative,* 104–5.
[22]Gerteis, *Civil War St. Louis,* 115–16, 118–25.

the north and the railroads, which forced General Price and Governor Jackson into southwestern Missouri.[23] John Charles Frémont was appointed major general in the U.S. Army and given command of the western military district based in St. Louis to replace General William Harney on July 3, 1861. Federal forces under Lyon clashed with Price's troops at Boonville (June 5), Carthage (July 5), and Wilson's Creek (August 10), where Lyon was killed in battle. Frémont was blamed for Lyon's death, having failed to send troops Lyon had requested. Frank Blair tried to assist Frémont in dealing with the mounting problems in Missouri, but the situation worsened. In July, the state convention declared all statewide offices vacant and appointed Hamilton R. Gamble as provisional governor, creating the strange situation of Missouri having two governors. In August 1861, Frémont issued a proclamation instituting martial law in Missouri, confiscating property of secessionists, and freeing slaves. President Lincoln rescinded part of the orders and eventually relieved Frémont of his command.

In the midst of this turmoil, Franklin Dick started to write his journals, never intending for anyone else to read them. He began looking over the events of the previous nine months and recorded his introspective and outspoken views. His life had rapidly changed from that of an intellectual St. Louis attorney and businessman to that of an ardent Unionist in the midst of a turbulent Civil War. Dick always spoke up for what he felt was fair, honest, just, and the right thing to do, and he acted on his views without regard to the consequences on his career. His notebooks, interspersed with details of his daily routine and his views on what unfolded around him, provide a graphic eyewitness description of life on the home front, public morale and opinions, and how people coped with the war. Dick wrote bluntly of his private thoughts about the country, the state, and politicians and military leaders he knew. He also wrote of his private

[23]Brownlee, *Gray Ghosts of the Confederacy*, 14–17; Parrish, *History of Missouri*, 3:22–35; and Meyer, *Heritage of Missouri*, 355–59.

worries and concerns, the morality of the war, and the Unionist cause. His account of how history changed his life begins on September 4, 1861, when he was visiting his family in West Chester, Pennsylvania.

JOURNAL No. 1

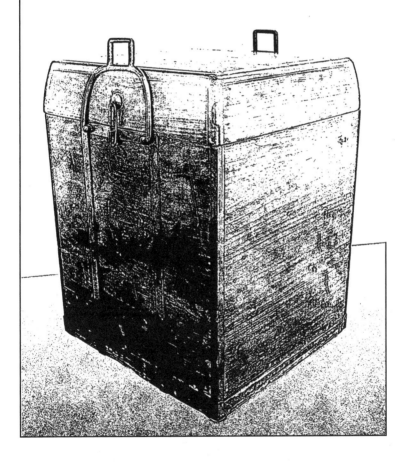

Franklin Dick's journal, notebook #1. Photo by R. L. Geyer © 2007.

September 1861

"The Rebels are doing enormous mischief in Missouri— rising up all through the State."

West Chester, Penna., Sept. 4, 1861 Memo of F. A. Dick

I have intended for some time past keeping a record of the rebellion. I regret not having begun it before. At this end of this book, I will make a short sketch of some of the past events. (I went back to St. Louis in fall of 1861 on a/c of necessity of making money to support my family.)

Claiborne F. Jackson,[1] the Rebel Governor of Missouri, with a villainous Legislature passed a law in January, 1861 for the election of a State convention in Missouri, to take the state out of the Union. The election was held in Feb'y. & Convention met in Jefferson in <u>March, 1861</u>, & adjourned to St. Louis— Sterling Price[2] was elected President, professing to be a Union man— Hamilton R. Gamble[3] secured his election—

[1]Claiborne Fox Jackson (1806–62) was elected governor of Missouri in 1860 and tried to pull the state into secession.

[2]Sterling Price (1809–67), was selected presiding officer of the Missouri State Convention in February 1861. He had opposed secession, but after Blair and Lyon seized Camp Jackson, Price was furious. Governor Jackson assigned him to command the Missouri State Guard in May 1861 and he led his troops in a campaign to secure southwestern Missouri for the Confederacy.

[3]Hamilton Rowan Gamble (1798–1864) tried to keep peace between Northern and

3

otherwise John D. [*sic*] Henderson[4] of Pike County would have been elected. The Convention proved to be Union by about 60 to 33— Jackson convened the legislature in May to pass laws giving him military control of the State. It passed such laws in secret session.

At that time, Camp Jackson[5] in St. Louis was gotten up. The 10th May, Genl. Lyon[6] took it. I was present, acting as Assistant Adj. Gen. I had counseled that movement— It was decided upon, on consultation at the St. Louis Arsenal, between Captain Lyon, Frank P. Blair, Jr.,[7] Col. 1st Regiment Mo. Vol., Oliver D. Filley[8] & F. A. Dick.

I first proposed taking that Camp, and reasoned strongly in favor of it. Captain Lyon fully agreed with me. Colonel Blair inclined the same way. Mr. Filley did not express his opinion. This camp professed to be a peaceable thing, & got up by authority of the State merely for a camp of instruction and drill— It was under the command of Daniel M. Frost, Brig. Gen'l—[9] It was in the west edge of St. Louis.

We had watched it closely, & learned that the morning of the 9th, heavy cannon, boxed up shot, mortars, muskets, &c. had been secretly

---

Southern factions, and worked to keep Missouri in the Union. In 1861, he was elected to the state constitutional convention, which appointed him provisional governor of Missouri when Claiborne F. Jackson joined the secession party and was forced out of office.

[4] John Brooks Henderson (1826–1913) served two terms in the Missouri legislature (1848–50; 1856–58), and was a brigadier general in the state militia in 1861.

[5] Each year, the Missouri Volunteer State Militia drilled at Lindell's Grove, located just north of St. Louis. In 1861, the annual drill was called Camp Jackson in honor of Governor Jackson. That year, the volunteer militia included members of the Minute Men, a pro-South paramilitary group.

[6] Nathaniel Lyon (1818–61), served in Kansas during the border conflict known as Bleeding Kansas, and became a fervent abolitionist. In March 1861, he was sent to Jefferson Barracks in St. Louis, where he worked with the Committee of Safety. Lyon drilled and organized the Home Guards, who were mustered into federal service to protect the arsenal and its approaches.

[7] Francis Preston Blair Jr. (1821–75) served on the Committee of Safety, raised troops to help Lyon at Camp Jackson, and rose to be a major general in the Union Army.

[8] Oliver Dwight Filley (1806–81) became a leader in the Republican Party and was elected mayor of St. Louis in 1858. He was a member of the Committee of Safety with Blair and Dick.

[9] Daniel Marsh Frost (1823–1900) supported Governor Jackson's secessionist views and worked secretly with him to set up a militia training center at Camp Jackson. He was also part of the plot to capture the St. Louis arsenal. Frost was arrested along with other men at Camp Jackson, but was paroled and exchanged. In 1861, Frost became a brigadier general in the Confederate Army.

before day light, carried from the Steamer J. C. Swan to this camp. But the U.S. Marshall, D. Rawlins, who was instructed to inquire into the facts, persistently alleged that this report was false— Therefore I was in doubt as to the fact, & was in favor of taking the camp as an original proposition.

On the 10th May perhaps about one o'c., we marched out of the Arsenal— the 1st Reg. Mo. Vol. Col. Blair had to march up from Jefferson barracks, 12 miles & we were compelled to wait for it. Because Capt. Lyon wanted the backing of Col. Blair in this momentous act, the 2nd, 3rd and 4th Reg. Mo. Vols. & about 250 U.S. Regulars, being Capt. Lyon's company 2nd U.S. Infantry, Capt. Totten's[10] Artillery Comp'y. (acting as infantry) & others. We drew up in order of battle. I was with Lyon— his Adj. Bernard G. Farrar[11] went to the enemy with a demand for their unconditional surrender—

The enemy, to the number of about 1,200, was in a camp— with six brass field pieces— Their camp was between Grand Avenue on the west and Olive Street on the North— in Leidell's pasture— Lyon's staff— myself, Farrar, Conant and Sam Simmons with a company of Regulars— & Siegel's Regiment—[12] & a battery of 4 brass field pieces were on Olive Street. The battery was run up on high ground and guns unlimbered— On the East was Schulterer's Regiment with a Comp'y. of Regulars under Lieut. Lathrop, U.S.A. & a battery of 4 or 6 brass field pieces— Boernstein's[13] Regiment was on Grand Av. on the west— & Blair's Regt. on Olive Street just east of Grand Av. We expected a fight.

In 20 minutes, Farrar came back with Genl. Frost's surrender— An hour passed before the traitors were ready to march out— They were passed out between the lines of Blair's & Boernstein's Regiments— Just as the last were coming out, or had got out, shots were fired from the rabble in the enclosure upon our troops— at part of Boernstein's Regt. not

[10]James Totten (1818–71) was chief of artillery at Camp Jackson, Booneville, and Wilson's Creek, serving in the First Missouri Volunteers under Lyon and Frémont.

[11]Bernard Gaines Farrar Jr. (1831–1916) was a major and aide to General Nathaniel Lyon at Camp Jackson. Later, he was provost marshal.

[12]Franz Sigel (1824–1902) organized the Third U.S. Volunteers, who carried a U.S. flag with "Lyon's Color Guard" stitched on it in German. Sigel attracted Germans to the pro-Union cause and served under Lyon at the capture of Camp Jackson.

[13]Henry Boernstein (1805–92) became the influential German editor of the *Anziger des Westens* in St. Louis, and led the Second Regiment of U.S. Volunteers under Lyon at Camp Jackson. He was a good friend and supporter of Frank Blair.

required to escort the prisoners. One rascal fired 3 times at Lieut. Santer, U.S.A. The third shot, one of his men pierced the scoundrel with his bayonet— A captain in Boernstein's Regiment was shot in the knee (of which wound he lingered a week and died) & then he gave the order to fire.

The firing was into the enclosure & upon the rabble, for the prisoners were all out— from twenty to thirty of them were shot and 6 or 8 of our soldiers. I was on my horse when the firing began— I did not know why or how it had begun & my first impulse was to get out of the way & moved my horse 20 or 30 yards back from the line, along with the retreating crowd— I then looked about me, as my horse was moving, & I saw Capt. Lyon at the head of the line, trying to stop the firing— I rode up & passed before him (he was then on foot) & went along the <u>front</u> of the line that was firing, commanding them in name of Capt. Lyon to cease firing— I rode on 50 to 75 yards, when the firing ceased & I returned to where I had been— Just before dark, the two Regiments with the prisoners moved on passing down through the City to the Arsenal.

Capt. Totten stepped up to Capt. Lyon & whispered. After that Lyon rode up to me, saying Totten had said that he was watched & would probably be shot if he went through the City— & he proposed that we should return to the Arsenal by the out-skirts.

We then, that is Lyon, Farrar, Conant & myself, rode in a gallop through the out skirts to the arsenal & got back there just before dark; where we met Cary Graly, Dr. Alexander & other officers awaiting our arrival— We told them what had happened & went into the arsenal.

Before leaving the ground, Lyon & I rode into the Camp where we saw the dead & wounded lying about— Lyon was greatly moved at the sight of the wounded & dying & said in a tremulous & low voice— "Poor creatures— poor creatures— How sorry I am for them"— His countenance & manner was that of a woman almost. He greatly regretted at the time the death of those people. A woman & child were killed & several unknown & innocent persons.

For about ten days before this I had been acting as Asst. Adjutant Genl. of Lyon. He had been elected Brigadier Genl of the 4th Missouri Regiments, the only ones then organized. He appointed as his staff, B. G. Farrar, Aid; Sam Simmons, Commissary Genl.; Chester Harding, Quarter Master; & myself, Assist. Adj. Genl— My appointment was the first he

made— It was a surprise to me— When he proposed it, I thanked him, &
said I would consider upon it— In 2 or 3 days he asked my decision— I was
not ready to accept & told him so; & I said therefore I had better decline.
But he would not take a declination so made— This was repeated several
times. When finding him extremely anxious for me to accept, I did so.

I was with Lyon all the time for many days. We talked together most
confidentially, & he expressed to me his great confidence in me— He did
this as a reason why he wanted me on his staff as his Asst. Adjt. Genl. My
acquaintance with Lyon began by my meeting him at the Democrat Office
one morning about 12 O'C. This was, I believe, in Feb'y. or March 1861.
He came in to inquire for the latest news. He was a small man, about 5 ft
5, sandy hair, & beard & mustache— wore a black slouched hat & his captain's uniform— not very neat— & carried a hooked old hickory cane all
the time. I opened conversation with him— found him well informed in
the latest occurrences & possessed of congeniality.

I asked him to meet me at my office in half an hour— He came & we
sat an hour talking over the Condition of the Country &c— We were of
the same opinions, feelings, & wishes— From that day we saw each other
often— He frequently came to my office— As the plot thickened, meetings of the leading Union men in St. Louis were held at my office & Lyon
was generally there. Amongst these men were Frank Blair, Oliver D. Filley,
Sam T. Glover,[14] Benj. Farrar,[15] R. L. Fay, Sam Simmons, Henry T.
Blow,[16] Giles F. Filley,[17] B. Gratz Brown,[18] & sometimes John D. Stevenson,[19] John Doyle, Henry Boernstein, &c.

[14]Samuel T. Glover (1813–84), friend of Franklin Dick, was a member of the St.
Louis Committee of Safety. He strongly advised Lyon not to attack Camp Jackson, but to
deal with it legally with a writ of replevin to reclaim stolen federal property.

[15]Benjamin Farrar was a good friend of Franklin Dick and Frank Blair. Benjamin's
father, Dr. Bernard Gaines Farrar Sr., a prominent St. Louis doctor, had five children:
John O'Fallon, Benjamin, Berhard G. Jr. (a Union general), James, and Ellen. Benjamin
Farrar was a pallbearer at Frank Blair's funeral.

[16]Henry T. Blow (1817–75). As a Blair supporter during the Civil War, Blow led a
group to Washington to have General John M. Schofield replaced for working too closely
with the governor of Missouri.

[17]Giles Franklin Filley (1815–97) was one of the 1848 organizers of the Free Soil
Party in Missouri. He was a manufacturer of cast iron stoves; in 1861, Filley made thirty
cannons for the Union.

[18]Benjamin Gratz Brown (1826–85) founded the *Missouri Democrat* with Frank
Blair, mobilizing Unionists in St. Louis.

[19]John D. Stevenson (1821–1912) served several terms in the legislature before the

The first serious meeting was held at night at my office, when the first above named with Lyon were there, including myself— We there discussed the probability of the traitors beginning their machinations. Lyon, Fay, Blair, Farrar, Blow & I from the first insisted that the enemy intended mischief— Our meetings were secret.

The enemy had begun their secret organizations to drill & arm— For weeks we mutually stood in fear of each other. Each expected the other party to attack. The possession of the St. Louis Arsenal was the great object of their designs. We got up a secret organization throughout the city & mustered over 2,000 men. But all our movements had to be secret, for we were denounced by the *Mo. Republican* & other hostile papers as incendiaries, & we were watched by Gov. Jackson & his spies & mercenaries in the City. The traitors got the Berthold Mansion,[20] N.W. corner of 5th & Pine, & there every day and night went on organizing the "Minute Men." Gov. Jackson furnished them with State muskets.

At first this was an unauthorized association, but afterwards they were secretly sworn into the service of the State. Finally General Frost acknowledged that he had mustered them into the State service. This place became the hotbed of active treason. Many of the young men of the City went into the organization as Officers— Hugh Garland,[21] Given Campbell,[22] &c &c. Tom Snead[23] and Wm. M. Cooke[24] were active in

---

Civil War, and one term as president of the state Senate. He raised the Seventh Missouri Regiment, and was made brigadier general of volunteers.

[20]The Berthold Mansion had been the headquarters of the Democratic Party in St. Louis since 1859. It became the center for Southern troops calling themselves Minute Men. Before the State Constitutional Convention, on the night of March 3, 1861, the Minute Men designed and constructed the first Missouri secessionist flags, and flew one from the front porch and another from the courthouse.

[21]Hugh Garland (1805–64) was captured at Camp Jackson, and later rose to be a colonel in the Confederate army. He was killed in battle at Franklin, Tennessee.

[22]Given Campbell (1835–1906) served as a captain under General Frost in the Missouri Volunteer Militia and was captured at Camp Jackson. After his release, he left St. Louis and joined the Confederate army, serving as a captain in the Second and Ninth Kentucky Cavalries.

[23]Thomas Lowndes Snead (1828–90) was a lawyer and editor of the *St. Louis Bulletin*, a secession newspaper, before the Civil War. He joined with the Confederates, becoming Major General Sterling Price's right-hand man and rising to acting asst. general.

[24]William Mordecai Cooke (1823–63) was sent in March 1861 by Governor Jackson as a commissioner to Confederate President Davis, but he returned to Missouri to serve on Governor Jackson's military staff at Boonville, Carthage, and Wilson's Creek. Cooke

increasing the organization. This was the beginning of the rebel army in St. Louis. These scoundrels afterwards made up part of the troops at Camp Jackson.

While the State Convention sat in the Library Hall, the Rebels raised the Secession Flag at their Headquarters, 5th & Pine— This created a great excitement in the city and there was imminent danger of a terrible riot, as the Union men were greatly outraged at it. The second day, O. D. Filley, then Mayor, was about issuing the order to his Chief of Police, Rawlings, to take it down. When I went into his office, & by my advice, he withheld the order. I knew it would lead to bloodshed & thought it best to let a little time pass, and see if it would not be taken down, for Snead and other influential men amongst them promised to get it down.

This was intended undoubtedly to influence the convention. But that body was true to the Union and voted against all disunion schemes. After Fort Sumter was taken & the Rebels showed their intentions, our active movements in St. Louis were no longer kept dark. We began our preparations with great decision. A meeting of our Party, the Republican, was called at Washington Hall[25] & we invited all Union men to join. We were notified through H. T. Blow that we were to be attacked by the Traitors in Arms. We armed ourselves, held the meeting and began our peaceful Union organization.

West Chester, Pennsylvania, Sept. 4, 1861
(Went to West Chester August 21st /Sept. 11)

News this A.M. but little— preparation of Rebels near Washington for attack going on— Their works seem to be fortified approaches on ours. Three weeks ago there was great uneasiness lest they should attack our lines— cross the Potomac and capture Washington— I was very uneasy then about it, & felt if ten days passed safely, that the impending danger would be over— More than the ten days have passed, & our troops have been pouring in, (but at what rate no one knows for the papers do not state

was elected to the Confederate Congress in 1861.
[25]Washington Hall was located at 50 South Third Street in St. Louis.

anything about it) in response to the public urgent call by the Secy. of War, and I suppose too, extensive defenses on the Potomac at the fords above Washington City (W.C.) have been made— so that the fear & excited anxiety has worn off. But yet I feel as though the attack must be a very dangerous thing to us; for if unsuccessful it will strike dismay to the Rebels, & my belief is a large part of their army would fall away.

They are as yet but a "Quasi" government & need established success to hold them together— Pay and subsistence are indispensable to keep up their army & if defeated at Washington City, with no means of paying and lessened means of subsisting their army, their cause is greatly shaken in their own States. Success is their necessary pabulum— They have subsisted on crumbs of it combined with great expectations— so that if the <u>reality</u> goes against them, their cohesive power and strength is severely injured. That is my view & the Common Belief. They started out to take Washington as soon as they got Fort Sumter, & can not well get off the track.

The danger of late has been that they would make the attack on W.C. while our force was small in consequence of the disbandment of the three months men, which has been going on during the last month— I am satisfied that Beauregard's[26] army was too much cut up, in fact too nearly defeated at Manassas to be able to follow over to attack Washington! Moreover, I do not believe that the Rebels at all knew how confused and used up our army was from fright— flight & a waste of organization at that time.

The great matter of interest just now, is what will happen in Kentucky— In that State, a Union Legislature has lately been elected by a large majority— It met on the 1st inst. but has done nothing yet. The Rebels there have been busy lately to get the State on the South's side— William Preston,[27] Breckenridge,[28] etc. are hard at work for the enemy—

[26]Pierre Gustave Toutant Beauregard (1819–93) joined the Confederate army, where he rose to the rank of general. He commanded the attack on Fort Sumter.

[27]William Preston (1816–87) served in the Confederate army, where he reached the rank of major general.

[28]John Cabell Breckenridge (1821–75), vice president under James Buchanan from 1857 to 1861, was elected to the U.S. Senate, but was expelled in December 1861 for supporting the rebellion. He entered the Confederate army, where he became brigadier general in charge of the Kentucky Orphan Brigade.

I feel confident that they will get up a terrific Civil War in the State— &
I anticipate a majority of fighting men there on the Union side.

EVNG.—

News tonight is that Magoffin,[29] Governor of Kentucky says he will
not resist the will of the majority of the People of the State, as it may be
expressed by the new Legislature— This Magoffin is a thorough traitor,
& has been very active in endeavoring to drag his State into the Rebellion. He has been threatened with impeachment and the late active measures of the President in arresting traitors have, I suppose, intimidated
him. Still Ky. is bound to be dragged into the war.

Mr. Holt of Ky. yesterday made a noble speech in New York— The
effect of his speech is a tonic to the Northern People. The brave patriot
General Nathaniel Lyon who fell at the Battle of Springfield arrived at
New York the 2nd inst. I knew him well and felt his death deeply. He was
a great strength to the cause in Missouri. Great blame rests somewhere
for not reinforcing him. He had but about 5,000 under his command. For
weeks he had been calling for reinforcements.

I find fault with the Secy. of War and also with Major Genl. Fremont[30] at St. Louis for the neglect. And yet there is no movement to find
out where the blame belongs. Our Missouri troops fought there bravely
against about 23,000 of the enemy, most of whom were Missouri Rebels
under command of Major Genl. Sterling Price, of the State Rebel forces
and Genls. Parsons, Rains, &c. and Arkansas & Louisiana & Texas
troops under Genl. Ben. McCullough.

[29]Beriah Magoffin (1815–85) was governor of Kentucky from 1860 to 1862. He
tried to keep Kentucky nonpartisan, supporting the Crittenden Compromise, but also the
Fugitive Slave Law. He issued a neutrality proclamation and attempted to call secession
conventions twice in 1861, but was blocked by a pro-Union legislature. He was able to keep
Kentucky uninvolved until September 1861, when the legislature declared allegiance to the
Union, reacting to a Confederate invasion in violation of the state's neutrality.

[30]John Charles Frémont (1813–90), with the help of his political connections, was
appointed major general in the U.S. Army and given command of the western military
district, based in St. Louis. Frémont replaced General William Harney, who had negotiated the Harney-Price Agreement to keep Missouri neutral. Lyon and other pro-Unionists were unhappy with the deal. Frank Blair sent Franklin Dick to Washington to lobby
for Lyon and ask for Harney's dismissal. Frémont was made commander on July 3, 1861; a
month later, Lyon was killed at the Battle of Wilson's Creek and Frémont was blamed for
his death, having failed to send troops Lyon had requested.

Lyon was wounded early in the battle, but gave no attention to his wound. His beautiful grey horse was killed. He led the Iowa 1st Regt. and was shot dead. Still our army defeated the Rebels, but we were so largely outnumbered that our army was compelled to retire, first twelve miles to Springfield, & then on to Rolla— The Rebels took possession of Springfield and all the country thereabouts. For a few days after that, great anxiety was felt about their marching on to Jefferson City, Fulton, &c. And if successful, they undoubtedly would have marched on to St. Louis. It was given out throughout the Rebel Army that they were to take St. Louis. Reinforcements were hastened down the S. W. branch of the Pacific R.R. to Rolla and the army— Had but two or three of the Regiments been sent in time to join Lyon, he would have been saved & the Rebels driven back, instead of their being able to ravage the whole Southern part of the State.[31]

A short time prior to that Fremont had sent large numbers of troops to Cain & Bird's Point & may have thought it more necessary to take care of those places than of Lyon. Pillow[32] was threatening Cairo & the S.E. part of Mo. For some time past the Rebels have been at New Madrid. They went up to commence around Cairo, but have been driven out of it. A considerable force— three or four Regiments have for some time been kept by Fremont at Cape Giradeau.[33]

West Chester, Thursday, September 5, 1861

No attack yet by the Rebels at Washington. They are still advancing their lines nearer to ours and seem to be erecting fortifications to sustain their advances. At Washington for several days they have expected the

[31]After the Camp Jackson incident, Lyon had rapidly occupied Jefferson City and Boonville, north of St. Louis on the Missouri River, and sent troops under Franz Sigel on the railroad to Rolla and Carthage to the south, which forced General Price and Governor Jackson into southwestern Missouri. Since he had moved so quickly, Lyon left pro-Southern men behind his lines.

[32]Gideon Pillow (1806–78), a Tennessee attorney and law partner of future president James Polk, was one of Jefferson Davis' worst political appointments. As a Confederate brigadier general, Pillow is best remembered for his actions in the battle of Fort Donelson, when he fled to avoid capture by Union troops.

[33]New Madrid, Missouri, was an important base for control of the Missouri River. North of New Madrid is the juncture of the Missouri and Ohio Rivers, and Cape Girardeau, Missouri. Bird's Point, Missouri, and Cairo, Illinois, are south of the point.

attack to be made. It is believed that they have provided a large number of boats and vessels on the Virginia side of the Chesapeake, with which to transport 5,000 men across to march thence upon Washington— And that they will attempt crossing the Potomac above, and at the same time attack our lines at Arlington. This is believed to be the plan. The statements from Washington are that our Army and the People are confident of our success. The impression exists that there is great distress in the Rebel Army there for want of the necessary supplies etc., and that they are compelled to attack Washington to keep their army together.

On Monday last (I believe) several U.S. vessels that sailed from Fortress Monroe went to Hatteras Inlet, a short distance below Cape Hatteras, bombarded and took two forts[34] of the Rebels lately built there. This achievement has given great joy throughout the North. The Navy has done so little, that the people had become dissatisfied with it. This thing will give great uneasiness to the Southerners, for they see the beginning of what they have so much dreaded. Day after day, news goes on, the nation awaiting with much patience for our army to accomplish something.

The defeat at Manassas Junction and Bulls Run has made the people feel that it is best to leave the commanders to move at their own time. General McClellan[35] has entirely taken the place of General Scott[36] in the public eye. He has not had any interference from the press or any other power. He has done much in reforming the want of discipline in the army. Under Scott, the army at Washington was a heterogeneous mass, undisciplined and inefficient. Old Scott was utterly deficient to perform his duties. He knew nothing of the state of the army, and seemed to be blind to the condition of things.

It is believed that McClellan has done all that was needed. If he has not, he is in fault, for all responsibility has been assumed by him. I believe

---

[34]On August 27–29, 1861, Union forces captured Forts Hatteras and Clark, which controlled the Hatteras Inlet, a busy North Carolina entrance for Confederate blockade runners.

[35]George Brinton McClellan (1826–85) was made a major general of Ohio volunteers at the beginning of the Civil War. In 1861, Lincoln made him general in chief of the Army of the Potomac.

[36]Winfield Scott (1786–1866) was the highest ranking military officer at the start of the Civil War. After the defeats at First Bull Run and Balls Bluff, he was replaced by McClellan and retired November 1, 1861.

now that the Northern mind is fairly confident as to our whipping the
Rebels at Washington. General attention is directed to that place. The
Northern people are subscribing pretty freely at New York and Phila to
the Public loan in shape of Treasury notes. The feeling prevails that the
U.S. loan is ultimately safe.

The Rebel Generals are taking time to prepare for the impending
attack. They are undoubtedly devising some able and ingenious plan.
They know that the danger of defeat is great and that the result is most
momentous to them.

Friday, Sept. 6ᵗʰ ¼ to 11 P.M.

Have expected to hear of a battle at Washington today— but none
yet. Rec'd a letter tonight from Simmons— has rec'd a Commission of
Commissary of Vol., rank of Capt. He writes his disgust of Gen'l Fremont— enclosed a letter to Postmaster Gen. M. Blair,[37] which I forwarded— as Sam left it to my judgment & I thought that Fremont's
failings ought to be made known. He represents F. as a great humbug—
given to bombastic swellings and surrounded with foreign officers and
California vampires. Benj. Farrar has written unfavorably of Fremont too.
His wife Jessie Benton[38] is silly & vainglorious & the man will prove
himself a fool before the Nation.   •

I wrote back to Simmons & then wrote to SM & Farrar— then
read in Dickens' *Great Expectations*[39] & now at eleven o'clock, when I
feel that the masses of people are asleep & I think of the great armies
lying in camps near the Potomac— armed with stores of military supplies— hundreds of cannon & thousands of muskets— over 200,000 of
men drawn up and seeking each other's lives. The power of the nation

[37]Montgomery Blair (1813–75) was Postmaster General in Lincoln's cabinet from
1861 to 1864, and practiced law with Franklin Dick after the war.
[38]Jessie Benton Frémont (1824–1902) was the ambitious daughter of Thomas Hart
Benton, leader of the anti-slavery Democrats in Missouri. She eloped with John Frémont,
and actively supported his career.
[39]*Great Expectations* had been serialized in Dickens' popular magazine, *All the Year
Round*, from December 1860 to August 1861.

there concentrated— The Southern masses seeking the destruction of the nation! The Northern assembled to defend it, & anxious to rush southward & carry death, devastation, and destruction with them— what a fearful sight it appears to me.

At night, I can in my mind's eye, see these opposing armies & behind them, the two divisions of the country, opposed to each other. And what a sight for this nation thus to be standing before their God.

The gov't is daily arresting Traitors everywhere. It has cut off all traveling southward, & no one can leave the country (except to Canada) without a pass-port; and no letters can now be sent south. Until within a few days, letters south were mailed to Louisville and carried thence by Adams Express. But the Gov't has stopped this. The refusal of passes to cross our lines at Washington & a strict guard along the Potomac, I think must have cut off the Rebels' means of information. Our newspapers have not for a month reported any movement of our troops East of the mountains & no one knows the force at Washington, nor where it is stationed, nor even what defensive works have been constructed below Washington & Harpers Ferry— nor can we get any information of the movements or force of the Rebels. They seem to be advancing towards our lines at W. C., but all is secret, & when & what they will strike is scarcely hinted at.

The Rebels are doing enormous mischief in Missouri— rising up all through the State— They seem to be ubiquitous. In N.E. Mo., Martin Green[40] keeps his 2,000 men together & goes about devastating. But a small force is there to oppose him & has not yet met him. Fremont does not accomplish anything. It is said that McCullough[41] has gone south towards Arkansas, Rains[42] towards Kansas. Trains on H. [Hannibal] & St. Jo. [Joseph] [Rail] Road are fired into nearly every day—

---

[40]Martin Green (1815–63) became a Missouri guerilla fighter at the outbreak of the Civil War. Frémont was blamed for not stopping Green's marauding in northern Missouri.

[41]Benjamin McCulloch (1811–62) joined the Confederate forces in Texas and fought Lyon at the Battle of Wilson's Creek. McCulloch had various commands in Arkansas, marauded into Missouri, and tried to enlist Indians to fight for the Confederacy. As a brigadier general, he was killed at the Battle of Pea Ridge in March 1862.

[42]James E. Rains (?-?) was a Missouri senator before the war, then brigadier general in the Missouri State Guard fighting at Dug Springs, Wilson's Creek, and Lexington.

Monday Night — 10½ — Sept. 9th

The last two days the events have been the usual ones, not narrated in the papers, & making quiet unexcited days— Today has been the same— Preparations for the great battle at Washington have been growing— I saw it stated today that a Person from W.C. says McClellan has 150,000 troops— but there is no reliability in any statements on the subject. Nor do we know anything about the number of the Rebels in Va., therefore they are put down by some at under 100,000 but commonly believed to be largely over that— Which side has the largest number is not known, but the Rebels are supposed to exceed.

In Ky., the decision is unmade as yet. The Rebels have entered the State on the S.W. and Gen'l. Grant[43] has sent troops of the U.S. to Paducah; & a battle is expected. Benj. Farrar writes me that the commencing of martial law in Missouri begins to show in the trepidation of the Traitors. I should like to hear that Fremont had executed a number of leading ones in St. Louis. Gov. Gamble having turned out the Rebel Police Commissioners, St. Louis ought to be very safe now for true men & very hot for traitors.

I have been feeling rather tired today at the protracted inaction I am under. I have many business letters to write; but I want congenial companions or active employment. Today I have felt a little like going to St. Louis; though I believe I would soon tire of it there. The weather here has been delightful ever since we came here which was Wednesday, August 21st. We have had very little rain & clear, cool, delightful days and not a single warm night. There is not nearly so much excitement as I supposed there would be at Fremont's proclamation of Martial Law in Mo. & freedom to the slaves of Rebels. The loyal papers all I believe approve of it— The Admn. has not pronounced upon it; & no doubt will leave it to the General as his own matter.; for in the face of the general approval of it, the President could not safely disapprove it.

---

[43]Ulysses Simpson Grant (1822–85) was named a colonel in the Illinois Infantry at the start of the Civil War. He was then sent to Missouri, rising from colonel to brigadier general, with great success in battles. As commander of the Union armies, he finally forced Lee's surrender at Appomattox, giving generous terms. Grant was commissioned the first full general since George Washington.

Before the Battle at Bull's Run, I bought 1,000 U.S. $ Missouri 6 per c. bonds at 44 c.[44] I have just sold them at same price— for ever since then, they have been below that— in the present distracted condition of the State, I see little chance of its paying anything for a long time. But the effect of freeing the Rebel's slaves is the rise of the State bonds from 40 to 44½ within four or five days. This is also in connection with the feeling of growing confidence in the North, from assurance of safety of W.C. & the successful result of the U.S. fleet in capturing Fort Hatteras.

Every day the People are subscribing to the Gov't loan of Treasury Notes at 7‰ interest. Frank Blair, since the adjournment of Congress, has been in St. Louis staying at Ben Farrar's & Ben writes that as Fremont is so absorbed by getting up his bodyguard and making a swell, that Frank is sought after by those who go to St. Louis to make known the distress of the interior. The *N. Y. Times* today has a severe letter on Fremont from St. Louis on this conduct of his.[45]

West Chester, Sept. 21st, 1861, Saturday

On opening this book, I am astonished to find I have not written in it since the 9th. Since then, no great event in the field has occurred— during part of it, the expectation of a battle at Washington was great, but the last few days the Rebels have not shown signs of attacking— The lines of our defenses have now been so strengthened that an attack on them is regarded as very unlikely at Washn.—

The Rebels say they have several miles of concealed batteries at Acquia Creek,[46] by which they can any hour cut the navigation of the

[44]During the Civil War, both governments sold large numbers of bonds to finance their military expenses.

[45]Frémont was looked down upon in St. Louis for the gaudily uniformed Hungarian and Italian officers who protected him and kept him unavailable to the people of the state. On August 30, 1861, Frémont issued a proclamation of martial law, death to guerillas, confiscation of their property, and freedom to their slaves. This infuriated Lincoln, who was attempting to keep Kentucky in the Union. Frémont sent his wife to persuade Lincoln to support him, but her efforts made the situation worse.

[46]The battle of Aquia Creek (May 29–June 1, 1861) involved three Union ships firing on Confederate batteries near the mouth of Aquia Creek, a minor tributary to the Potomac near Fredericksburg. A rail line to Richmond ended nearby, protected by the batteries, which the Confederates later abandoned.

Potomac. This fact is doubted by us. An examination has been made there
& the report discredited. Our army has steadily increased at Wash. Cy.
and is now believed to be about 200,000, but the papers are not permitted
now to publish any fact that will aid the enemy.

The Rebels have been driven out of St. Joseph within the last few
days. Martin Green has also withdrawn from N.E. Mo. and crossed the
Mo. River— This looks as if the northern part of the State was being
given up by the Enemy, but they are threatening Booneville and Lexington— There has been a battle at both places, but the result is not known.

Last Sunday the 15th, Genl. Fremont had Col. Frank P. Blair
arrested— on charges for using disrespectful language & leaking complaints to Washn. Cty. of the Genl. The President has relied upon Frank
to keep him informed of the management of Fremont: & Frank has been
greatly distressed for some time past about it, for Fremont has totally
neglected the important duties of his station and given himself up to California speculators, flatterers &c— Frank made known the Genl's incom-
petency to the Pres. Jessie Fremont went on & got knowledge of the letter
Frank wrote, & and went back & had Frank arrested. M. Blair, Postmaster Genl. and Genl. M. Meigs went to St. Louis to look into the matter—
They returned to Wash. on Wednesday, since when the Cabinet have had
the matter under advisement.[47]

Wed., Sept. 25

The last few days have been anxious & distressing. I have been
much troubled about Frank Blair's position. The Cabinet have had Fremont's defects under consideration. The abolition papers have been howling in his favor on account of his proclamation freeing the slaves of
Rebels, & this has bolstered him up & made the President cautious about

---

[47]President Lincoln had asked Frank Blair to advise him of events in Missouri after
Blair's return from Washington in August. Frank realized that Frémont was not able to
command the Department of the West effectively and tried to help him. On September 1,
1861, he wrote his brother Montgomery about the dangers in Missouri, praising Frémont
but pointing out his incompetence. Montgomery showed the letter to the president, who
sent Blair and Quartermaster Montgomery Meigs to St. Louis to investigate and counsel.

touching him. In the meanwhile, Jesse Fremont is filling the papers with false reports.

And there has been a fearful battle at Lexington— The Mo. Rebels under Price with Claib. Jackson, 25,000 strong, invaded Lexington, & Col. Mulligan of Chicago, being cut off from water, was forced to surrender— his army was over 3,000— All the officers are kept prisoners & the men released, on oath not to fight again. This has produced a tremendous uproar against Fremont & on Tuesday, all the New York papers, even the *Tribune* included, came out strongly against Fremont.

I thought yesterday & today that the President would certainly remove him: but this Ev'ng's Paper says Fremont is to take the field, & that the President will give him an opportunity of redeeming his character.

Benj. McCullough has a large army & is marching to join Price at Lexington. Their joint forces, with such others as they can gather, under Rains, Monroe Parsons,[48] Martin Green, Tom Harris &c. will exceed 40,000 men. Sturgis[49] from St. Joseph was on his way to reinforce Lexington with about 4,000 men. His force, I fear, has been cut off. Several Regiments went from St. Louis towards Lexington by River, & I fear also for them— If their forces are cut off, there will be great probability of the defeat of Fremont. What force he will take to Jefferson, the point I suppose he will aim for, I know not, but probably 20,000 men; & it may well be expected that the victorious and numerous Rebel Army will defeat him. If so, St. Louis will certainly be in great danger. So much for Mr. Fremont's inefficiency.

This is lamentable, all of Missouri south of the Mo. River in possession of the enemy— What wretched mismanagement & yet the President dares to keep Fremont in his place. Is it not fearful and wretched to think of so much being perilled because the President fears to remove Fremont.

[48]Mosby Monroe Parsons (1822–65) supported Governor Jackson, served in the Missouri State Guard, and became a brigadier general in the Confederate army. He was commander of Price's van at Lexington and fought in the battle of Prairie Grove.

[49]Samuel D. Sturgis (1822–76), at the start of the Civil War, was ordered by Lyon to bring his battalion of trained Indian-fighting cavalry to reinforce Lyon's troops in southwest Missouri. He fought at Wilson's Creek and commanded the Union retreat to Rolla.

And along our lines across the Potomac near Washington, the
Rebels are erecting fortifications & it seems to me that McClellan must
attack them. I expect a great battle there every day. If the Rebels are successful there, what will be the result? Will the North give up the contest
& let the Secession States go? I can not answer, but for myself, I trust not.
Better fight on & draft men and enlist the Negroes and take even the
Slaves into the army, rather than yield to the enemy. For such a result
would, I fear, lead to a miserable cowardly submission by the North to the
South. They could ask anything and make any terms.

I believe the North will have to resort to drafting. The Rebels have
forced all into their ranks; & thus they keep up their army. But the Admn.
is slow & halting & always has been & never does anything at the right
time.

In the last few days, things in Kentucky have assumed a warlike cast.
Genl. Anderson[50] has taken the field; & the Rebels have invaded the
State. There will be terrible fighting in that State, which still stands to the
Union. This is a dark & gloomy time. I know not what to think.

I have hitherto felt great confidence in our strength; but it seems
that the enemy out-numbers us on every field, & we gain no victories over
them. When the troops from the free states were taken in to Missouri, I
felt that our success there was certain & would be speedy & thorough.
But by the most wretched mismanagement, we have lost & lost, until now
the odds are all decidedly against us. What Frank Blair is to do is all dark
to me. When Lexington fell, I thought that Fremont would fall— but
now that he retains command, how Frank is to be reinstated, unless after
fearful disasters, is what I can not see. Ab. Linc. [Lincoln] was miserably
in error when he had Fremont called from Europe to take command in
Missouri.

---

[50]William Anderson (1840–64) was called Bloody Bill for his habit of riding into
battle with Union scalps hanging on his saddle. He was raised in Missouri, and joined
Confederate guerilla Colonel William C. Quantrill on the Kansas-Missouri border in
1862 as one of his lieutenants.

October 1861

"Accustomed to peace all our lives & to feel perfectly secure against the effects of war raging in other countries, we felt as if we were forever safe & had no concern but that of our individual prosperity & happiness."

Philadelphia— Sunday, Oct. 6, 1861

We left West Chester on Wednesday, October 2nd, & came to Phila. to N.W. cor. Spruce & 9th. I was going to St. Louis to help Frank Blair, who was released & re-arrested by Fremont— but Benj. Farrar came on to Washington, & Tuesday telegraphed me that Frank was ordered to be released— Apo.[51] went out with Benj. on Tuesday night— On Thursday, I felt miserably depressed— The President fears to remove Fremont— & Missouri is bleeding at every pore— the abolitionists have made Fremont's cause theirs, & his dependents through the press & wires make his cause clamorous, so he is retained to waste money & sacrifice all our interests in Mo.

Kentucky too is being overrun by the Rebels— The Admin. is so slow & weak hearted— so old fogeyish & faulty that they never try to save a State until it is lost— Our army at Washington now is very strong, supposed to be largely over 200,000 but no forward movement is yet made— The truth is the Rebel power is enormous— Their activity &

[51]Apolline Agatha Alexander Blair (1824–1908) was the wife of Frank Blair and sister of Myra Alexander Dick, wife of Franklin Dick.

21

energy makes them truly a formidable enemy— It seems to me that the South is all energy & devotion to their Cause; while the North is dull, & slow & impassionedly indifferent—

I attribute this much to the fault of the President— He is emphatically, not a war man— he is for peace & easy blows, when he has any to strike— If we had a young, bold, & vigorous President, who was ready to sacrifice him-self to save the Country, he could lift up the People as one man & precipitate them on the Rebels. But Lincoln is always watching the lines of the Constitution, & looking for rays of peace & good intentions amongst a set of determined Rebels, & he does not act as if he knew the only safety was in subduing them. He believes Fremont is not a safe man, & yet he permits him still to control in Missouri. What is to be the result? I can not answer. I have not felt yet as if we will not conquer the Rebels, but yet the South is so completely under their subjection that I can not see through to the end.

We have had so little to encourage us, & they get & keep such large armies together all along the line— from Washington through Ky. & in Mo. & they rise up in such numbers wherever our troops appear, that thus far there seems to be no progress making against them.

Phila   October 7, 1861.

Willie[52] went first to school—

Phila   Tuesday, October 8, 1861

Yesterday went with Geo. Alexander[53] to see Jackson about making cartridges— Yesterday & to-day I feel much depressed about matters, & especially in Missouri. A few days ago I believed that Fremont would be superseded; but the last few days, it looks as if he would not— I think the President greatly in fault in not removing him, in view of the facts.

[52]William Alexander Dick (1855–1945) was the oldest child of Myra and Franklin Dick.
[53]George Alexander (1829–?) was Apolline Alexander Blair's and Myra Alexander Dick's brother and Franklin Dick's brother-in-law. Alexander and Dick were involved in a cartridge-making business at the beginning of the Civil War.

18   West Chester —   Phila.

What Frank. Blair is to do, is all dark to me,
When Lexington fell, I thought that Fremont
would fall — but now that he retains command, how Frank. is to be reinstated
unless after fearful disasters, is what
I can not see.
Mr. Frank. was miserably in error when
He had Fremont called from Europe to
take command in Missouri.

     Philadelphia —
   Sunday Oct 6. 1861
We left West Chester on Wednesday Oct 2d. &
came to Phila to N. W. Cor. Spruce & 9th.
I was going to St. Louis to help Frank. Blair who
was released & re-arrested by Fremont — but
Ben. Farrar came on to Washington & Tuesday
telegraphed me that Frank. was ~~released~~
ordered to be released —
Apo. went out with Ben. on Tuesday night —
On Thursday I felt miserably depressed — the
President fears to remove Fremont — & Missouri is bleeding at every pore — The abolitionists have made Fremonts cause theirs, &
his dependents through the press & wires make
his cause clamorous & he is retained to waste
money & I despair of all our interests in Mo.

Kentucky too is being over run by the Rebels —
The Admin is so slow & weak hearted — so old
fogyish & faulty that they never try to save a
State until it is lost —
Our army at Washington now is very strong.

Page 18 of Franklin Dick's first journal shows his handwriting. Photo by R. L. Geyer © 2007.

But the vice of the times seems to be in a great degree, the want of competency in the President to cope with the emergencies of the day— Oh how deplorable is the condition of the border slave states; & as I believe owing to Lincoln's faltering policy— the Rebels in the Southern States are not molested— Well, we must bear it. It is the Lord's will—

I have been so much perplexed what to do— My mind is kept in such anxiety that I can hardly read anything but the papers— I cannot settle upon any plans— I cannot take my Family to St. Louis with any assurance of continued safety there— for I fear still greater reverses there— with Fremont I fear that the Rebels may get full possession of the State— even of St. Louis, and while all is so uncertain; I do not feel able to decide upon any plans. And while matters in Virginia remain uncertain, it is difficult to decide upon anything.

Genl. McClellan is acting with great care & prudence, & rightly too. Should his army be defeated, the consequences would be most disastrous. It seems to be his object to await an attack, which becomes daily more probable— Lately the enemy have fallen back & his lines have been pushed out to Munson's Hill, Mann's Hill, Falls Church, &c. But he will not do more than that, but goes on increasing his army in number & efficiency & organization. He keeps his purpose to himself, & all that can be learned is, that he intends having no reverse— I give him honor for his prudence & moderation & great care & self-control. For the last ten days, there has been very little done.

Sunday Morning, Oct. 20, 1861, Phila. — 9th & Spruce

I feel so dispirited this morning instead of going to Church, I stay to write. I could have gone to St. Louis but have stayed on account of the powder business. Dr. Bartholow arrived here on the 18th & yesterday I got the papers executed. As it remains uncertain about that, that is the success of it, we therefore continue at this house— but for this, I believe I could take my family to St. Louis— though that is by no means certain— The last 3 months I have been awaiting the turn of events— Sometimes, I feel as if the rebellion will be put down; at other times I feel great doubt about it. This feeling of doubt has grown up comparatively of late, & is from the want of success of our arms, along with the increase of the secession feeling in the South— Large numbers of Union true men there have become secessionists, for the war to them is growing to be one of subjugation— and again— the Union men of the South are so weak & inefficient that they seem to have no power— even in Missouri, in the interim, the Rebels seem to carry all before them, & to meet with but little resistance from the Union men. If the Southern People are really united to accomplish their independence, the war is a very different one from what it was in the beginning, & it begins to look decidedly so. Hence the growing doubts in my mind as to the result.

Very much is said about interference by England and France, both here & in those countries, & the disposition of England is decidedly to acknowledge the South— mainly on account of its free trade principles; and the increasing opposite principles in the North— These various matters seem to render the final result of this struggle uncertain— the North has been in a state of suspense ever since the battle of Bull Run— Sometimes we get confidence & at other times become depressed— this feeling dependant in part upon the small successes or reversals of the occasional conflicts.

In Missouri, matters remain still miserable— Fremont has not yet met the enemy & it is uncertain if he ever will— though it looks somewhat now as if Price was turning southward to fall upon him, with Hardee[54] & others in overwhelming force. Cameron[55] & Adj. Genl. Thomas[56] went out to Missouri a few days ago to remove him, but left without doing it— Though I believe he will be removed in a few days— But the Admn. halts & fears to do it, while ruin overruns the State.

I look upon the Admn. as greatly deficient— they want the souls & hearts of men in this immense struggle— The People wait & wait upon them— but should we meet with any great reverse, it is impossible to tell

[54]William J. Hardee (1815–73) published a book that explained Napoleonic tactics of war and was used by both Union and Confederate troops. When the Civil War began, he resigned from the Union army and became a Confederate brigadier general.

[55]Simon Cameron (1799–1889) was Lincoln's secretary of war. He filled his department with inept political and personal appointments; he was charged with corruption, buying guns that did not work, and forcing General Winfield Scott's resignation.

[56]George Henry Thomas (1816–70) was born in Virginia and served in the army after graduating from West Point. When the Civil War began, he stayed in the Union army as a colonel, alienating his family, and rose to major general.

what effects it would produce in the north— possibly the rising up of a powerful anti-war party. But my belief is that such party would be overwhelmed— & the President called upon to resign & have a new President elected by the House of Reps., who should be a strong hearted war man—

My thoughts & feelings are mainly absorbed by these matters— I can think of little else; & others are like me— I am every day of late engaged in getting up the powder business & suppose we will hang on here as we are, while that remains unfinished— Oh how fearful & uncertain seems everything at this time. Europe is in an unsettled & threatening State— The Revolution in Italy hardly yet settled— The fate of the Pope, new shorn of his temporal power to a small compass; yet is confined. A war between Hungary & Austria not improbable— England & France watching each other: and both threatened with internal revolutions. Our prosperous country now frustrated & unhappy— And then all these dreadful things so unnecessary— No war was ever more foolish and unnecessary than this Southern Revolt— It is impossible to realize the full extent of this war on this country— or to anticipate its effects.[57]

Accustomed to peace all our lives & to feel perfectly secure against the effects of war raging in other countries, we felt as if we were forever safe & had no concern but that of our individual prosperity & happiness. When now, no one can tell where the war is to run to— To yield the independence of the South, would be to establish a foreign hostile wicked & ambitions nation alongside of us. We would not have peace with them, & a peace now made would only give them ample opportunity to strengthen themselves to wage a future war upon us—

They detest democracy— & are in every way opposed & hostile to us. So that if we let them go, they will turn upon us with hatred & rage— If we hold on to them, & subdue them, we have a continued strife with them, while our Democratic Constitution stands. They will oppose the North always, complain of it— & compel the North to treat them with

[57]There was little news from Europe in the censored newspapers, and Dick was concerned that England and France might recognize and support the Confederacy. The Italian city states had been a battleground for centuries between France and the Hapsburgs, and the war to liberate Italy had been going on since 1848. German unrest came partly from William I of Prussia and Bismark, his prime minister, scheming against the Austrian Empire.

intolerance & severity. Indeed, the prospect is a sad one— The will of the Almighty is inscrutable— It looks as if he was letting the Devil loose amongst us— I do not wonder at it, for I think the Nation deserved it. My only comfort is in the belief that the Lord reigneth. Hope in Man's power, I have none—

My daily prayer to God is that the Nation may be preserved, & turned unto Him— & that all the earth may acknowledge the precious Lord & Savior, Jesus Christ— In the mercy of God alone, have I any hope— that the People may become sensible of His power & their dependence upon Him is my only hope for them.

Phila., Oct. 27, — 1861 — Phila. 9th & Spruce

The past has been a week of anxiety & gloom & sorrow— the dreadful slaughter of our men at Ball's Bluff near Edwards Ferry— & the blockade of the Potomac— The strain upon the public mind— the incessant daily expectation of a general battle across the Potomac— & the interest about our naval affairs— all have kept us anxious & incessantly concerned— The Rebels showing themselves in such force at the extremes of their lines, looks as if they are very strong in the centre— & their active & effective operations at these extremes; along with our having accomplished nothing during the past week— & the rumors of disagreement between McClellan & Scott— all make us fearful and wretched— Then the hesitancy of the Admn. about Fremont— I have believed in the last week four different ways as to his removal— & that has been so, for the last many weeks—[58]

Great dissatisfaction exists with the Admn.— They accomplish nothing & are almost hidden from the public eye. It is their vascillations, rather than their actions, we hear of— I feel compelled to say that during

[58]The Battle of Ball's Bluff on October 21, 1861, was a Union disaster. The battle took place on the Potomac where Harrison's Island divides Maryland and Virginia with a seventy-foot cliff on the Virginia side called Ball's Bluff. Union Colonel Edward Baker, without checking the Confederate troops and with insufficient boats, led his men across the Potomac. Meanwhile in the woods above the bluff, Confederate Brigadier General Nathan G. Evans fought with Union Colonel Willis A. Gorman's brigade, driving them back to the bluff. Baker was shot, and many Union troops were killed, wounded, or missing.

the past week I have often thought upon the subject whether or not we can put down this rebellion— It is so assuming the shape of a war between hostile nations— that this doubt increases. It is getting so amongst the People of the South— & is so taking the shape of conquest, that the probability is changing every month. There being no union party as such— & all union feeling being now treason in the South— it seems to me that it will be impossible to conquer the South, unless we have the most astounding & thorough victories over their armies, so as effectually to annihilate them— They as a war power have certainly grown stronger each month— and when I know that this is a war in which their gentlemen are concerned so numerously— a large proportion of their society— & very many from the necessity of not standing opposed to their States—

When all officers are on that side (civil as well as military)— and I bear in mind their vigor— and proficiency in war— their determination & desperate purposes— their intolerance at home to any show of opposition to the Southern interests— and feeling that a real belief in the cause exists amongst their <u>ruling men</u>— the hatred & deep rooted prejudice against the north— their untiring activity is always presenting to us a formidable line of troops & batteries— the fact that they are to perpetuate their existence as a nation, always, by being here eminently warlike— & maintaining an immense standing army— therefore seeing that if every officer feels that his present calling is for his life— & the same spirit spreading amongst the soldiers—

When so many millions of men— with such interests, all— all at stake, are embarked in the war— and thus forming a military government which can maintain it-self by <u>taking</u> with strong hand the means of sustaining it-self— O— I can see no destruction of it but by the destruction of the army.

(above— written at noon)

later— night

Since writing above, I have heard from Horace Furness that some weeks ago, Genl. McClellan was so disheartened at the slow enlistments, that he serious contemplated a public appeal to the country, to come forward & enroll themselves— At that time, the enemy was believed to have 3 to our one. Now they outnumber us— & from Lieut. Hays, just arrived from General McCall's division, we hear that McClellan does not intend attacking the Rebels at their entrenchments—

I am relieved to hear that!— for to do so, would be to great a risk— and they, when satisfied of it, will I hope, move off, or else come out & attack our troops from behind their entrenchments— Here then, we are to have probably weeks of delay & comparative inaction. But as our navy is rapidly increasing, & the Southerners suffering from being cut off from all the world, they must suffer more than we. And if the great fleet of about 80 sail about to start from Hampton Roads shall be successful & achieve a great victory by taking some important place, it will it is hoped, have the effect of bearing off a considerable part of the Rebel army from Va.

In Mo., Fremont still follows Price towards the S.W. It seems that Price is really falling back; & so far as I can tell, the Confederates are not sending troops into the State. There seems now to be good hope that their army will be driven from Missouri. How wretchedly the State is cut up by their maraudings— For some time past, North Missouri seems to have been quiet.

Apo. writes that Frank Blair is thinking of coming on to Washington in hope of getting something done for Missouri— I suppose she means getting Fremont removed. Frank is greatly disheartened; for he is lying in St. Louis, trying to recruit his Regt., which has now but a few companies filled— a part of it is in one place & part another— But Frank is not ordered to any active duty— Apo. writes that Frank ought to have commanded the companies that lately went to Pilot Knob and had part in the successful conflict at Frederick Town. Frank is in a most unfortunate position— The Germans[59] uphold Fremont; & they are our mainstay in St. Louis— It some time since, was a constant subject of pain to me to think about his unfortunate position. Fremont's strength through his proclamation[60] is the difficulty in removing him.

---

[59]Many German immigrants joined the anti-slavery "Republican Wide-Awakes," organized by Frank Blair. They paraded through the streets and caused many pro-South citizens to fear mob violence. The immigrant populations were large and powerful, and both the Unionists and Confederates wanted their support.

[60]On August 30, 1861, General John Frémont declared martial law in Missouri, ordering that secessionist's slaves be freed and their property seized. Lincoln criticized Frémont's proclamation, telling him to amend it.

I find that those I talk with, my friends— the strongest war people— have, of late, been growing uncertain of the final result— & today,
Uncle E.[61] said that he has money on hand, but the last few days has not
decided whether or not to further invest in Government loan— & he says
it is the first time he has had doubts in the subject— He is so firm—
when he begins to doubt, the doubting may well waver—

The question is, will we be able to put down the rebellion? I am in
serious doubt about it— If we only could know the numbers the enemy
have under arms— & the means they control, I could better judge. How
they keep such large armies paid & subsisted is what cannot be understood.[62] We know very little about them, & nothing accurately. The probabilities seem to me not to be in our favor at this time. If they succeed,
whether or not they will get Missouri and Kentucky, can not be
answered— but I strongly believe that they will not— But all is uncertain
& my only trust is in God. This evng. dear little Frank[63] is right sick—
threatened with pneumonia.

[61]Dick named one of his sons for his uncle, Evans Rogers, an iron merchant.

[62]McClellan's critics charged him with overestimating the number of Rebel troops
against him, but it was not known to be true until he had fallen from favor. Faust, *Historical Times*, 456.

[63]Frank Madison Dick (1860–1936) was the fourth son of Franklin and Myra
Dick.

November 1861

1 Lincoln appoints McClellan as general-in-chief of all Union forces

2 Lincoln relieves Frémont of this command, replaces him with Hunter

4 Pro-South legislators meet at Neosho, pass ordinance of secession and elect congressmen and senators to Confederate Congress

7 Union troops occupy Fort Walker and Fort Beauregard at Port Royal, South Carolina

8 Two Confederate officials sailing toward England are seized by the U.S. Navy

9 Henry W. Halleck takes over command of the Department of Missouri

18 Hunter relinquishes command to Halleck

28 Missouri admitted to Confederacy, but state still under Union control and not considered part of Confederacy by Union

"Oh, what a dismal, dreadful thing this war is."

Tuesday, Nov. 5, 1861   Phila. — Cor. 9th & Spruce

I have felt a good deal dispirited since I last wrote— War matters stand about as they did— The naval expedition sailed this day week Oct. 29th & even its destination is not yet known. We hope it will accomplish something— but we have met with so many disasters, that hope does not rise very high—

Genl. Winfield Scott retired three or 4 days ago from the Army, & McClellan elevated to his place. That is a great gain, I believe— Fremont's order of supercision has gone out— but as he is near Springfield, we have not heard yet of its delivery to him. It is somewhat doubtful what he will do— He has so many foreigners dependent entirely upon him under him, they may induce him to revolt.

I have felt somewhat dispirited about the powder business. Our little lever machine is just finished today but the moulds not made for it, nor can we get them for a few days— The pistol cartridge moulds we got today & this P.M. will make sure of— But we have been waiting on the little machinery & on Dr. Bartholow's experiments; until I have gotten to feeling almost dispirited about them.

Geo. Alexander got home Saturday night from Washington & goes next week to Paducah to leave his wife there. He seems to think we can not do much until Congress meets. The sale of the cartridges in the market here, does not promise much to me; & is a small business I could not consent to carry on. But for this cartridge matter, I could take my family to St. Louis— & yet I do not feel at all disposed to go there, excepting to have something to do.

I keep the time running away fast enough— but the uncertainty about the cartridge keep[s] me suspended— Going about to Jackson's & to Hollingsworth's a while every day, keep me interested wearily in the business— but the slowness & uncertainty keeps me dispirited—

Frank & Apo. got here on Wednesday last. He went to Washington & goes to St. Louis in a few days— She goes with her children to Silver Spring tomorrow—[64] No one knows at all whether or not there will be a battle at Washington— The armies lie there— The Potomac continues blockaded by the Rebels & little stirring occurs— In Missouri, Fremont has been straggling down towards Price in his retreat towards Arkansas—[65] Meanwhile the marauders through the State devastate it. James S. Rollins,[66] Willard P. Hall,[67] Bob Wilson and others as Refugees are

[64]Silver Spring was the country home of Francis P. Blair Sr. The Blair family moved back and forth between the Blair/Lee houses in Washington and their place at Silver Spring.

[65]Lincoln sent Secretary of War Cameron to St. Louis to decide whether to remove Frémont. Cameron gave Frémont one more chance to capture Confederate troops or to be replaced. When nothing happened, Lincoln sent General Hunter to succeed Frémont unless he had won a battle or was fighting one. Luckily, Hunter arrived before Frémont could lead his troops to battle the next day, as he had promised. Frémont did not know the Confederate forces were farther than sixty miles away at that time.

[66]James S. Rollins (1812–88) was a friend of Frank Blair's from Kentucky.

[67]Willard Preble Hall (1820–82), a Yale attorney, was lieutenant governor when Hamilton Gamble died in January 1864. Hall completed Gamble's term of office, resisting Sterling Price's raids on the state. He had the state legislature authorize the voters to call a

staying in St. Louis— Gov. Gamble is in Washington asking arms for his State troops— It is very gloomy now—

Yesterday we dined at Fairman Rogers[68] & in evng. to Sister Mary's—[69] This evng. Myra & I go to Aunt H.'s to tea— We went there to tea tonight week; & we were all at Uncle Evans' Saturday evng. to tea—

Phila Wed Evng. November 6, 1861   Corner 9th & Spruce

This has been a cloudy, gloomy day & this evng., it pours rain— I have felt discontented & gloomy today— I feel so tired of waiting & waiting— Our powder business drags on so slowly, that I cannot help feeling dispirited & today I talked of giving up my interest in it & taking my family back to St. Louis to stay— There I can do some professional business, whereas the longer I remain away (if I do return at all) the worse it will be.

This A.M. & P.M. George & I went down to Jackson's & had young Jackson at work making the pistol cartridges with a single mould. He made them at the rate of 33 in 10 minutes, which is 200 an hour & 2,000 in a day, viz 10 hours— George glued 125 to the balls this morning & they make quite a good appearance.

The Mifs. Biddles have telegraphed from St. Louis that they want my house— but I declined to let them have it as I do not know as yet whether I will go back soon—

News from the fleet today is that it was near Bulls Bay, in neighborhood of Charleston— Its destination is probably Beaufort— Heard today that Fremont had read a letter retiring from Command of the Army of the West, & started for St. Louis. I am glad he did not cut any fool tricks in doing so— Good riddance of him— Hunter[70] for the present takes command there & I hope will soon drive the Rebel forces over the Arkansas line—

---

new constitutional convention to decide on emancipation and the electoral franchise oaths.

[68]Fairman Rogers (1833–1900) was a first cousin to Franklin Dick, related through Franklin's mother, Hannah Rogers.

[69]Franklin Dick's sister, Mary, was married to Peter Hill Engle.

[70]David Hunter (1802–86) served in the Union army and was severely wounded in the First Battle of Bull Run. He took over command of the Western Department from Frémont and later controlled the Department of the South, where he started the first

The Army still lies at Washington. McClellan is busy just now as commander of the Army, in getting an understanding of the entire army of the Country— I shall look for vigor and efficiency under him. It is a matter of entire doubt whether he will move on Manassas, & I must say I do not want him to do it. Should the Southern expedition strike such an effective blow as to diminish Beauregard's army much, then McClellan will probably attack him—

But the expectation rather seems to be that he will take part of the army to some other point for offensive operations— As to the great question, can we put down the Rebels, I remain in doubt. If we can defeat their Grand Army of the Potomac, I shall hope to suppress them; but while they have a large undefeated force, we cannot do it.

Whether the war will be long or short, is not much talked about now— There is some impatience that McClellan shall strike; but generally the feeling seems to be to leave it to him. It is published, that he says he intends to be uninfluenced by any power or persons— I hope so— The British newspapers of late seem much more friendly than they were 2 months ago & it now comes out that we were 3 months ago on the verge of a war with England on the privateering question. Russell[71] says so in his letter.

Whether the U.S. will be able to borrow as much money as it needs if the war lasts longer is a serious question; but not much is said about it. I think the subscription to the loan of late has been rather slack. One thing is very certain, that but for this cartridge business, I could go to St. Louis to stay. It seems to me now that my family could stay there in safety—[72] Aura Farrar writes that since the autumn returners have got back, it seems pretty much as it was. I do not believe now that there will be much more fighting in Missouri. Slavery there is I think about ended— Valuable Negroes cannot be kept there with any safety—

Negro regiment to be used as guards on plantations and towns.

[71]William (Billy) Howard Russell (1820–1907) was an Irish reporter for *The Times* (London). His dispatches covering the Civil War were published in Union and Confederate papers. Scorning Americans, he became an unpopular correspondent in both the North and South.

[72]Franklin Dick rented a house for his family in Philadelphia, at the corner of 9th and Spruce streets, for the winter. Missouri and St. Louis suffered from the guerilla raids during the war, and he was concerned about his family's safety if they moved back to St. Louis.

Oh, what a dismal, dreadful thing this war is— I am so, so tired of it & of the state of uncertainty— May God in his mercy protect and preserve this nation.

Sunday Evng. Nov. 10, 1861 — Cor. 9th & Spruce

The last few days the feeling has been rather better. Hope for success to the fleet which we have learned has reached Port Royal Harbor, S.C. has kept the public mind interested— An attack from Cairo on Belmont opposite Columbus, Ky. has interested the People & not being a downright disaster, has given some relief. The change of Scott to McClellan & Fremont's removal, have also given relief— of late I have been feeling a good deal the want of some position— Here in the East, I have none— and I have felt perhaps I ought to go back to St. Louis— But that is of small weight with me— but I have been feeling it was necessary for me to be looking after my business interests in St. Louis & on Friday & yesterday I made up my mind to go back there to see whether or not it will be worth while for me to remain there during the winter—

I believe the powder business will be successful; but as it will be some time perhaps mid-winter before that can be known. I feel that it is unsafe for me to risk losing my business relations in St. Louis, for this uncertainty. From the looks of things, war will not reach St. Louis, and there is some business there for me to do— & as I must be making some money or spend capital, I therefore have felt that it is safest for me to go back. I could remain here until the powder business is settled, were it not that the longer my absence from St. Louis, the worse it will be for my business there. Therefore, reluctantly, I feel that it is best for me to go back, & leave George Alexander, assisted by Lewis, to work along the powder business.

Myra seems much averse to going back, but is willing for me to do what I deem best— So I will go out on Tuesday & expect to have her come in a week or two afterwards. One matter that has had a slight influence with me is the probability that Missouri will ere long become a free State— But I long for some home— a house in which we can rest again & feel that we have a home.

December 1861

"I see now, as things appear to me, very little prospect of reconstructing the Country."

St. Louis Dec. 26, 1861 Thursday

Mem. Did not write any in this book last night. I wrote in small book having left this one at my office until today—[73]

On Monday, Nov. 11 at night left Phila. for St. Louis— arrived here Wed. night Nov. 13— went to Ben. Farrar's & stayed there till Myra came out the… [date not filled in]

I found much excitement in St. Louis— Frank Blair got here the next day, Nov. 14 & stayed at Ben's & the army officers & crowds of others came to see him— & for a while we lived an unnatural kind of life— In 5 or 6 days I determined to stay here & telegraphed Myra to come— & at her request moved up to Frank Blair's house, 241 Washington Av. two doors E. of 12th. Until the last 2 weeks, things have been moving on rather evenly— but since England's menacing attitude we have been much concerned.

---

[73]This book has been lost.

36

Today I have felt depressed— & wrote a letter (copied) to Mr. Blair[74] urging the emancipation of slaves— Phil. Lee[75] has been up this evng.— it is now ¼ to 12 at night— & we have been talking over affairs gloomily— the chances of putting down the south begin to look evil— Until lately I have felt free from trouble about it since I left Phila. But lately & especially the last 2 days I feel great anxiety on that account. The Traitors in St. Louis are very confident of the success of their cause— and are in great hopes from England's course—[76] Well if England forces us, we will have to fight her as well as the South— how long we can stand it no one can foretell— but I trust that with a brave people & Right on our side, we may prosper.

St. Louis   Friday night ¼ to 12, Dec 27, 61

This has been another gloomy day— all loyal people continue to feel most uneasy about England— No definite news from there. Genl. Scott has just arrived in Washington from Paris, but we have no knowledge of the object of his return— The N.Y. Papers rec'd today have many extracts from English & French papers, but nothing encouraging— The Unionists say nothing out as yet; waiting to see what shape the demand of England will be in, & all seem willing to even give up Mason & Slidell,[77] rather than have War. I am decidedly in favor of it—

Today I have felt that the probabilities of putting down the South are against us— more strongly than at any previous time I believe.

[74]Francis Preston Blair Sr. (1791–1876) was a journalist and politician. As editor of the *Washington Globe* and advisor to President Andrew Jackson, he was politically very influential. In 1855, Blair was a founder of the Republican Party and presided at its first convention. He supported Frémont at the 1856 convention and Lincoln in 1860.

[75]Admiral Samuel Phillips Lee (1812–87) was the husband of Elizabeth Blair Lee (Lizzie) and brother-in-law of Frank Blair. He served in the Union navy during the Civil War. Franklin Dick represented Lee on several salvage cases.

[76]The British focus was on menacing the Union. The North feared they would send troops to invade from Canada, enabling the South to win the Civil War.

[77]James Murray Mason (1798–1871) was expelled from the U.S. Senate in 1861 for his support of the rebellion. As Virginia's delegate to the Confederate Congress, he was Commissioner to Great Britain in 1861. John Slidell (1793–1871) represented Louisiana in the U.S. Senate (1853–61). He was Confederate Commissioner to France in 1861. Mason and Slidell were traveling from Havana to England on a British ship, the *Trent*,

Sunday Morning Dec. 29, 61   10½ A.M.—

Did not go to Church this morning— Yesterday Seward,[78] Secy. of
State, gave up Mason & Slidell to Lord Lyons—[79] Thus England is
appeased, as to the present moment. I am glad of it & I feel no regret at
the humiliation of the U.S. in this thing— Our nation has been arrogant
& swaggering & I hope to see it become moderate and decorous— News
of still more bridge burning up the North Missouri & on the Hannibal &
St. Jo. [Rail] Roads— the uprising through this State is distressing— The
exasperation of the Rebels is unbounded— How we are ever again to conquer these People I can not see— They will not be conquered without a
most desperate assistance— as yet our 18,000,000 against their
8,000,000 has not availed us at all— Amongst the Traitors in St. Louis,
is the most defiant feeling, & they would rise upon us & put us to death if
they had the strength— as it is, they have come out in a protest against
Halleck's assessment[80] which is bold & denunciatory— I have not any
assurance at all now that we will put down this rebellion, but it seems to
me that we will not....

Cameron does not enter into it to put them down, but only to plun-
der, & provide for his future— that being such total lack of vigor in the

---

when they were captured by the Union navy and confined in Fort Warren in Boston Harbor. The British government viewed this as a flagrant violation of international law, and
threatened war if the two diplomats were not released. British business was sympathetic to
the Confederates, and England sent an army of eight thousand soldiers to Canada.

[78]William H. Seward (1801–72) was an ambitious contender for president against
Lincoln, who named him Secretary of State. Seward felt he was a "prime minister" to govern for the inexperienced new president. Seward wanted war with England over the
Mason and Slidell incident, but Lincoln said, "One war at a time," and sought peace so he
could get the saltpeter he had secretly bought from England to make gunpowder.

[79]Cabinet members Welles and Cameron cheered the actions of the Union general
who captured Mason and Sliddell, but Montgomery Blair and Seward said international
law was violated, and the prisoners should be returned. Going against public opinion, Lincoln followed Blair and Seward's advice.

[80]Henry Wagner Halleck (1815–72) was commissioned a major general U.S. Army
in 1861, succeeding Frémont as commander of the Department of Missouri. He declared
martial law in St. Louis and assessed disloyal persons, creating a Board of Assessors in
December 1861 that compiled a list of 300 names to contact. If the people named did not
make a contribution to support refugees in St. Louis, they were assessed an amount based
on three degrees of disloyalty: joining the Confederate army, giving direct aid to the Confederacy, and supporting the Confederacy in print or speech.

admn., & our army being composed so largely of politicians, while on the other hand the Rebels act with such vigor & activity & sacrificing every thing for the cause, and being able to meet us every where with armies at least equal to our own in numbers & efficiency— consolidated by hatred & pride & a feeling that they are fighting for their independence— with resources far greater than we supposed they had. In arms they are well supplied— in clothing & other necessaries for their troops also— In heavy guns we know they are amply supplied— they have held their defensive positions every where— and they have successfully acted on the offensive— they have kept the Potomac blockaded the last two months & they hold us in check at all points—

Acting in principle, as they maintain that they do, on the defensive, fighting for their independence, they will not submit. How they get their supplies I know not— but with a strong government, a fully aroused & desperate & bold People— with the issue independence, or subjugation by a People they hate to the death & also despise— with a nation's grandeur of wealth & proud dominion before them, which dazzles & delights them— with an aristocratic principle at the basis of their organization, begun through the exercise of power gained by the violence of a minority— & this aristocratic principle built up & protected & sustained by an extensive military organization; which is its heart & right arm— with a system of compulsive labor, which supports the power which keeps it down— an organization which thus forces labor from one class, which is kept ignorant & deprived of all opportunity, to sustain the other, has originated with an aristocracy, which is bold, energetic, intelligent, unscrupulous, sees the future & understands the present— always seizing weakness in time to keep it down— skilled in exciting & moulding the passions of the non slaveholding whites; & through their passions, making them their complete instruments— & combining the interests of this ignorant & prejudiced class with their own, by placing them in the army & there controlling them by military law: all this combination is formidable and will not yield until power of resistance is gone—

The Southern People act as if they knew no fear & had no weakness— I need to believe that the poor whites would leave the South in great crowds— but it has been so managed that none of them leave: I believed they were attached to the Union, & would appreciate real liberty

& virtue— but Southern management has worked it so that their armies are composed of that class— I believed that in all the States, the union men had a large majority & that the U.S. would when the war begun, send forces into these states with which Southern Union Men would unite— but the U.S. has not done this; & tens of thousands of union men have thus been forced by necessity to go over to the South—

I thought they would have a divided Country with the real strength against them— but the weakness & dilatoriness of the Admn. has been such, that the South is now practically one & united— The policy of their govt. is such that doubtful or suspected men are used by them for the war— when I look...

Sunday Evng.

I feel very sorrowful for my thoughts are almost all the time upon the miserable condition of my country & at the sad prospect for the future— Since writing this morning I had a long walk with Ben Farrar this P.M. & we talked over this subject— & he too has been feeling as I have; & he thinks perhaps more strongly than I do that the prospect of subduing the South is against us— He thinks emancipation is the only remedy, & does not know precisely how that can be carried into practice—

Captain Phil. Lee left here this P.M. for Washington. During his stay here about ten days, he & I have had many talks on this, & he thinks the only success is through the slaves— & I believe by arming them— but whether he is in favor of that he did not distinctly say; though I believe all of us are in favor of any thing necessary to ensure success. The truth is, if we conquer the South, their independence as States can not be allowed; but we would have to govern them as a subjugated People— and that Ben thinks is impossible, excepting by liberating the slaves, which he believes would expel the whites from that part of the country—

I see now, as things appear to me, very little prospect of reconstructing the Country— Months ago the defeat of the Southern army followed by our invasion of their territory would have raised up a large Union Party in the Rebel States, to whom power could have been given, sustained by our armies; but now, even if we could defeat & scatter their armies, unless by the most overwhelming success, which would so dispirit them as to cause them to seek for quiet in submission, I doubt very much if a suffi-cient Union Party would rise up to act as a nucleus around which to build up a new power.

Why even here in Missouri; the Rebels are overrunning the State, & late reports represent the whole interior of the State as under dominion of the Rebels; & I know that there are many Union men amongst them; & our troops have been going through the State & endeavoring to put down the Rebels for months past! & the Southern Govt. has given little or no aid in men & none in money to the Rebel cause in Mo.

Unless we shall soon have most considerably decisive victories, the real question will soon be one of boundaries; & I am almost forced to the belief that it will not long be deferred. Oh the horrors of this Civil War— Who could have anticipated them— if it goes on & on the spirit on our side must become as it is on the Other, Wolfish. Why the Rebels in this City would dance at the Execution of such strong Union men as we are; so bitter & malignant is their hatred.

Monday Night 11¼ O'C. Dec. 30.61

Another day of sadness & evil forebodings— Every passing day adds strength & solidity to the Southern Govt. amongst their own Peo-ple— accustoms foreign nations to it also & increases our debt. Saturday all the Eastern Banks suspended specie payments— so we go drifting now with only paper money— That is a sign of weakness & opens the door to the greatest disasters—[81]

Unless we have extraordinary success with our army, the indepen-dence of the South will be forced— I do not want to have the North give up the fight; but my opinion is that they will do so before long— the North has not yet suffered much & the excitement of going soldiering has

[81]All but one of Missouri's banks had suspended specie payment in November 1860, and the Eastern banks followed on December 28, 1861. Early in the war, stamps were used for small denominations, but heat made them stick in people's pockets. In August 1861, against the law, the Bank of St. Louis had issued paper cents, which ranged from three to fifty cents and were called shinplasters. The federal government issued paper-cent currency in 1862.

kept up the war movements; & it has been aided not a little by the money making spirit of those who have had the management of things.

Well it is distressing & humiliating to see our great Govt. torn in two— but yet the country has not aroused its-self to prevent it. In the North the army is officered by Politicians, & the men are largely made up of those who have gone into it to get employment— The yeomanry of the Country are not in the army; so far as I can see.

I am much inclined to think that in the Western States back north of the line that there must be a good deal of the feeling that it will be good riddance to be free of those blustering, troublesome Southerners, & the everlasting wrangle over the extension of slavery—

I see none of that great uprising which I looked for of patriotic men— but I may be mistaken in my opinions upon this point.

There is one remarkable thing: that the man of property in Missouri; those who have always been old Whigs, are nearly all in favor of the South— proving that they are opposed to universal suffrage, & real democracy. This class of People are really in heart with the Southern Cause & hail with satisfaction the exclusion of the common masses from equality of rights with the wealthy—

Monday Night 10 O'C. 31st Decr. 1861

This is the last night in the year— I have felt better in mind & heart today— This Evng. the English news is less discouraging & there seems to be some reason & traces of proper feeling left in G.B. There seems now to be some prospect of our troops advancing, which even arouses some cheer in my heart— This long inaction & the severe trials we have passed through almost bore the National heart down— But today, & especially this Evng. I feel decidedly more cheerful. By God's mercy each member of my Family is well & we enjoy all the blessings of a well supplied home— For the coming year in God alone do I trust—

January 1862

"In starting in upon the new year, I feel that all is uncertain & have no lights by which I can judge of the future."

St. Louis   Thursday night 11 O'C. January 2ᵈ. 1862

Yesterday was a quiet and gloomy day— rather cold & chill— the sun not shining— I spent most of the morning at home & did not feel cheerful at the prospect of the future— No particular event to note— Today the same— it is the first real wintry day & the earth is covered with sleet, which will add to the hardship of the soldiers— The Eastern papers have come with their comments in the release of Mason & Slidell & they try to make a good thing of it. The tone of English papers is more moderate, as those opposed to war with us are speaking out & those in favor of it, having accomplished their purpose of enforcing the Ministry to make a preemptory demand, have therefore held up somewhat. But still it seems that preparations for war in G.B. go on— & I suppose will continue. There is such a strong war party there that another cause may soon occur, which it may not be in our power to remove.

I fear all the time the recognition of the South by G.B. & France— & then how war is to be avoided I do not know. Our People have taken the surrender of these two Rebels with good spirit: but it will leave a deep impression, & if other insults are given, their spirit may rise up and brave the danger— I hope this may not be so— for if a foreign war is added to the present we can scarcely maintain ourselves.

This is a long season of suspense that we have had. At this time our troops in the interior are busy in trying to capture the bridge burning & marauding Rebels. Yesterday we heard that Price has left Osceola and started in haste southward, and our troops from Rolla have started off to try & cut him off— I hope they may succeed— The desperate determination of these People is shown by their adhering to him in the difficulties that he has to encounter— It is believed that his purpose is to keep Halleck from sending troops south against Columbus.

All this suspense is truly hard to bear up under; & from the East we see daily now the Govt. is pressed to get money to carry on the war. It has stopped paying out coin and relies upon its Treasury notes. Secy. Chase[1] is out with a plan to have U.S. Bonds used as a basis for banking all over the Country; but a great difficulty is that banking capital is not now wanted. If the business of the Country needed more money, then his project might work; but when there is more banking capital now than can be employed, it is too artificial an invention to stand; & especially to become the basis of the currency for a nation.

It is palpable that this matter of money is becoming a serious embarrassment— & it will get worse, unless we have some great success against the Rebels. If the Southern States go off, will the free States hold together— I believe they will; but that is a contingency, which no doubt affects the credit of the Govt. Look whichever way we may, & all kinds of difficulties are before us.

I do not know what is the situation of the armies near Washington— So far as we know the Southern troops remain there, & are well

[1]Salmon P. Chase (1808–73) was named secretary of the treasury in 1861, despite his having no financial background. To finance the war, Chase first used private loans, then war bonds marketed by Philadelphia banker Jay Cooke. As sources of capital disappeared in 1862 and the government spent about $2.5 million a day for the war, Chase printed federal paper money, called greenbacks, backed by Treasury gold under the Legal Tender Act in 1862.

provided— Genl. McClellan has been sick for several days past— the Rebels there keep so quiet, that little is known of them or if known does not get out. Military movements on the Potomac are very little said about now in the Eastern papers.

In starting in upon the new year, I feel that all is uncertain & have no lights by which I can judge of the future.

Friday night 11 O'C. Jany. 3ᵈ 1862

Another day has passed of the same kind & no decisive or important event. The New York papers contain copious extracts from London papers, written in a spirit of the extremest hostility to the U.S. Speedy & large preparations for war with us go on; & the stoppage of the *Trent*[2] seems to have been not so much the cause, as the occasion of their malignant outbreak towards us.

With such a spirit as they evince, I do not believe that they will let us off without a war. They have their naval preparations all ready, & with sufficient troops thrown into Canada to protect it, they believe it will be a handsome piece of business to batter down our Cities & sweep out of existence our Navy & establish the South—

And so far as human vision can penetrate, it looks as if this might well happen— but this Nation must trust in God, & maintain its integrity & uprightness. If we are overthrown & perish, let it be so endeavoring to maintain our honor & integrity.

I have long felt that the prosperity of our People had led them into the weakest follies & vices; & this chastisement of the Lord is surely needed to cure us of our National errors— May this have the effect to make a Godly People of this Nation. I believe that we will have the war with G.B. Then beyond that I can anticipate nothing.

This has been another stormy wintry day— Sleeting & all covered with sleet— Spent the day in my office writing— Congress is not passing any laws of importance; but the Committees are considering the measures of finance, & the slave question too.

---

[2]See entries for December 27 and 29, 1861, and notes 77 and 79 (1861).

Saturday night 11½ O'C. Jany. 4, 1862

Another day of waiting & suspense. Winter continues swift & cold— the ground covered with sleet— We have no intelligence today of any movements— Rumors that Genl. Halleck is to take command on the Potomac under McClellan, who I fear is very sick. The papers speak of Burnside's large expedition about to start from Annapolis— its destination unknown— vague hints of a forward movement of the army— but such intimations have been given so often that they go for naught.[3] Congress does nothing as yet— I feel so impressed at the earnestness of the South, & the want of it in the North— & yet, I cannot but suspect that there is a suppressed feeling at the North, which will upon occasion break out in majestic overpowering action. If it is not so, then has the North settled down into almost apathy— The Rebels work, night & day, earnestly & effectively; while we accomplish nothing. I am sick & weary at the inefficiency of our troops.

I feel all the time that something must be done to restore our expelled Government; the fact that our troops are in the judgment of their commanders, not ready to move on the Enemy, is a most discouraging one. Passed this day writing in my office.

St. Louis Saturday night 11 O'C. Jany. 11th 1862

A week has passed swiftly away since I have written— Nothing of moment has happened. I have become so accustomed to waiting, that I almost cease to feel impatient at it; & yet I cannot help feeling so. Burnside's expedition from Annapolis just started or starting I believe is intended to move on the rear of the Rebel army on the Potomac; & when it strikes, I think McClellan will move forward. This I think from a letter I saw today from 77 G. Arth.— McClellan has been very sick & is now

---

[3]Ambrose Everett Burnside (1824–1881) entered the Union army in the first wave of three-month enlistments and served at the First Battle of Bull Run, then was made brigadier general. Dick refers here to an expedition Burnside took down the east coast to attack Confederate seaports. He captured Roanoke Island, New Berne, Beaufort, and Fort Macon, and was made major general.

just getting about again. Just now too there is a movement southward from Cairo of our fleet— & of our army in Kentucky— & altogether it looks like a general movement about to take place along the lines. I know not what to anticipate— if we can but have victories in these battles, our hopes will rise— if defeat, it is very probable that Europe will interfere & the war be ended against us. The past week Genl. Halleck appointed me to act on the Assessing Comn.— & I find the secessionists are very bitter— I am inclined to think that the ensuing will bring some very important, if not effective events. I trust that Providence has not in store our national downfall. Nothing important has been done in Congress— nor any military events of importance anywhere— In western Mo., our troops under Jennison[4] are marauding & laying waste— horrid to say, it gives me bitter satisfaction to know how he is devastating that part of the state.[5]

Sunday afternoon 4½ O'C. Jany. 12th 1862

It is cold today, very cold & I am glad to sit in the house with a strong fire going. I have been reading in the papers of Burnside's expedition & other war matters, & I recd. today a letter from old Mr. Blair, in which he endeavors to take a hopeful view of things; but his whole case is our having a large army of patriotic men. It is cloudy & has been most of the time for two weeks; & all together, I cannot help feeling badly & dispirited. The papers are full of schemes for raising money, but all is based upon extending credit— taxing the people is not resorted to— well it is disheartening & sad enough. A letter of Russell's I read today intimates that McClelland [*sic*] has not advanced, on account of the slaughter such a battle would make. How evident is it, that the North & South after such a war can never be united under our present form of government. If

---

[4]Charles Rainford "Doc" Jennison (1834–84) was the leader of "Jennison's Jayhawkers," a fanatical abolitionist hero of the Free-Soilers and the guerrilla war. He was colonel of the Seventh Kansas Volunteer Cavalry. When Halleck complained about Jennison's military behavior, Jennison was transferred from Missouri to Humboldt, Kansas.

[5]In the winter of 1861, General Price's Confederate troops had frightened a few thousand inhabitants of southwest Missouri, who fled to St. Louis. General Halleck issued General Order 24 on December 12, 1861, which said that the refugees were to be quartered, fed, and clothed by Southern sympathizers. The second assessment committee, on which Franklin Dick served, was to review and change unsuitable fines.

the South is part of the U.S., it can only be as a governed part of the nation— Is that not impracticable. I can see no way out of this dreadful war— The power of the two sections, actuated by the hatred and conflicting interests may prolong the war very long & then end in a peace from exhaustion, which will leave us two hostile nations. Of late I have often felt that this has become but a war for boundaries.

Tuesday night ¼ to 10, Jany. 14, 1862

No battle yet. The indications are that in a few days there will be— In Kentucky I believe the U.S. troops are moving towards the Rebels— and troops from here have gone to Cairo— Burnside's Expedition has started— its destination unknown— It has gone South from Ft. Monroe. I hope it has gone to take Charleston— & then I think that T. W. Sherman[6] from Port Royal can take Savannah. I believe I was wrong in supposing Burnside was to move in the rear of the Rebels at Manassas— In St. Louis I feel troubled about the Germans—[7] they are a restless set & their hatred to Frank Blair is deep rooted & persistent—

The telegram says that Cameron has resigned as Secy. of War— of this I am truly glad— & if Seward, Chase & Welles & Smith and Bates[8] will go out too, & a young set of men take their places, I should have new & strong hope for the future.

---

[6]William Tecumseh Sherman (1820–91) took command of the Thirteenth U.S. Infantry Regiment at the start of the Civil War, and served at the First Battle of Bull Run. He then was in Kentucky, at the battles of Shiloh, Vicksburg, and Chattanooga, taking command of the western theatre after Grant went east. He invaded Atlanta, laid waste across Georgia to Savannah in his March to the Sea, and then fought his way north to join Grant.

[7]The large German population was powerful in Missouri politics. Prior to the Civil War, Frank Blair had sought their support for the Union, which they gladly gave. After Frémont arrived, the Germans felt he represented their best interests. When Blair backed President Lincoln in opposing Frémont's proclamation, the Germans turned against Blair as the enemy of their hero, Frémont.

[8]Lincoln's cabinet consisted of Secretary of State William H. Seward; Secretary of War Simon Cameron (replaced by Edwin M. Stanton); Secretary of the Treasury Salmon P. Chase (replaced by William P. Fessenden and Hugh McCulloch); Postmaster General Montgomery Blair (replaced by William Dennison); Secretary of the Navy Gideon Welles; Secretary of the Interior Caleb B. Smith (replaced by John P. Usher); and Attorney General Edward Bates (replaced by James Speed).

Sunday Evng. 7 O'C. Jany. 19, 1862

It is raining & dismal weather tonight— It has been very cold since I last wrote & the river stopped by ice— The troops that have started from Cairo southward not yet heard from & the object of the movement in Ky. is not yet known.

Burnside's Expdn. not yet heard from. The papers say they believe it has gone to North Carolina— but up to this time we do not know. The last several days, we have been in expectation, & therefore not felt up or down, but inclined somewhat to be up in hope of hearing of victory. Geo. A. writes me of a new patent for a cartridge which he fears will injure the success of ours— He has been all winter in Washn. pushing this matter on— A few days ago the country was taken by surprise at the Removal of Cameron & the appt. of Ed. M. Stanton[9] of Ohio & Penna.— & the papers say S. is a vigorous war man.

The Assessment Comm. has acted here, & the parties fined, neither appeal nor pay. I am inclined to think that Genl. Halleck will have to resort to Extreme measures with them— He ought to send them all South. Increased evidences of the intention of the Germans to make mischief continue to unfold.

Sunday Evng. Jany. 26, 1862 — 7½ P.M.

This week passed away in expectation— Excepting our victory at Somerset, Ky. where Zollicoffer[10] was killed, the week has produced no events in the war. We do not yet know where Burnside has gone— his Expdn. not yet heard from. Secy. Stanton, it is given out is energetic & a vigorous war man &c— I hope he is— I do not feel at all in great hope as

[9]Edwin Stanton (1814–69) served as legal advisor to Secretary of War Simon Cameron, and wrote the section in the annual report about freed slaves being armed to fight against the Confederacy, which caused Cameron to be fired and Stanton to be named War Secretary.

[10]Felix K. Zollicoffer (1812–62) advanced into neutral Kentucky in late November 1861. On January 19, 1862, as he was backed up to the rain-swollen Cumberland River, Brigadier General Zollicoffer was ordered by Major General George B. Crittenden to attack Union Major General George H. Thomas at Mill Springs. Zollicoffer, who was very nearsighted, rode in the advance; he was killed and the attack failed. The Confederates, after losing 533 men and officers, retreated from Kentucky and fled to Knoxville.

to the result. There is, I fear no such thing as restoring the Union— the authority of the U.S. can be restored only by force, & then the rebel states, can be governed only by Military power— & with Lincoln's disposition & Seward controlling all, I fear the Govt. will shrink from that position. I begin strongly to fear that Seward & Chase & other ambitious men, knowing they can never be supported in the South, want to divide the country, & that even McClellan feels the same way—for the war is not conducted as if the purpose was to conquer the South— Well, my hope fails when I think of such things.

I feel utterly disgusted with Lincoln— upon him do I throw all the blame— He is in my opinion a paltry coward. The past week Benj. Farrar has been seizing the chattels of the assessed Traitors in the City & they are howling in suppressed tones— Sam Engler sued out a replevin—[11] & was arrested with his atty. & one security & thrown into prison by Farrar, & Genl. Halleck sent him yesterday to Cinti. [Cincinnati] & issued an order prohibiting all events &c. interfering with his military orders.

I have contracted additional hate from these bloody Traitors here by acting on this Comm. & our weak kneed' Union people shake their heads at it—

Tuesday night Jany. 28, 1862 12 o'clock

Today has been a dull & gloomy wet day & news yesterday & my spirits have been greatly depressed— I have felt very badly the last 2 or 3 days— No progress seems making— though I believe now our forces are beginning to accumulate in Ky. & I suppose the purpose is to concentrate an overwhelming force there & move southward by early Spring. Yet the long, long continued inactivity is hard to evidence. I hear a good deal of the hatred of these Rebels in St. Louis. Exasperated by the seizure of their chattels by the Provost Marshall Gehl for the assessments our Board makes on them.

This Evng. for the first the Burnside Expdn. heard from as at Hatteras Inlet, where many of the vessels have been wrecked— it seems there

[11]Legal term for an action for the recovery of goods or chattels wrongfully taken or detained.

has been a furious storm— The account this Evng. is so vague I do not understand it.

Today rented our House on 5th St. to Dr. Philip Weigel for 13 months from 1st Feby. at $500 a yr.

Congress has yet passed no money, nor confiscation bill. I feel greatly dissatisfied with that Body— they seem unable to agree upon any important measure— I suppose they are awaiting the result of military action. News has come from England 3 days ago of the reception there of the release of Mason & Slidell. The particulars of the late Battle near Somerset, Ky. are coming in, & it is cheering to know how bravely our troops fought there, & what a great victory it was for us; yet it seems to me that it was managed badly by the Rebels. It is reported that the rebel Genl. Crittenden[12] was in command and <u>drunk</u>— As he was an inveterate drunkard when in our army, I suppose the report is true. The Tennessee & Virginia newspapers[13] lately are very dolorous in tone, showing great fear as to the result. The South is certainly much discouraged, & they seem astonished at the still increasing forces of the North.

Friday night Jany. 31. 1862 11¼ o'c.

Nothing especial has happened since I last wrote— additional news from Burnside, tells of the long continued terrific storm that they suffered, & yet comparatively few of the vessels were lost. His landing not yet known. The particulars of the battle at Somerset, makes our victory there an important one. Secy. Stanton seems to be acting with energy & honest zeal— The papers since his appointment have not had a word of news about the condition or movements of the army anywhere, & I think he has stopped all such publications. The indications seem to me are of a very formidable concentration of our forces on the Rebels in all directions. Burnside invading N. Carolina— Sherman & Dupont moving on

[12]George B. Crittenden (1812–80) joined the Confederate army and was assigned to liberate Kentucky, causing a family rift when both his father and his younger brother, Thomas L. Crittenden, stayed with the Union. After the defeat at Mill Springs and rumors of his drunkenness, he was transferred to Mississippi.

[13]During the Civil War, it was difficult to obtain war news, since Union newspapers did not give out facts about troop movements. Information was more readily available from Southern newspapers and from the English newspapers.

Savannah— troops going into Ky.— Buell making no noise, but moving forward steadily— Halleck has been sending troops South from here every day nearly for 2 to 3 weeks. I met Major John S. Cavender in the street today & he goes to Cairo tomorrow with 3 batteries of Blair's Regt. A large body of troops have moved from Rolla & Sedalia towards Price at Springfield, & he must either fight there or be driven into Arkansas— Genl. Hunter in Kansas preparing to move South too—.

This morning just before breakfast our house was discovered on fire— but put out with small damage— I have felt troubled in mind today— at 2, our Comm. met—

February 1862

"Our papers are not permitted to publish much,
so I suppose little of military movements will
be known until something decisive occurs."

Thursday Night Feby. 6 1862—10 O'C.

Since I last wrote, until today, I have felt rather hopeful. The news from England of the satisfactory reception of the news about the Trent— the march of our troops in large force to drive Price from the State— the Expectation of hearing that Burnside would strike a severe blow in North Carolina— the probable advance of Dupont & Sherman to take Savannah— the knowledge that Phelps was in large force in Louisiana— the good aspects of the victory at Somerset— the preparations for advancing in Ky. towards Bowling-Green— so many progressing movements produced expectation of good results.

But tonight I feel extremely anxious— This morning we have news of the advance of our troops to Fort Henry on the Tennessee River, & that the Enemy are there in great strength— Beauregard is there I believe, & heavy Rebel reinforcements going there from Columbus & other points— Our troops not being in sufficient force, had to wait for reinforcements— I fear that the enemy will have a much larger force than ours— and that we may suffer a serious reverse there. I am most anxious tonight as to this.

For several days past, the finance bill has been up in the House— the leading feature of it, making U.S. Treasury notes a legal tender. Those who press the bill insist that this feature is necessary to the credit of the Govt. I cannot concur in that belief & yesterday wrote to Blair against it. I cannot but believe that the Govt. can better sustain its credit, without than with that provision. The foreign papers still press the recognition of the South— & I fear that the strong hostility to the U.S. will lead them to it at an early day— Unless we seriously cripple the Rebels in a short time, that event will happen— & then the war must sooner or later end disastrously.

Saturday night Feby. 8 1862 9½ P.M.

Yesterday morning came the good news of the capture of Fort Henry by Commodore Foote[14] with his Gunboats— with that of the Rebel Garrison under Genl. Tilghman.[15] The Garrison was only 100, enough to serve the guns of the Fort. The supporting army had gone— fled before & to what point we do not yet know— nor have we heard anything more about it. Fort Donelson, on the Cumberland, 12 miles from Ft. Henry we have not yet heard about. This victory is very cheering, & raises some hope that we may make good progress now. Halleck is sending forward to the place all the troops he can gather together— & I hope that Buckner[16] will be compelled to fall back from Bowling Green to Nashville, & that Buell[17] can move forward— If so, Columbus will be

[14]Andrew H. Foote (1806–63) was put in charge of naval defense on the Upper Mississippi River, building and refitting ships, manning and supplying them for service. He and his flotilla of seven gunboats, together with General Grant, captured Fort Henry, one of a string of small, low-lying Confederate forts on the Tennessee River.

[15]Lloyd Tilghman (1816–63) inspected the forts on the Tennessee and Cumberland rivers; he reported that Fort Henry was badly maintained, but received no help. When General Grant approached, Tilghman sent most of his men to Fort Donelson and defended Fort Henry with a small number of soldiers against Flag Officer Foote and his gunboats, until forced to surrender on February 6, 1862.

[16]Simon Bolivar Buckner (1823–1914) organized the Kentucky State Guard. After failing to keep the state neutral, he became a Confederate brigadier general. He led a division to reinforce Fort Donelson.

[17]Don Carlos Buell (1818–98) was an early organizer of the Army of the Potomac. He served as head of the Department of the Ohio and helped Grant defeat the Confederates at the Battle of Shiloh.

taken in the rear & the enemy evacuate it & fly, or be attacked front & rear— If we can hold our own in Tennessee & follow it up, we will have pierced the center of the enemy, & commenced a forward movement that it seems to me can be kept up to the Gulf— This disaster I hope will discourage the Rebel forces, whose terms are about running out from re-enlisting— No news from the army of the Potomac since Stanton went in. He seems to be energetic— & it is rumored that McClellan's time will be taken up with active movements of the Potomac army, & therefore Stanton takes charge of all the general movements. I hope that may be so, for I have lost assurance of McClellan's force— I think he fears to do anything aggressive. I do not want him to attack on the Potomac, as at Bull Run, but there are numerous other ways & places, where he could have kept some forward movement going— So I think, & therefore my wish—

Congress lags & loiters— I know not what to think of the House of Reps.— They do not move towards confiscating the Rebels property— The House has just passed a Try. [Treasury] Note & loan bill, with the fatal vice in it of the legal tender principle—

Notwithstanding our victory at Ft. Henry,[18] yet I have felt badly today— Unless we now have a succession of telling victories, I fear difficulties from our finances— In St. Louis, I feel that we have in our midst a damnable, wicked & treacherous set of bloodhounds— Their hatred at me for being on the Asst. Commission is deep & exasperated— and I feel pointedly the stupid weakness of Congress in permitting these Traitors to remain openly defiant & hostile here, where they do so much injury—

The end of this dreadful revolution I do not pretend to see— I stay here in St. Louis as a temporary arrangement— for I have business matters to attend to, & can do service to the cause of the Union; but unless our Traitors here be crushed, I can not continue here.

It is miserable, fearful & wretched to have such a state of things— I am looking most anxiously for further news from Tennessee— Should the enemy combine a large force & attack our troops successfully, our inchoate victory may prove a fatal defeat to us. Therefore I shall continue anxious

---

[18]The Battle of Fort Henry, Tennessee, took place on February 6, 1862. Tilghman surrendered to the Union navy, then to Brigadier General Ulysses S. Grant, who was approaching by land.

until I know that our troops are in strength & position too strong to be
beaten by the Rebels.

Sunday night Feby. 9th 1862 11 O'C.

I have not been to church today, & have not felt satisfied at it, but
this evng. I have just read the 6th chap. of Matthew in the plain commentary, on the blessed Lord's prayer. I would have gone this morning to hear
Mr. Post, (for there are so many Traitors at the Episcopal Churches, that I
hate to go amongst them) but I went down to the Alton Packet, to see the
several hundred Prisoners of War that have been confined at McDowell's
College,[19] sent to the Alton Penitentiary.[20] They are most of them a
rough looking set of fellows— not particularly ill looking, excepting a few,
who do look like scoundrels.

No news today from Tennessee— I see that 4 Regts. have just
started to Cairo from Inda. [Indiana] & Ills. [Illinois]— The Nebraska
First has just come in & starts for Cairo. Halleck is hurrying his troops
forward there. I have been looking back over the papers, & at the map. I
do not think that the Rebels can bring any large force against ours. Some
days ago, an expedition sailed south from Port Royal, & from what I hear,
probably has gone to add to Phelps's force against New Orleans.

It looks to me now, as if we are pressing the Rebels on so many points,
that we must break them down very badly— Whether they will be able to
rise up again is a great question, which I do not feel able to answer. Their
papers are showing great concern. Where Beauregard is, we do not know.

I hope tomorrow that Fort Donelson on the Cumberland is ours—
That will open the River for us to Nashville, so far as I know— But I suppose the Rebels will fight there. We don't yet know where the army they
had at Fort Henry went to—

---

[19]In December 1861, the McDowell Medical College was cleaned and renovated
for use as the Gratiot Street Prison. The first 1,200 Confederate prisoners arrived on
December 24, 1861. There were a few escapes, since the building was not designed as a
prison. Political prisoners, Confederate soldiers, Union criminals, and deserters were
housed together.

[20]Alton Penitentiary, in the steamboat port of Alton, Illinois, was the first state
penitentiary built. Major General Henry W. Halleck, commander of the Department of
Missouri in St. Louis, had it refitted and opened for prisoners of war in 1862.

Wed. night, Feby. 12, 1862 12 ¼ o'c.

No news of a battle yet at Fort Donelson, though it is likely it has been fought— I feel almost certain we must be successful there— Genl. Grant has invested the Fort— but what number of troops he has, I do not know— a large force— & the number increasing constantly— Every Reg't. from here & the States East of here are pushing forward— & I suppose we have nearly double the force the enemy has— we do not know whether our Gun Boats have gone up the Cumberland— Learned today that 3 of our Gun Boats that went up the Ten. River, got as far as Florence, Alabama & cleared the River of Rebel Gun boats, & brought 2 or 3 back with them— The Union feeling along the Ten. River reported very strong—

Yesterday was a repeat of the fighting of Burnside at Roanoke Island— & this evng. comes the glorious tidings of our magnificent victory there— the capture of the Island & the entire Rebel Army— the capture & burning of Elizabeth City— This is all from Southern Papers via Norfolk & Fort Monroe. They say we captured 2,000 men— but when our account comes, it will show a much larger force. This threatens Norfolk in the rear, & will give us possession of the Southern Rail Roads. We learn also that Genl. Thomas is moving in Tennessee, to attack Bowling Green on the East Flank. Curtis & Sigel are moving from Lebanon in Mo. on to Price near Springfield & by this time a battle may have been fought there—

These great victories have raised my spirits very much & if we meet with continued successes, we will soon crush the Rebellion. Burnside & Goldsborough captured Roanoke Island last Friday the 7th.[21]

Friday night Feby. 14, 1862. 11 o'c.

News today of the arrival of our army under Curtis at Springfield, & a small fight there, & Price retreating, & our Flag flying in Springfield—

[21]The Battle of Roanoke Island took place on February 8, 1862, when 100 Union ships commanded by Brigadier General Ambrose E. Burnside and Flag Officer Louis M. Goldsborough landed troops under Confederate fire on Roanoke Island. Outnumbered and fighting to the sea with no escape, Confederate Colonel Henry M. Shaw unconditionally surrendered with 2,500 men.

No further news— This shows Price intended fighting there— I expect to hear that our troops will continue on after Price, & use him up—

This evng. our account of the Capture of Roanoke Island— but no definite particulars yet— No news from Fort Donaldson— but that our Gun Boats have gone up the Cumberland— I suppose they needed repairs & the delay in attacking may have been from that cause— the cause assigned is the bad roads. Our troops are pouring into Ky. up the Tennessee & Cumberland Rivers.

Well, it looks now as if we could sweep the Rebels away— I should look for some defeats, but for the fact that so far as I can tell, we will largely out-number the Rebels wherever we strike them. No news of what they are doing at Columbus. Their newspapers show great alarm. We are hopeful— strongly so— at Norfolk the Rebels are much alarmed—

Sunday night Feby. 16. 1862 10 o'c.

Yesterday we had no particular news. This morning we learn that the Rebels have evacuated Bowling Green & that Genl. Mitchell had reached there & was making a Bridge to cross the Barren River; the Rebels having destroyed it— Where they have retreated we do not know, nor have we any further information—

This evng. a dispatch from Genl. Curtis says he has pursued & over-taken Price's army, captured nearly all his baggage, & a large number of Prisoners— News comes tonight of the continued battle at Fort Donel-son— It began on Thursday— Friday our Gun Boats attacked the fort— there were 3 tiers of batteries & the fire of the Rebels tremendous, & our boats retired— renewed again yesterday and several of our Gun Boats dis-abled, & Com. Foote wounded, & had gone to Cairo— It is reported that our army surrounds the Fort, extending up the River to Dover, & cuts off reinforcements; also that we have taken one of their out-works.

This far it seems that the Rebels have pretty well held their own. But the acts are so meager that I can form very little opinion about it. If their reinforcements are cut off, I think they must be reduced, but it will cost much more hard fighting yet to do it. But few of our Regiments are yet engaged— Nor do we hear of our artillery doing much. I feel much anxious about the contest— though I suppose they must be reduced, sooner or later. It cannot be very long before Buell gets there, which will cut them off entirely—

With Donelson reduced, & Bowling Green ours, the Rebels will be in a bad way— though Donelson is costing our Navy heavily— all anxiety now hangs on the conflict at this Fort—

This morning I went to Benj. Farrar's office to see him about carrying out Halleck's Circular of the 14th as to arresting Secessionists— then to Ben's— Ben came up this evng. & brought the 'Extra' with news of the fight at Donelson, & Curtis' exploits— I do feel most anxious tonight— a good deal wrought up— I can not well doubt our success at Donelson, for it is reported that we have 40 to 50,000 men there— But knowing no particulars of the engagement & having no knowledge of the strength & nature of the place, & not certain that they are cut off from reinforcements, makes me feel most anxious & concerned— for with Donelson, defended by 15,000 men, with Genls. Johnson, Buchner & Floyd there, down will go the Rebel cause.[22]

Monday night 12½ o'c, Feby. 17th 1862

This has been the day of days— a great day of rejoicing & hope & thankfulness to the Lord God Almighty.

This morning came the great news of the capture of Fort Donelson— on Sunday morning at 9 o'c. it surrendered— Our brave troops took it— we captured, it is reported 15,000 men, 20,000 arms, over 40 heavy guns— 3,000 horses— but these particulars are estimates— and we took Genl. Simon Buckner, the base traitor who acted the spy— and Genl. Albert S. Johnston—[23] Genl. Floyd[24] fled in the night with 5,000

[22]Union Brigadier General Grant and Flag Officer Foote attacked Fort Donelson by land and river. Confederate Brigadier General John B. Floyd and Major General Gideon L. Pillow escaped with around 2,500 soldiers, leaving Brigadier General Simon B. Buckner to surrender. This led to the capture of Nashville on February 23, giving control of Kentucky and western Tennessee to the Union.

[23]At the outbreak of the Civil War, General Albert Sidney Johnston resigned, but did not leave his post in the west until his successor arrived, giving him the reputation of the finest soldier in the North or South. He was made the second-ranking Confederate general in charge of the western operations. He held the line of defense in Kentucky from the Appalachians to the Mississippi River until defeated at Mill Springs, and Forts Henry and Donelson in 1862.

[24]John Buchanan Floyd (1806–63) was a Confederate brigadier general at Fort

troops— We have no further particulars yet. The City today has been in a whirl of excitement— I could not stay in my office, more than a little while, and passed a good deal of the day with Ben. Farrar.

It looks now as if the rebellion could suddenly crumble away. I think that the Rebels must evacuate Columbus— & that we must be able at once to take Nashville & Knoxville— Reports from Port Royal indicate a movement upon Charleston & Savannah— and I trust soon to hear of their capture.

Oh my God, the Gracious Lord of Mercy, now are we in the hollow of thy hand. May this nation turn to Thee in love & faith, & never forsake Thee. Our loss tonight at Donelson reported at 700 wounded & 300 killed—

Tuesday night Feby. 18. 1862 — ¼ to 10 o'c.

Today we hear of no battles, or advances— our troops are rapidly passing into Ky.— & I suppose the next movement will be upon Nashville & Columbus— Genl. Hunter is rapidly collecting a large army at Fort Scott, Kansas to move into Arkansas— We have further particulars of the battle at Ft. Donelson, but not any full or clear a/c yet. I have been reading this evng. an account of the battle at Roanoke Island, and am struck at the weak defense & poor fighting of the Rebels there & at our bravery— also the Rebel Report of the engagement at Port Royal— & am surprised at the inefficiency of the Rebels there & at their poor way of managing the defense— I believe had Genl. Sherman pushed on, he could have captured Charleston or Savannah.

It feels now as if this Rebellion is being crushed with good management & brave conduct. I do not see where we can meet with defeat— though nothing is more uncertain than the result of battles— Yet the late fighting has shown us so greatly superior to the Rebels, that we ought to whip them everywhere. St. Louis today seems like a real Union City—

Donelson, where he commandeered river steamers and fled across the Cumberland River with Brigadier General Gideon Pillow, a political appointee and inept soldier. Wanting to avoid the shame of being the first Confederate officers to surrender, they left Confederate Brigadier General Simon B. Buckner in command.

The miserable Secesh keep out of the streets, & have slunk into their dens.

Wed. Night Feby. 19, 1862 — 11 o'c.

Today we have additional particulars of the Donelson battle, but not accurate ones— The Prisoners are so many, they have not been able to count them yet.

News of the evacuation of Clarksville, Ten., where the R.R. crosses the Cumberland— This place was strongly fortified— this removes every obstruction, I believe, between Ft. Donelson & Nashville, where the Rebel forces have fled— & they will make a stand— A Report also of the destruction by the Rebels of their works at Columbus—

Curtis still pursues Price's army & has captured his son, Brig. Genl. Price,[25] and several of his staff— Price's army & Curtis after him, have crossed over into Arkansas—

It looks now as if the Rebellion was fast dying away. Yesterday 2,000 Rebel troops arrived at Fort Donelson, saying they came to <u>re-enforce it</u>!

Our Secessionists are gasping woefully. Benj. Farrar arrested D. Robert Barclay[26] & Dr. J. B. Burnett & Professor Swallow under Halleck's circular of the 14th. Glover, Broadhead, Giles Filley, Dick, Thward, and Ben & Briney met at my office this morning about the April election.

Thursday night Feb. 20, 1862 11½ o'c.

No battles reported today, nor statements of movements of the enemy— The rumors of the evacuation of Columbus not yet confirmed, though I am much disposed to credit it. No war news from Tennessee—

---

[25]Edwin M. Price (1834–1908), son of Sterling Price, served in the Missouri State Guard and as a Confederate brigadier general. He was returning from northern Missouri when he was captured near Stockton, Missouri. He was sent on to Rolla, then St. Louis.

[26]D. Robert Barclay was a St. Louis attorney who lost two library cases of books in the first assessment by Henry Halleck. The assessment board set total fines of $16,340, collecting $10,913.45, most of which came from auctioning the seized property of disloyal persons who had refused to pay their fines.

Several 1,000 of the Prisoners came up in Boats today & go by the cars to the North—

Passed this evng. with Ben. Farrar & we talked over the prospect with great satisfaction. I am looking with great interest for news from Savannah & the Gulf— The news from Europe is favorable— The tone in England improved, & Napoleon's late declaration that he will wait, has given the impression in France that there will be no intervention. If things continue so, until our late victories reach there, I think danger from Europe may be considered as ended. I feel happy & hopeful today.

Saturday night Feby. 22nd 1862 10 ¼ o'c.

No advances or battles yesterday or today, excepting Curtis to Bentonville, Arkansas, & so Price is driven from the State, and Arkansas entered by our troops for the first time— The dispatches from Curtis are very meager— the latest look as though He might overtake Price, & force him to battle— Nothing especial from Tennessee— Our papers are not permitted to publish much, so I suppose little of military movements will be known until something decisive occurs— What the Rebels are doing at Columbus, we do not know, but it looks as if they are preparing for a battle there— I suppose when Buell has taken Nashville; for they abandoned Clarksville, & Genl. Smith is there in force; then Halleck may move across behind Columbus to cut it off, & it seems to me, as if the Garrison there can be reduced, without a battle—

The enemy made great havoc of property at Bowling Green when they fled from it— We have not a word since, of the movement of Buell's forces— I suppose he is moving on Nashville— Nor have we for a long time had a word from East Tennessee— Nor word from McClellan, nor the Rebel army at Manassas— Whether it still all stays there, or not, I do not know at all— Nor do we know what Sherman is doing at Port Royal, though the last several days, rumors are that he is very close to Savannah. How the Rebels are to hold out, & permit our troops to enter the Southern States, is for them to answer. We hear that their troops will not re-enlist. My best information is, that their troops are a mean low set of men, not uniformed— those from Donelson are a hard lot, in their mean cheap home-spun.

At Donelson & Clarksville we got immense supplies of army provisions— at Bowling Green the Rebels destroyed enormous supplies of theirs that they had accumulated—

Com. Foot has gone up the Cumberland, but not heard from yet— probably to co-operate with Buell. It may be that the Rebels have a very large force at Columbus, & will attack Cairo, when we move into Tennessee— but Halleck, I suppose will keep a large force there— The European news promises for the present non-intervention. The movements of England, France & Spain in reference to the Mexican Affair, begins to look as if they intended appropriating that Country— so that we may have another war, to defend Mexico, as soon as we finish this Rebellion.[27]

Congress has not yet passed the finance bill— The Senate & House disagree on Senate amendments, Missouri Stocks in the last few days have gone up from 40 to 47 & Tennessee from 42 to 55. The Country seems to regard the late victories, as almost decisive of the War.

Last evng. had Benj. Farrar, Genl. Schofield,[28] Jim Broadhead & Capt. Meigs to a supper— Today all St. Louis turned out in a grand celebration of the day— The procession was 2 ½ hours passing our house, & in it were many hitherto secessionists. I find that a considerable number of the People, are ever ready to fly from the weak side— They are base wretches who do not seem to care what government they have— The stern union People amongst the better classes, are but few. The want of patriotism amongst this class of People has surprised, and disgusted me. I have just concluded arrangements to renew 90,000 of James H. Lucas' bonds for 5 yrs. that fall due in April— One of President Lincoln's sons died 2 days ago & another is ill.[29] Secretary Stanton is attacked with vertigo, & unable to attend to business a second time.

---

[27]The Mexican Affair was started by Napoleon III to detract attention from his failures with Italy and Poland. In the fall of 1862, Napoleon III sent 30,000 French soldiers to Mexico. Eventually they captured Mexico City in June 1863, after which Napoleon III set up Archduke Maximilian as emperor of Mexico in 1864.

[28]John McAllister Schofield (1831–1906) rode with Brigadier General Nathaniel Lyon to disband Camp Jackson. As a brigadier general, he was appointed, removed, and then reinstated as head of the Department of Missouri. In 1862, Schofield and Governor Gamble reinstated assessments of disloyal persons (as well as banishment) in St. Louis and the state.

[29]Willie (age 11) died and Tad (age 8) was ill with "bilious fever," which was probably

Genl. Halleck devotes all his time to work. He seems to know every thing here & yet I do not know whom he consults. He is an able man— perhaps the ablest in the Country— His management matters in this State, indicate the greatest ability.

Sunday night Feby 23rd 1862 ¼ to 10 o'c.

The paper today is without a particle of war news— Preparations for great events are no doubt pushing forward, and I trust in God, that they may be favorable to us. The Rebels are now in such severe straits, that they must make some aggressive movement; for to fall back & await attack, is of its-self disastrous to them— Seven of their Gunboats, from the South, are reported at Columbus, and as our Gunboats are so much cut up, it will not surprise me if they attack Cairo—

If they rely on the defense at Columbus, that will not avail them; for they can not always hold on there, & in the meanwhile our movements below them go on. It is therefore simply a question, as it seems to me, of their making an attack on Cairo, or falling back— & to fall back is to get to a weaker point, & open more of the Country to our occupation, & to greatly diminish their services for supporting their armies. And get what advantage an attack upon Cairo can be to them. I do not see— for they cannot hold it— & at best, they would gain a battle, devoid of strategic results— and incur great danger of being themselves cut off from retreat—

In Congress they are talking about the disposition they will make of the Conquered States. I am inclined to think we ought first to ascertain the political condition of the states. If the loyal men so out-number the disloyal, that they can keep them down, then let them govern the states as heretofore— if not, the state of facts disclosed, will enable Congress to know what they would do. Emancipation, unless necessary as a measure of conquest or subjugation, should not be resorted to. If loyal men govern the slave States, there will be no occasion to fear the slavery influence—

---

typhoid from contaminated water from the Potomac River, the source of water for the White House. Washington was overcrowded with troops, and sewage ran directly into the Potomac.

Many difficult questions will arise, out of the new State of things— & it is the part of wisdom to defer measures, until the ends necessary are disclosed. The pure abolitionists are pressing the matter, but they will be found a minority of not much voting power. The North will never permit slavery to spread where it does not exist; but as it is not responsible for slavery in the South, it ought not to touch the subject, where loyal citizens have the control. If in certain sections, disloyal men prove impracticable, their slaves should be taken from such, and sent to Central America, or some other proper climate and region.

Monday night Feby. 24, 1862 12 o'c.

No news of a battle today— Our troops have Cumberland Gap, without opposition— Reports from Cairo indicate a proposition of the Rebels to retire from Columbus— No news as to what advances have been made.

Read a parcel of intercepted letters[30] tonight, from St. Louis— they do not indicate much hope— We all feel very confident of further successes.

May God protect & preserve us.

Wed. night Feby. 26, 1862 12 o'c—

We have had rumors of our having Nashville the last 2 or 3 days— but today it is confirmed & the Rebels reported to be making a stand at Murfreesboro, 30 miles south of there— but we have no particulars— preparations to move in large force from Cairo have been made, & it is said a few days will show some great achievement— Our Gunboats 3 days ago went to near Columbus— & a flag of truce came out— &c.— but the meaning of it has not transpired— very little information comes from below— a stop is put on the Reporters— so that we can not foresee

[30]Postmaster General Montgomery Blair had stopped postal service to the South on May 31, 1861. The South then adopted the North's system for itself. Both North and South intercepted and confiscated any mail from their opponents, looking for news and information. Franklin Dick's St. Louis friends must have passed on these letters for him to read.

results. No news from Savannah, nor New Orleans, nor the Potomac—
Burnside seems to be trying to work his way towards Norfolk.[31]

Went tonight with Myra to Drake's— It seems as if the Rebels can
make no stand against us in the West— our troops are pouring into Cairo
& the Cumberland River— the Rebels are drafting— a pretty bad sign
for them—

Thursday night Feby. 27, 1862 — 11¼ o'c.

We are completely in the dark as to the coming military movements— The Gov't. has taken pos'n of the telegraph, & interdicted the
press— so that nothing can be printed not supervised & approved by the
Military. Today we have no information of any kind from below— we
hear that Curtis has followed Price to Fayetteville, Arks. and has stopped
there— having gone to near the mountainous regions. Price's force is
pretty much scattered, & has gone into the Boston Mountains—[32]

I read this evng. Jeff. Davis's[33] inaugural— it lacked spirit & tone—
The Treasury note bill has just passed, making notes a legal tender. The
effects of this I cannot foresee, but I see no reason to depart from my
views as written to Blair several weeks ago, against the measure.

No movements on the Potomac— the Rebels there must feel rather
uncomfortable, at seeing themselves threatened with being cut off from
supplies— It seems to me that process will force them in a short time to
an attack on our army there, or to a retreat; which I suppose is McClellan's great plan.

I got a letter from John Hickman today saying that the Negro was
the obstacle to the passage of a confiscation bill.

[31]The Battle of Stone's River (Murfreesboro, Tennessee) did not take place until
December 31, 1862, through January 2, 1863. Union Major General William S. Rosecrans battled Confederate General Braxton Bragg, who finally retreated.

[32]The Boston Mountains are in the Arkansas Ozarks, southeast of Fayetteville,
where the Confederate army under General Earl Van Dorn rallied before the battle of Pea
Ridge.

[33]Jefferson Finis Davis (1808–89) resigned from the Senate after secession and
hoped for a military post in the Confederacy; instead, he was surprised to be elected president. As president, he personally supervised military affairs, squabbled with generals, and
had six secretaries of war in four years. Stubborn and uncompromising, he was totally loyal
to the South, and convinced he was right.

In St. Louis there is a strong influence looking to the end of the war, & to manage things so that the Republicans here shall be crushed— I find myself disapproved by a certain class of union People, for the secession assessments— It is very offensive to me, to find that class of quasiunion people, prominent, & recognized as such— The hypocritical Hugh Campbell acting on the Commission of Claims, & associated with Mr. Holt— Bob. Campbell[34] the traitor— a year ago, now constantly entertaining our military men— & figuring as a prominent Union Man— Yeatman,[35] President of the Sanitary Committee— a traitor and that class of cringing deceitful People, prominent as Representatives of the Gov't. they did not dare stand up for in the beginning, & turning away from men like me, because I am too strong, radical &c.— When I look around & see Every day, & every where, our Union People on the most friendly terms with the secessionists, I turn from all of them with disgust—

[34]Robert Campbell (1804–79) became a prominent businessman in the elite society of St. Louis and stood as a Conditional Unionist when secession began, supporting the Crittenden pro-slavery compromise, but not advocating secession. Campbell presided over a Conditional Unionist meeting in front of the courthouse on January 12, 1861, which endorsed slavery or Missouri joining with the South.

[35]James E. Yeatman (1818–1901) was a slaveholder, but a Unionist. He was an important force in St. Louis with civic posts such as president of the library. On September 5, 1861, Yeatman became president of the Western Sanitary Commission, serving with Carlos S. Greeley, Dr. J. B. Johnson, George Partridge, and the Reverend Dr. William Eliot. The commission worked with the St. Louis Ladies' Union Aid Society to help sick and wounded soldiers, families, and refugees; establish soldiers' homes and hospital steamers; and provide relief for freedmen and former slaves.

March 1862

6–8 Battle of Pea Ridge, Arkansas; Union victory

8–9 Battle of Hampton Roads—Confederate Ironclad *Merrimac* (rechristened CSS *Virginia*) battle with USS *Monitor*, sinks two wooden Union warships off Norfolk, Virginia

11 Lincoln temporarily relieves McClellan as general-in-chief and takes direct command; McClellan in command of Army of Potomac is ordered to attack Richmond

"The events of the last few days have been momentous."

Saturday night March 1st 1862 10¼ o'c.

The last two days bring news of no battle— but the movements show the closing in of our army around the Rebels. Burnside has gone up the Blackwater & Nottaway Rivers & cut off Norfok from Weldon,[36] & I believe also from Richmond— it is so reported— also a report of the burning of a R.R. bridge at Lynchburg— it seems therefore that Virginia is cut off from Knoxville & the West— & nearly so from the South— Our navy is growing fast— The Monitor,[37] an armed vessel put in Commission, & another just launched in Conn. The news comes from

[36]The terminus of the Wilmington and Weldon Rail Roads was in Petersburg, Virginia, from which it ran 162 miles into North Carolina. It was a major supply line for Confederate forces.

[37]The ironclad USS *Monitor* was a flat armored ship with a revolving turret and two eleven-inch guns, sitting eighteen inches above the water, 172 feet long and 41½ feet wide. The USS *Monitor*, under Lieutenant John L. Worden, arrived and fought with the CSS *Virginia* under the command of Confederate commodore Franklin Buchanan, on March 9, 1862. The battle was inconclusive, and the *Virginia* left for Norfolk. The long-term effect was that the blockade remained intact.

England that all Parties are settled not to recognize the South— also in France— & the matter ceases there to be agitated— this feeling will be greatly increased when our victories are known there. Buell is moving from Nashville on the Rebels at Murfreesboro— Halleck is, I suppose trying to cut them off at Columbus— The Southern papers are full of fears, bombast— & schemes. The Rebel congress at Richmond opens with a fierce attack on their adm'n., & especially their Secys. of War & Navy, & the demand for an aggressive policy— The call is for an increase of their army— Memphis is all excitement & fear— The Rebels talking about fortifying Island No. Ten &c.

Soon we must hear from Savannah— where our forces have got in between Ft. Pulaski & Savannah & erected batteries, & cut off communication between them— & from David Porter's[38] expedition of Mortar fleet, which has gone somewhere— a large force has & is collecting at Ship Island for a movement on New Orleans— Burnside is, I suppose, to be re-enforced largely— so the present is a time of many great points to be seized about the same time.[39]

Today we hear that Banks has crossed the Potomac and taken pos'n. of Harper's Ferry again & finds no enemy to resist. McClellan prudently lies still & hold the Rebel Army there— if they stay much longer, all their resources, & means of retreat will be cut off, & they must fall into his hands, without a battle— It begins to look very much that way to me, already. It is said that the Rebel army there is not over 60,000, & I am beginning to think it has been enormously exaggerated— in truth, I will not be surprised if we find they are not all told 200,000 men under arms—

It looks now certainly like a great hollow structure, crashing in at all places, under a resistless pressure— & I am strongly inclined to believe that, in this month, we will have military possession of every fortification & strategic point in the Country.

Little Frank is sick today—

[38]David Dixon Porter (1813–91) had the brilliant idea of putting mortars on flatboats to attack river forts, and was a major contributor to the Union's later naval successes.

[39]The Battle of Forts Jackson and St. Philip, Louisiana, was on April 18–28, 1862. The two forts were built of strong masonry, protecting the Port of New Orleans.

Sunday night Mch 2nd 1862 — 11¼ o'c.

Dear little Frank is well today, & running about.

The paper this morning has absolutely no war news. Under the late act of Congress to that effect, the President has taken power of the telegraph lines & not a message is sent, unless first approved by the Govt. & today there is not a war dispatch. I approve such measures at this time— The N.Y. Post of the 26 has copy of an order of Secy. Stanton prohibiting papers from printing war intelligence— & now we have none.

The Wash'n. letter of that paper of the 25 says, everything there indicates a movement of the Potomac army & Apo. writes that her brother Andrew says the army starts tomorrow. As it has been raining the last few days, that may stop it; but I suspect not, & I suppose that tomorrow McClellan will commence his forward steps. I pray to God, that he will give victory to our arms. Not a word as to Columbus. Halleck has sent a large force, from Commerce to go around to New Madrid, and cut off Columbus from the South— This week will probably see great events. I trust that Providence will guard & uphold our just cause. I do not feel any fear that the Rebels can stand up against us at any place. We have our troops now in such positions & force, that I think we can crush them in. Perhaps by telegraph tomorrow, orders will be given to go upon them at all points.

The House of Reps. has just passed an important bill to prohibit the Army & Nvy. from being used to return fugitive slaves. The Bill was introduced by Frank Blair & passed the same day, the 25th ult.[40]

Monday night Mch 3rd 1862 11¾ o'c.

The papers being cut off from printing war news, we have none today— It is strongly rumored that Columbus is being evacuated & I

---

[40]Congress had passed the Fugitive Slave Act in 1793 to protect Southern "property" rights. The Compromise of 1850 made Northern officials responsible for returning fugitive slaves to their masters and stated that anyone assisting a runaway slave would be sentenced to six months in prison, charged a fine of $1,000, and had to reimburse the owner. The Federal First Confiscation Act in July 1861 authorized taking slaves from disloyal masters. Blair's bill, the Act Prohibiting the Return of Slaves, effectively annulled the Fugitive Slave Act, although the act was not officially repealed until June 1864.

believe it— The Rebels have fled from Murfreesboro & are at Chattanooga— & Buell is after them— The R. Road from Louisville to Nashville
will be running tomorrow— Part of the R.R. bridge has been burned at
Lynchburg, Va.[41] No news from the South— nor Charleston, nor Savannah— The Rebel papers say we have batteries on the Savannah River cutting Ft. Pulaski off from the city—[42] Not a word from the Potomac today,
but I feel certain that McClellan is already on the move— his advance may
be retarded by weather— Last night & today has been freezing cold— ice
in the gutters frozen solid— I feel extremely anxious to hear from the
Potomac.

Tuesday night Mch. 4, 1862 10 o'c.

Had neuralgia today and came up early— cold & cloudy— No news
at all from anywhere, until this evng. at 9 when Capt. Meigs came up &
told us that our old Flag is flying at <u>Columbus</u>— This is cause for great
rejoicing & thankfulness— Thus the miserable Rebels retreat from one
strong place to the rear— Where they can expect to make a stand, I do
not know. No particulars at all.

Wed. night Mch. 5, 1862 10 o'c.

Today has been extremely cold & bleak & snowing at times— Some
particulars of the Evacuation of Columbus— It was immensely strong,
said to have 200 mounted guns— The garrison supposed to be 20,000—
Part went down the river & part by land— but no reliable facts, nor
details. Not a word of war news from any other point—
Jeff. Davis is out with another message, speaking distress. Cannot
believe so large a number of Southerners w'd. surrender as at Donelson—
and says the surrender at Roanoke was humiliating—
Well, we are very anxious to hear from the Potomac— the papers

[41]Three railroad lines intersected in Lynchburg, Virginia, but no real battles
occurred until June 16–18, 1864.
[42]To reach Savannah, Union Captain Quincy Adams Gillmore attacked Fort
Pulaski in February 1862. Confederate Colonel Charles H. Olmstead surrendered the fort
on April 11, 1862, to Gillmore, closing the port of Savannah to blockade runners.

east grumble at being cut off from printing war movements. I wait in hope & trust for a victory there— the Rebel papers are trying to talk themselves up; but their honors are very plain.

Thursday night Mch. 6 1862 11 o'c.

No particular war news today— nothing of our advances on the Potomac— nor from Gen. Buell— nor where the flying Rebels have gone— a slender a/c of Columbus, gives some little particulars about the strength of the place. Nothing from Genl. Curtis, since his arrival in Fayetteville.

Andrew Johnson[43] has been appointed & confirmed a Brigadier Genl.— Military Governor of Tennessee & goes out to start proper measures in the State, to enable the loyal people to take measures to constitute a loyal Civil Gov't. This is a most important thing & Johnson is the very man to lead & manage the reform. A considerable number of our Brig. Gen'l.s have been promoted to be Major Generals & Colonels to be Brigadiers— those selected being the officers who have distinguished themselves in the late victories.

This morning I rec'd. a telegram from Geo. Alexander in Wash'n. for me to go & meet him in Phil'a., that he had gotten a contract for the cartridges— As I intended going on to arrange the $100,000 for Jas. H. Lucas before 1st Apl., I determined to start at once & will leave in a day or two, to see also to this cartridge business.

There are rumors of reinforcements for the Rebels at Manassas—[44] I am very anxious to hear of the condition of things there. Banks has crossed over in large force at Harpers Ferry & I believe finds none of the enemy nearer than Winchester. Gen'l. McClellan went up to Harper's Ferry & was present when Banks' forces crossed, & returned to Wash'n. the same night by 2 A.M.

---

[43]Andrew Johnson (1808–75) served in the U.S. Senate (1857–62) as a pro-Union Democrat. After Tennessee seceded and was a divided battleground, Johnson remained in the Senate and Lincoln named him military governor of Tennessee.

[44]Manassas Gap Railroad linked with the Orange and Alexandria Railroad at Manassas Junction, then ran west for 60 miles to Strasburg. It was used to transport Confederate troops for the First Battle of Bull Run, then equipment and food. When Johnston retreated from northern Virginia in early March 1862, the Confederates destroyed the track.

Saturday night, Mch. 8, 1862 9 P.M.

Yesterday & today I have been extremely busy in working to be
ready to start for Phil'a. on Monday P.M. & I am nearly through— have
today closed up the cancellation of the $400,000 Lindell Hotel Co.
Bonds— for their new sizes & rec'd. my fee $250. for it— No battles, or
important movements since the evacuation of Columbus— Porter's mortar fleet had nearly all arrived at Key West by the 27th ult. & Capt David
Porter himself had arrived— a large number of new powerful war vessels
were reported in the Gulf— one vessel there very active & capture[d] a
good many prizes. I expect every day to hear of Porter's attacking New
Orleans, & perhaps Mobile too. We have now 3 batteries between Savannah & Ft. Pulaski. The Southern papers show great consternation in
Richmond, & other southern Cities— they do not seem to have any plan
of defense—

Andy. Johnson has left Washington for Nashville to start his new
movement— he goes as Military Gov. under the power of the Pres't.
establishing martial law— Gen'l. Fremont has just come out with a copious defense & yesterday Frank Blair made a speech on it in the House—
This is the first of the Fremont matter in Congress. It looks as though
Congress would not pass laws of confiscation. Of late, Tenn. Bonds have
gone up to 60 & Missouri to 52— This State keeps pretty generally quiet
now. Nothing lately heard from Genl. Curtis, in his pursuit of Price. No
news at all from the Army of the Potomac— Banks is continually pushing
on slowly, & has met with no resistance. The Rebels are believed to be in
large force at Winchester.

It seems now if the rebellion is going backwards & downwards. The
news from Europe is that all excitement there has stopped & no disposition existing to recognize the Rebels— & this too, before hearing of any
of our great victories— The only one heard of was that of Mill Spring—
In Richmond they speak of the defeat at Roanoke as discreditable. It is
surprising that the Rebel fleet permitted us to erect batteries on the
swampy islands above Ft. Pulaski; all the enterprise & bold achievements
are upon our side now; & the neglects & failures on side of the Rebels. I
suppose they are discouraged & worn out standing inactive & on the
defensive so long.

I thank God for our successes, & the strong hope I feel that Our National Integrity will be perceived.

St. Louis Sunday night Mch. 9, 1862 — 8½ P.M.

This morning mild & cloudy— at 1 commenced raining— & has continued to rain— warm. I have felt right badly— I always feel unhappy when I am about to part with my Family— Have nearly determined to take Evans[45] with me to Phil'a.; for he has been running down in health for some time past, & looks pale & thin, & I believe it w'd be of great benefit to him.

No war news today excepting that the Rebels are reported to be near or at New Madrid in some force, & probably surrounded by our troops— Gen'l. Pope may have got in the rear of them on this side— & Grant on the Ky. side— Rec'd. a letter of the 5th from Sam Simmons, from Ft. Henry— he speaks highly of Gen'l. Grant— wrote him tonight.

Philadelphia— Thursday Night   Mch. 13, 1862 — 2¼ o'c. at night

Although it is so late, I must write a few lines to keep up with the times

Left St. Louis Monday Evn'g. 10th at 4¼ o'c. & arrived in Phil'a. at 11½ at night Wed. night— bringing Evans & his nurse Marie—

Today in A.M. went to Jackson's & was surprised & gratified at the increase of our cartridge works— found them in successful operation on the late order for 1,444,000 army pistol carts. At $15.50 a m & making an excellent article— Geo. Alexander here—

Not until tonight at 12, could I get opportunity to read the newspapers— The events of the last few days have been momentous—

1st Curtis' great battle at Pea Ridge[46] about 5 days ago, defeating the combined forces of Price, Van Dorn, McIntosh & Ben. McCullough,

---

[45]Evans Rogers Dick was the third son of Franklin and Myra Dick, born in 1858.

[46]The Battle of Pea Ridge, Arkansas, began on the morning of March 7, 1862. The Confederates under aggressive Major General Earl Van Dorn marched north from Fayetteville, joining troops under Brigadier General Sterling Price, Brigadier General Benjamin McCulloch, and Brigadier General Albert Pike with his Native American troops. They

who was killed— Curtis' report shows the battle to have been a severe one
& a great victory for us— We were attacked— loss heavy on both sides &
no particulars yet—

Next comes the great naval contest between the U.S. ironclad vessel
the Monitor & the Rebel ironclad vessel the Merrimac—[47] with victory
to us, as the Merrimac retired, & somewhat damaged— The Merrimac,
before the Monitor arrived, destroyed the Cumberland & Congress & w'd
have destroyed the Minnesota & St. Laurence—

Next— the evacuation by the Rebels of Manassas & Leesburg &
their escaping— Our army moved forward & took possession. The
Rebels evacuated Manassas on the 9th & it is said were doing so a long
time before— It appears that their force was very small there— The facts
revealed astonish the Country & McClellan's utter ignorance of their
condition, & his allowing the remnant of them to get off & carry off all
their guns & pretty much everything, indicates, & almost proves McClellan's inefficiency— Nearly all the papers denounce him— severely & I do
not know whether he is a fool— a traitor, & miserably incompetent from
some other cause—

The President by orders first published today, on 27 Jan'y. issued
orders for a general advance of all our armies on 22 Feb'y.— & just now he
has issued an order taking McClellan's command of all the army away &
composing him to the command of the Army of the Potomac—[48] Giving
Halleck an enlarged Dpt. of from Knoxville west— & Fremont the inter-
mediate or Mountain Dpt.

---

charged three times, driving the Union forces under Major General Samuel R. Curtis
beyond Elkhorn Tavern. A fourth charge pushed them farther back, but reinforcements
arrived. Curtis, with Brigadier General Franz Sigel, successfully attacked the morning of
March 8, thinking correctly that the Confederate ammunition would be low. McCulloch
was killed and Van Dorn ordered a general retreat.

[47]The South had ten major ports which the U.S. Navy tried to block: New Orleans,
Mobile, Pensacola, Fernandina, Savannah, Charleston, Wilmington, New Bern, and Norfolk. The *Monitor/Merrimac* battle was in Hampton Roads, near the port of Norfolk, after
which the blockade remained intact.

[48]President Lincoln lost his patience when McClellan ignored his presidential
General War Order No. 1 for an offensive, after eight months of successfully organizing
and training the Army of the Potomac. Lincoln wanted McClellan to march straight
through Virginia to Richmond, but McClellan chose to go by water and up the peninsula
from Hampton Roads to Williamsburg to the Confederate capitol.

I wonder that Lincoln has not put some one else in command of the Potomac & let McClellan go. However the Pres't has made 5 grand divisions of the Army of the Potomac, & assigned officers to their command— thus he has shorn McClellan of a large part of his command & power. It is amazing to me that McClellan could have been so utterly incompetent— These 3 Major Gen'l.s now each report to the Secy. of War—

Phil'a. Friday night 12 o'c. Mch. 14, 1862

No stirring events reported today— the papers are full of accounts of the advance of our army into Va.— & finding desolation— & of the battle at Ft. Monroe— The Merrimac is injured & repairing at Norfolk— the Monitor, uninjured, lies waiting for her to come out— A part of the Rebel plan was an attack on Newport News & Ft. Monroe. Gen. Wool[49] called at once for reinforcements, which are going to him—

Gen'l. Burnside not heard from— & no news from David Porter, except his fleet have left the rendezvous for their destination— no news from Savannah— nor New Madrid— We do not know anything of the advances being made in Tennessee— but it is reported that Gen'l Smith is moving on Corinth, Miss.

Wrote 2 letters to my precious wife today— had 1 from her— this morning with Uncle E.[vans] & at Exchange & to see Jos. Swift, Mr. Blanch and Jos. Jones— then to Jackson's— after dinner to Jackson's— Evn'g. at tea at Phebe's—[50] then to Continental to Geo. A's room— then back & wrote to Myra & read papers— Darling Evans bright & happy—

Phil'a. Saturday Evng Mch 15, 1862 — ¼ to 10 P.M.

Been very busy all day— A.M. talked with Lewis about cartridges— then to Jackson's— then to Exchange to meet Uncle E. Closed up list of Lucas bondholders to be renewed— Then at ½ past 2, with Geo. Alexander, to Lewis Store to meet a Gentleman who proposed to

[49]John Ellis Wool (1784–1869) in 1861, as Union senior brigadier general, secured Fortress Monroe (an important supply depot) for the Union.

[50]Phebe was Franklin Dick's second sister, married to James H. Castle.

get the cartridge adopted by the War Department— Met him & had a talk over it— at 4½ he came up to Lewis' to see, as with Mr. M., agreed an arrangement— Evn'g. at Mary's to tea— Uncle E., Geo. A. time in evn'g.— wrote to Myra & now am to start to Washington tonight at 11, so as to be there Monday for the patent business in Pat. Office on Monday—

The weather so bad, I cannot take Evans with me— he is happy & bright here— News today of our taking New Madrid[51] & the Rebels leaving behind them their heavy guns, field guns, munitions & large supplies— This done under Gen'l. Pope— Rumors of the removal of Gen'l. Grant— do not understand it —

Phil'a Sat. night 11 o'c. Mch. 22nd 1862

Got back from Washington last night. The past has been an eventful week—

The great battle at Pea Ridge, Arkansas, I learn began March 7th.

Naval battle at Hampton Roads between the Merrimac & Monitor, the 9th Mch.

Mch. 11th. Fort Marion & St. Augustine taken poss'n. of by DuPont.

Mch. 14. Newburn, N.C., captured by Gen'l. Burnside—

Mch. 15. Battle at Island No. Ten in Mspi. River begun, and continued to this time— Now a week. Foote says the place is stronger than Columbus was—

Gen'ls. Grant & Smith marching from Savannah on Tenn. River to some other point not known.

McClellan's army has been for several days embarking at Alexandria— point of destination not known.

The abolitionists are howling against McClellan to have him removed.

I passed all my time in Wash'n. at work at the patent cases— Evans has been well & happy while I have been gone—

[51]Union forces led by General John Pope and Navy Flag Officer Andrew H. Foote with a fleet of ironclads fought the Confederates at New Madrid, Missouri, on March 13 and 14, 1862. Confederate troops and gunboats were unable to hold New Madrid and retreated to Island Number 10.

Phil'a. Wed. night Mch. 26/62 11¼ o'c.

After taking Newburn, Burnside went to Beaufort, N.C., found it evacuated & Fort Macon blown up by the Rebels— but to this time we have no particulars from there— The siege at Island No. 10 still continues— no result there yet— Grant & Smith in very large force are near Savanna, Ten. And the Rebels in large force near Corinth, Miss, & a battle there is near at hand—

No information at all as to movements of McClellan's Army by ship from Alexandria— The Merrimac not out yet, therefore all continues quiet at Fort Monroe— A severe battle has been fought near Winchester Va. between Gen'l Shields & the Rebel Jackson— Banks also there. We won, but no definite particulars—[52]

I have been busy in going to Jackson's, & to Howard's on 18th near Market, to get a machine contrived to mould the carts. [cartridges]—

Today Lewis & I went to Chester, to see if a place for manufacturing there can be got— found a suitable place on the Pier— of Mr._____ Crook. Which we can have at $50 a month— took refusal of it— Sent yesterday 120 boxes, 600 each, carts. to Wash'n.— today 60 boxes— making sent about 300,000 of the 1,400,000 ordered—

Phil'a. Friday night Mch. 28/62 — 10½ o'c.

Yesterday after breakfast, had long talk with Lewis about the cart. business— Then to Jackson's— came up with Geo. A. & proposed to let Lewis in at ¹⁵/₁₀₀— he agreed— then wrote long letter to Bartholow about it— P.M. went to see Henry Lawber & Dick Sergeant. Evn'g. Geo. & Mary & Phebe & I at Mary's to tea—

---

[52]Union troops under Major General Burnside captured New Berne, North Carolina, on March 14, 1862, as Confederate Brigadier General Lawrence O. Branch and his men fled to Kinston. Fort Macon, below Beaufort, North Carolina, was besieged from March 23 to April 25, 1862, when Confederate Colonel Moses J. White surrendered it to Union Major General John G Parke. The Battle of Corinth, Mississippi, did not take place until October 1862. The battle near Winchester was the First Battle of Kernstown, Virginia, on March 23, 1862, with Union Major General Nathaniel P. Banks defeating Confederate Major General Thomas J. "Stonewall" Jackson, who retreated.

This morning busy about the Lucas business— getting up the bonds— & also want to have Evans' photograph taken— P.M. filled up Lucas notes— at Continental to tea—

No battles today— We had a real victory at Winchester— The report of the capture of Beaufort & burning the Nashville & blowing up Fort Macon all false— Beaufort not taken & the Nashville escaped. No news yet of McClellan's movements— I suppose he is sending large numbers of troops from Alexandria, but we have not a word of it— Island No. 10 still holds out— Porter has arrived at the mouth of Mississippi, but no news of his progress— Troops gathering near Corinth— We have our troops at Florence & several points on the Memphis & Charleston Road, but no battle yet. No news from Savannah. Butler[53] not heard from since his arrival at Ship Island— The Rebels have taken Santa Fe, New Mexico—[54] The Merrimac is reported as ready to come out again, & is daily expected— It is said that we are prepared for her, but the particulars not given— Have not yet heard from Mr. Wm. J. Murdoch, Washington—

Phil'a. Saturday, Mch 29, 1862   2½ P.M.

This has been a horrible day— This morning about 8 o'clock Jackson's factory exploded, and many of the men & girls killed & many more dreadfully burned— I was on my way down there at 10 o'c. with Uncle Evans when we met Geo. Alexander, who had just come from there & told us of it— Geo & I then went down to Jackson's House— where were several other victims— Well, I will not describe it—

My feelings are indescribable— I try to feel thankful to God that it did not occur while I was there— Poor wretched man— What a world of pain, & sorrows, & accident— and the providence of God, how mysterious— The danger of this factory had been apparent to me, & I had every

[53]Benjamin Franklin Butler (1818–1893) was an ambitious politician who entered the Union army in 1861. Leading the Eighth Massachusetts Regiment, he was first assigned to occupy Baltimore and reopen vital railroad connections between Washington DC and the Union States. He led an expedition to capture North Carolina coastal forts.

[54]The Confederates planned to conquer the Southwest and had occupied Fort Bliss (Texas) and Fort Fillmore (New Mexico). Confederate Brigadier General Henry Hopkins Sibley defeated Union Colonel E. R. S. Canby at Valverde in the New Mexico Territory. Sibley took Albuquerque and Santa Fe by March 1862.

day cautioned them there about it— & I had kept away myself from it.

I will now give up all connection with this business— I have had more pain & anxiety about it than money can compensate me for. I telegraphed Myra at 12 o'c.

Night — 10½ o'c.

I have been feeling greatly distressed all day at this most sad disaster— It fills my mind & heart with sorrow to think of the afflictions of so many of these poor persons— I think that I will start back to St. Louis Monday night— I will go no further in this cartridge business. I have felt reluctant in it from the first, and never any confidence that it would be successful— There is now about enough money due from the Govt. to pay all expenses and refund what I have advanced— nearly $4,000— and I want to get out of it— It has given me much trouble & anxiety— cost me much time; and at best might not be profitable— It is not unlikely that I may lose 2 or 3,000$ to get out of it— but out of it I am determined to get— that is certain and determined upon.

I had a talk with Lewis about it tonight, & told him he might dispose of my interest if he could, to anyone who, with him, would repay what I have advanced—

Frank Blair & Apo. with George came up this P.M. from Washington— No war news today— The Southern papers show that the Rebels are making most desperate efforts to defend themselves, especially in building iron war steamers & drafting armies—

April 1862

"How many bitter enemies amongst the traitors have I made, by my activity for the cause of the union."

St. Louis Friday Evng. 9 o'c. Apl. 4, 1862

Left Phila. the 1st Sunday at 11½ A.M. Stopped at night at Altoona, & arrived in St. Louis last night at 12— All my time in Phila. after the fearful disaster was greatly distressed— the public excitement is considerable & there is a disposition to censure us for this dreadful thing— My feelings have been horrible— to feel that I have furnished the means which had drawn together to be so fearfully burned & killed so many unsuspecting young people— I left $550 with Lewis to be distributed amongst the sufferers—

Friday night, I wrote from Altoona to Lewis, authorizing him to use $2,500, in paying damages to adjoining property injured— Today the Jury of Investigation was to sit again in Phila. to give their report— About 7 or 8 in all were dead by the time I left Phila. I fear that many more will die—

All the way out, I could think of little else than this horrible matter— The money loss does not much trouble me— I have already
advanced for all purposes, $4,561.56 including $550 left with Lewis for
the relief of these sufferers— and how much more it may cost me I can
not tell— damages & claims may come in one shape & another to the
extent of several thousand dollars more—

I feel as if God had given me a most solemn warning in this blow.
True, I did not seek out this project— and I was reluctantly & not until I
had refused several times, induced by George Alexander to go into it—
and when I did, I moved in the dark, & never looked forward to getting
up in manufacturing, nor did I expect to put in more than a few hundred
dollars— But I have found it a vexatious, tedious, worrying, wearing,
profitless, and at the finale, a fearful thing—

It is God's visitation upon me for desiring to make money at this
time— I was easy in circumstances— But I must do myself the justice to
say, that I went into it against my inclination & my judgment; at the
pressing urgency of George, and partially to benefit him— nor did I at all
appreciate the dangerous nature of the work to the employees, until the
last few days when I saw them crowded together, with the powder all
around them— I feel no moral responsibility for these poor people, for I
had nothing to do with the work, & constantly remonstrated with Jackson about the risk and danger he was subjecting them to. He is the
responsible man for it, & fearfully has he suffered— the death of a fine
son, 23 years old— 2 daughters severely injured—

All the time in Phila., before I went to Wash'n., I was very unhappy
about this business— I have suffered torments, lest it would run away
with the money I had accumulated— I put in all the money & had also to
direct the management, & got but ¼ the profits— I felt that it was a mistake— I suffered in it daily— And when this stunning blow came, I
instantly resolved to end my connection with it—

On Monday morning, I so informed George Alexander, & urged
him to have nothing more to do with it; & told him it was a failure— &
w'd ruin him— But he is infatuated with it, & went to work to get someone else to take my place in it— I have some consolation in believing that
I convinced Lewis that he ought to have nothing more to do with it—

I have prayed to God continually now that my heart may cling to him & his cause for its support & confidence— But a few days before, I had bewailed that this thing so distracted my mind & heart, that until I was through with it, I must postpone my former conferences with his Holy Spirit— how little did I then think how soon, & how dreadfully this termination should come—

And oh the Mercy of God in my abandonment of Him, that He did not then abandon & throw me off from Him—

I feel sincerely that whatever loss I may suffer in future, or trials that may be before me, in consequence of this disaster, I can and ought meekly to bear, as chastening from the Lord to me, as one whom he wills to so draw unto Him— I pray now that God will in this spirit keep & preserve my mind & soul.

At this moment I knelt down, & earnestly prayed to God as above. I ask of him not worldly gifts, nor ease, nor worldly peace— but the meek, contrite spirit that faith gives. Come what may in his Providence to me in this life, I pray for faith, contrition & the Holy Spirit for myself, my precious wife & children.

And now, tonight, I feel, here in St. Louis, almost separated & isolated from all around me, but my own house-hold. Ben. Farrar has just removed to the Country, & tonight, I do not think of a Friend that I have in this City, that my heart draws me to— There are here, many good hearted Union men who are friendly to me; but there are no associations or intercourse of friendship between me & them— How sad & dreary is this life— here have I lived nearly 20 years, & not a solitary person but Ben's People, who warm my heart—

Can I wonder, that I do not enjoy life in St. Louis— If my circumstances compelled me to work to get my every day's support, I could not think of going anywhere else— But as I have an income of from 3 to 6 thousand dollars, & therefore, am not compelled so to work, I do not feel anything holding me here; excepting that I hardly feel safe to leave, as the war might cut off my income— & then I be left to begin to labor at an other place, where I might not be able to make a support.

But tonight, as I sit here, & think in this City of 150,000 People, where I have so long lived, I might leave forever, & not be regretted by many, & leave no sympathizing friends, the world, as it is here, is cold &

sad & cheerless— and too, how many bitter enemies amongst the traitors
have I made, by my activity for the cause of the union; & how many
seeming or half way Union men avoid me, lest their countenance might
bring upon them the displeasure of the Traitors.

No war news yet. The siege of Island No. 10 continues, with no
result yet. The Merrimac has not yet come out, though expected for many
days past, & the Monitor still lies waiting for her. No news as to McClellan's movements in Va., excepting that a large force is going by water from
near Wash'n.— Ft. Pulaski, not yet taken—nor Fort Macon— both are
besieged. We are concentrating an immense army on the Tennessee River,
near Savanna, and the Rebels at Corinth, Miss., and the pickets of both
armies close together; a great battle there impending. Some days ago it
was reported that Porter is ascending the Mi'ppi towards New Orleans—
In many quarters I expect daily to hear of great battles— The Rebels are
making every effort, & the Reports are that they are pressing large numbers into arms. The Senate yesterday passed a law to abolish slavery in the
District of Columbia— I approve of that— The House of Reps. has long
been & still is working on the tax bill.

The Missing Journals

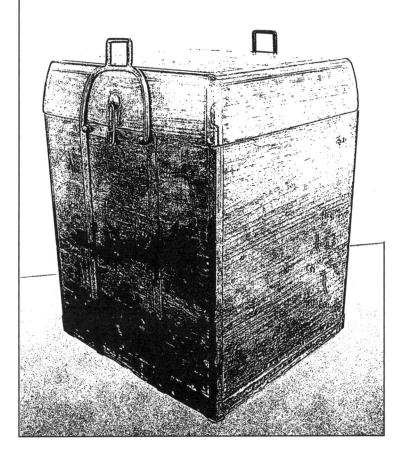

Franklin Archibald Dick.
Painting by D Frun[?], 1850[?]. Photo by Elizabeth Smith © 2007.

April 1862 through September 1864

Franklin Dick's journals from April 1862 through September 1864 (numbers 2 through 9) are missing, but other sources provide information on what he was doing during this time. Dick had returned to St. Louis in December 1861 and began serving on the assessment board in January 1862. The Board of Assessors had been formed in December 1861, consisting of two officers and several citizens known to be loyal to the Union. The board's purpose was to raise money for the Western Sanitary Commission to support civilian refugees in St. Louis. Southern sympathizers who did not voluntarily donate money to the commission were required to pay an assessment based on the value of their property and the degree of their disloyalty (those who had joined the Confederate army; those who gave direct aid to the Confederacy; and those who supported the Confederacy in print or speech). The board compiled a list of known or suspected secessionists and determined the value of their property. Their first list contained three hundred names. In December, the board selected sixty-four names from the list and assessed fines that varied from $100 to $400, giving them five days to pay their "Christmas Greetings."[1] Some of those assessed denied supporting the South, and some protested the legality of the fines.

In January 1862, when Franklin Dick was serving on the Board of Assessors, new assessments were drawn up and General Henry Halleck ordered that the property of anybody who refused to pay should be seized and sold. The highest unpaid assessments belonged to Dr. William

---

[1]Parrish, *A History of Missouri*, 3:68. Much of the information in this section about events in Missouri was drawn from the Civil War St. Louis timeline available online at http://www.civilwarstlouis.com/timeline/index.htm.

McPheeters of $800, for which his furniture was taken; and J. Kennard & Sons, merchants, whose fine of $800 was satisfied by carpets. D. Robert Barclay, an attorney, lost two library cases of books; and Sam Engler, another merchant, had $700 worth of candles taken, which did not yield that amount at the auction which followed.[2] On January 26, Dick wrote in his journal "I have contracted additional hate from these bloody Traitors here by acting on this Comm[ission]," and on January 28, he wrote that the rebels were "exasperated by the seizure of their chattels by the Provost Marshall Gehl for the assessments our Board makes on them."

Despite the contempt that Franklin Dick and his family were shown by the Southern sympathizers, Conditional Republicans and Old St. Louisans, he continued to follow his conscience and serve on the board until it was dissolved in March 1862, when Halleck ended his post as Commander of the Department of Missouri.[3] Missouri was a sharply divided state during that time, so that even Southern children were taught to walk around a Union flag, and Union children to keep near their flag.[4] Dick had been practicing law in St. Louis since 1844, but he had stepped over the line of social and political etiquette, and he and his family suffered from his actions.

Dick was also involved in other affairs in St. Louis. On March 5, 1862, he wrote to his brother-in-law Frank Blair, Chairman of the Commission on Military Affairs in the U.S. Congress, about the problems of paroling Confederate officers.

> Dear Frank:
> There is one thing that at first was inexplicable to me— it is the feeling or policy that induces U.S. officers to grant extraordinary privileges to the rebel officers who are taken as prisoners, such as releasing of a number of them in this city on parole by General Halleck, thus giving them the opportunity of going freely among our wealthy secessionists. The consequence of this was that these home rebels ran after the officers, dined and feted them, encouraged them to stand firm in their disloyalty, and so bold and defiant did they become as I am

[2]Gerteis, *Civil War St. Louis,* 174–76.
[3]Gerteis, *Civil War St. Louis,* 175.
[4]Parrish, *A History of Missouri,* 3:62

informed that General Halleck has revoked the parole, gathered up the officers and sent them to confinement at Alton.

I was surprised that so judicious a man as Halleck should have fallen into this error; but with his usual correctness he soon saw his mistake. From what I have learned of the feelings of the regular officers I am inclined to believe that Halleck fell into this error through their influence. I have heard most loyal and sensible officers of the U.S. Army say that they had no personal feeling whatever in the war nor toward the officers whom they captured. This I suppose because these officers of ours have kept aloof from political contests and do not recognize in the rebel officers the instigators and workers up of this rebellion. In our eyes Buckner, Floyd, Jo. Johnston, &c., are traitors, and none the less so because they hold in this rebellion the place of officers. If the rebellion had been less formidable and soon put down these men would not have been treated as officers but as felons if captured. There are necessary reasons why to a certain extent we have to treat them as conducting a war and therefore according to the rules of war. The only reason that I recognize for this is that we may save our own soldiers from severe treatment when captured by them. Beyond this there is no necessity for our going, and I say that it is only necessity or in other words our inability to do so that prevented us in the beginning from hanging them all as traitors. The privates and non-commissioned officers in the rebel armies are mostly ignorant men who enlisted as they believed to protect their country from an unjust aggressive war. The proper treatment for them—all I believe concur in this—treat them fairly, correct the errors they have been educated in, inform them of the truth and let them go back home when it can be safely done. But these men who under a mock government are called officers, who are but political desperadoes in military garb and disguise, must be punished; if not for their misdeeds certainly for the sake of the country. Will the privates, the masses, believe their leaders criminals or in the wrong when they see them set at large on their honor and allowed to associate with the wealthy rebels who so openly honor them?

I call your attention to this matter at this early day hoping that you will think it worth while to bring the matter before Secretary Stanton. The officers of the Army do not feel the effects of this rebellion as the masses of the people do. To them (the officers of the U.S. Army) it is a war merely, and not a political struggle—maddened, desperate, and aimed to destroy rather than submit to a political defeat. Believing as I do that the practice I have spoken of is a serious evil and that the only way of remedying it is for the Secretary of War to make general regulations upon the subject, to be departed from by commanding officers only for pressing reasons, I therefore suggest that you call his attention to the matter. I have no fear that General Halleck will again fall into the error, but in my opinion few of our officers are equal to him in correctness of judgment.

Yours, very truly,
F. A. Dick[5]

Reading Dick's letter to his close friend, Frank Blair, it is important to remember that the home rebels, wealthy secessionists, and rebel officers were their former friends and business associates. Both Blair and Dick had invested twenty years getting to know the people of St. Louis, becoming a part of the community and setting up their law practices. Each day, the divisions of the Civil War further separated Dick and Blair from all they had strived to create.

In the East, McClellan led Union forces against Confederate forces led by Joseph Johnston in the Peninsula Campaign. Near Richmond, Johnston's army attacked McClellan's troops in the Battle of the Seven Pines. Johnston was wounded and Lee assumed command of the Confederate Army. On July 25, the two armies fought the first of a series of battles near Richmond that came to be known as the Seven Days Battles. Losses were very heavy and McClellan retreated toward Washington, DC while Lee withdrew north toward Richmond.

In July and August, General Pope led the Union forces in a series of battles in Northern Virginia, ending with a Confederate victory at the Second Battle of Bull Run (August 29–30). After this loss, President Lincoln relieved Pope of command. In early September, Lee invaded the North and headed for Harpers Ferry, pursued by the Union Army under McClellan.

[5]Franklin A. Dick to Frank Blair Jr., March 5, 1861, *The War of the Rebellion: A Compilation of the Official Records of the Union and Confederate Armies*, 2.3.379–80 (hereafter cited as *OR*, with series, volume, and page number). Frank Blair sent a copy of Dick's letter to Secretary of War Edwin M. Stanton; Blair to Stanton, March 15, 1862, *OR* 2.3.379.

A Union victory at the Battle of Antietam in Maryland on September 17 helped to restore morale in the North, and gave Lincoln the opportunity to announce his preliminary Emancipation Proclamation, which would free slaves in areas that had rebelled against the United States.

In September 1862, General Samuel Ryan Curtis took over command of the Department of the Missouri, replacing General John Schofield, who had succeeded Henry Halleck in July 1862.[6] When General Halleck had replaced Frémont in November 1861, he insisted on a clear chain of command and well-defined authority and responsibilities, and had declared that he would take decisive action against disloyal persons. Franklin Dick felt that Halleck was too lenient to prisoners who were rebel officers, believed that prisoners from the lower ranks should be treated fairly, and that many prisoners, when shown their error, would return to being loyal citizens of the Union. In early November, Curtis appointed Dick as provost marshal general for Missouri,[7] making him responsible for carrying out orders for banishment or assessment of disloyal persons, and for overseeing the military prisons and dealing with prisoners. On November 20, Dick wrote about conditions in the military prisons to the commander of the prison at Alton, Illinois.

St. Louis, November 20, 1862
Col. J. Hildebrand, Commanding at Alton, Ill.
　　　Colonel: The military prisons here are overcrowded and sickness prevailing amongst the prisoners and is rapidly increasing. I desire to know the number of prisoners that the Alton prison is capable of receiving and the number now confined there. There are many prisoners sent to Saint Louis under sentence of imprisonment for the war, and it has become necessary to remove them from Saint Louis to relieve the crowded conditions of the prisons and to make room for other prisoners daily coming forward from the interior of the State. Will you let me know the number you can now receive, and also from time to time let me know when room has been made by discharges or removals to another point, stating the number that you can receive? Will you detain at Alton such prisoners as

---

[6]Faust, *Historical Times*, 198–99; and Denney, *The Civil War Years*, 85, 137–38, 477.
[7]Gerteis, *Civil War St. Louis*, 357; Freehling, *Road to Disunion*, 151–76; and Parrish, *History of Missouri*, 3:65–77.

have been sent here who have not been committed for the war until finally disposed of by me? In the future I will endeavor not to send any to Alton excepting those to be imprisoned for the war or a long term, but there are some prisoners now in Alton sent from here whose cases have not been finally acted upon. Have you any prisoners of war which you intend soon sending to Cairo to be forwarded to Vicksburg for exchange? I will send about fourteen from here in a few days, and if you send can it not be arranged to send them under the same guard from here? Please inform me if letters to prisoners are thoroughly examined before passing into their hands.

I am, colonel, very respectfully, your obedient servant,

F.A. Dick,
Lieut. Col. and Provost-
Marshal-General Dept. of the
Missouri.[8]

Dick wrote to Hildebrand again on November 27 about the transfer of prisoners. He began, "I send you to-day about 400 prisoners. The precise number I cannot this moment state, as the list is not corrected, but with them will be a list stating names and numbers.... Gratiot Street [Prison] has nearly 1,000 prisoners in it, and of this number over 200 are sick."[9] What should have been a simple transfer of prisoners from one facility to another became a problem. As Dick explained in a letter of December 8 to Colonel Hoffman, Commissary-General of Prisoners, when he took office, "the Gratiot Street Prison held about 800 prisoners. Its maximum number should not have exceeded 500." Dick had repairs made to the Myrtle Street Prison and transferred 150 prisoners there, but prisoners continued to pour in, "coming in daily from the country at the rate of from 30 to 100 a day." The number at Gratiot Street soon rose to 1,100, and sickness began to spread through the prison. Dick reported that:

within a week it ran up to 235 so that a large number of sick and dying men were lying on the floors. Every morning men would be found dead on the floor in the common rooms who had received no attention because from the crowded condition

[8]Dick to Hildebrand, November 20, 1862, OR 2.4.739–40.
[9]Dick to Hildebrand, November 27, 1862, OR 2.4.762.

of the rooms it was impossible with the ordinary hospital atten-
dance. With this condition of things it was impossible to
observe the ordinary police and sanitary regulations. The men
could not be even taken out of doors, for the prison has no yard.

He determined to transfer to Alton "several hundred of those whose cases
would not probably be disposed of at an early day." Looking at the records,
he determined that there were 400 prisoners of this category, but the actual
number turned out to be 276. He explained:

> Upon the lists were a large number who were found too sick to
> go. Some had died, some been discharged and two pages of
> names were duplicated. Had the books of this office been in
> proper condition such inaccuracy would not have existed, but
> for that I am not in fault for half my time has been occupied in
> overhauling the confused state of things found by me in this
> office.[10]

In a letter of November 29 to Colonel Hildebrand, Dick wrote:

> All such irregularities are being corrected as rapidly as possible
> but order cannot be brought out of confusion instantaneously.
> What made the matter appear worse the officer in command
> of the guard left at the prison the rolls of the prisoners actually
> sent. This will be sent to you at once."[11]

Franklin Dick felt that a large number of the prisoners would gladly
be exchanged to be sent South, which would relieve the prison over-
crowding. As an attorney, Dick was careful and concerned with ensuring
that each prisoner's case was dealt with legally and properly; as a businessman, he understood the ramifications of the mass of incorrect records in
the provost marshal general's office, and how important it was to keep
accurate official information. He worked long and hard to excel at his
post to support the Union, but was continually hampered by past mistakes, disagreement, and incompetence in his subordinates. Dick always
spoke out for what was fair, honest, and best to his way of thinking,

[10]Dick to Colonel W. Hoffman, December 8, 1862, *OR* 2.5.48–50.
[11]Dick to Colonel J. Hildebrand, November 29, 1862, *OR* 2.5.50.

despite the consequences to himself and his family.

One of the most difficult tasks for Franklin Dick was to ferret out and remove disloyal people, especially those able to speak their views to large groups, such as ministers. In December, Dick wrote to Montgomery Blair, asking him to give a letter to President Lincoln regarding a certain prisoner.

> St. Louis, Mo., Decr. 12th 1862.
> Dear Sir.
> I enclose an important letter to the President, which I ask you to place before him— I take this course, that it may receive his attention. This man Farris is well known here as just the kind of a Rebel that can do most harm. The Preachers in St. Louis, with few exceptions, are miserable enemies of the Government, and I am urged upon all hands to send them out of the State, for under their protection and countenance disloyalty flourishes. Farris is a persistent, persevering Rebel, and I trust that the President will not sustain Him, and so, strike a serious blow at our cause in this State. I had nothing to do with the charges against Farris— I find him sentenced by Genl Merrill, who is now sustained by Genl Curtis & myself— Col. Gantt also refused to interfere in his behalf— His disloyalty is of the most injurious kind, for he is man of talent, education, good address and untiring perseverance. From what union men tell me, he has done great injury to our cause in Missouri.
>
>> I have the honor to be Your
>> Obt. Svt.
>> F. A. Dick
>> Lt. Col. Provost Marshal Genl[12]

> St. Louis, Mo., Decr. 12th 1862.
> To the President
> A certain Robert P. Farris, a Preacher, residing at St. Charles Missouri, was ordered by Brig Genl. Merrill, commanding that District of the State, to be imprisoned for the War. His sentence has been modified by consent of Genl Merrill, to leaving this State, during the War. I learn from Judge

---

[12]Franklin A. Dick to Montgomery Blair, December 12, 1862. Abraham Lincoln Papers at the Library of Congress. Transcribed and annotated by the Lincoln Studies Center, Knox College, Galesburg, Illinois.

Office of the Provost Marshal General,
DEPARTMENT OF THE MISSOURI.

St. Louis, Mo., Decr. 12th 1862.

To the President

A certain Robert P. Farris.
a Preacher, residing at St. Charles Missouri, was
ordered by Brig. Genl. Merrill, commanding that
district of the State, to be imprisoned for the war.
His sentence has been modified by consent of Genl.
Merrill, to leaving this State, during the war.
I learn from Judge Barton Bates, presiding justice
of our supreme court, (son of Atty. Genl. Bates) that
Farris is one of the most impudent, persistent and ominous
Rebels in the State, and as a Minister, has wielded
a powerful influence in aid of the rebellion.
undoubtedly he ought to be removed from this
State during the war. I understand, that he
has a strong hope, of procuring an order from
your Excellency, rescinding the sentence
against him, and therefore I send this
Statement, that it may be known that such
action would encourage a dangerous and
influential class of cunning aiders of
the rebellion in Missouri.
I have the honor to
be your most obedient
Servant

F. A. Dick
Lt. Col. Provost marshal Genl.
Department of the Missouri

20110

Franklin Dick's letter to President Lincoln, December 12, 1862.
Abraham Lincoln Papers at the Library of Congress.

Barton Bates, Presiding Justice of our Supreme Court, (son of
Atty. Gen. Bates) that Farris is one of the most impudent, persistent and ingenious Rebels in the State, and as a Minister,
has wielded a powerful influence in aid of the rebellion.
Undoubtedly he ought to be removed from this State during
the War. I understand, that He has a strong hope, of procuring
an order from Your Excellency, rescinding the sentence against
him, and therefore I send this statement, that it may be known
that such action would encourage a dangerous and influential
class of cunning aiders of the rebellion in Missouri.

> I have the Honor to be Your most
> obedient Servant
> F. A. Dick
> L. Col. Provost Marshal Genl.,
> Department of the Missouri

Farris did live in the County of my residence & I well know his
general course. For God's sake dont let him return to Missouri.
His banishment from Missouri is a very slight punishment for
his misdeeds.

> Barton Bates[13]

A week later, Dick wrote to Montgomery Blair again, this time
about permission to send Confederate sympathizers South and enclosing
a letter to Lincoln.

St. Louis, Mo., Decr. 19th 1862.
Dear Sir.

I enclose a letter to the President, which I beg you to
read, and present to Him. It would be most disastrous, for a
different course from that advised by me to be pursued.

I desire very much to obtain leave, to send our bad Rebels
South.

These fashionable Women Spies are working the most
serious mischief to the cause, & yet I can not handle them,
unless allowed to send them South— They and the disloyal
Preachers, keep the fire burning briskly in Missouri, and cost

---

[13]Franklin A. Dick to Abraham Lincoln, December 12, 1862, endorsed by Barton
Bates. Abraham Lincoln Papers at the Library of Congress. Transcribed by the Lincoln
Studies Center, Knox College, Galesburg, Illinois.

the Govt. much money— many lives. Today I send off Revd Sam. McPheeters and his Wife & turn his Church over into the hands of the Union men of his Congregation.

If the President will sustain me, I will rid the State of Rebel Preachers,— send them to preach to their Southern Bretheren. Genl. Curtis has told me to send off McPheeters— & I expect soon that he will direct me to send the other less open, but more wicked Rebel Preachers—

I do most earnestly ask that the President will let Genl Curtis know that he may use his discretion in these matters.

I press this subject, for it is most important at this time.

Unless I can work, there is no use in my holding this office. I took it at on Frank's strong appeal to me— which he urged because he believed I could accomplish Good— But unless sustained by the President, I can do nothing.

> I have the honor to
> be your Most obt. svt
> F. A. Dick
> Lt. Col. Provost Marshal Genl
> Dpt. of the Mo.

I ask that the President himself, or through you, will favor me with an immediate reply.

[Endorsed on Envelope by Lincoln:]

McPheeters— Preacher at St. Louis. Also, about allowing rebels to go South.[14]

St. Louis, Mo., December 19th 1862.
To the President

I submit most respectfully to the consideration of Your Excellency the following remarks. I was informed to day by Major Genl Curtis, that the President had telegraphed him to inquire, if it would be advisable to suspend martial law in Missouri.

---

[14]Franklin A. Dick to Montgomery Blair [With Endorsement by Lincoln], December 19, 1862, Abraham Lincoln Papers at the Library of Congress. Transcribed and annotated by the Lincoln Studies Center, Knox College, Galesburg, Illinois.

Officially I have most complete and reliable information as to the condition of this State. I have been in Missouri nearly all the time during the rebellion, and I say positively that at no previous time have the efforts and evil purposes of the Rebels in this State and City, been more active and hopeful than now.

All through the portions of the State, occupied by our troops, Traitors are indefatigable in their efforts to aid their Southern Friends. The successful military efforts of such brave men as Genl Merrill, who has captured thousands of those Traitors, have made them somewhat cautious for a time: but their hopes never die, and their purposes and efforts remain the same.

Appeals and representations to the contrary may be made by Major Rollins, and Judge Hall, & other Gentlemen who live in the worst part of the State— but those Gentlemen are not regarded in Missouri as fair Representatives of the Union men, who uphold the Government.

It is not unfair to say, that those Gentlemen were elected by the votes of disloyal men.

I make these statements, not from a desire to injure them, for I esteem them both as Gentlemen; but that their dependence upon disloyal men may be known.

I have daily evidence, that in the interior & in St. Louis, secretly information & material aid is being furnished, by many of our most respectful Citizens to the Enemy.

The most bitter hostility exists between them & the Union people— I have daily appeals from the interior for the adoption of a more stringent policy, that Union men may have security from their rebellious neighbors.

I have instructed Provost Marshals in the interior to select out the leading, dangerous men and banish them from the State, during the War.

Genl Merrill, & the other Generals in the interior, are pursuing the same system—

I came into this office on the 5th of November— I then found Genl Curtis, in consequence of the persistent appeals of pretended Union men at times really in doubt as to what course to pursue— but the powerful evidence of this active disloyalty, daily furnished him through my office, & other sources, have completely satisfied him of the <u>necessity</u> of a vigorous policy with so malignant an enemy.

No one who has contended with these people as we in Missouri have done, & who is a true friend of the Government, is in doubt as to this.

But pretended Union men, who never work for the cause, and encounter no hardships, nor risks, can well cry out in behalf of the Rebels.

I therefore most respectfully ask of the President, that he will not require that we relax in our Efforts to fight this Enemy in the most effective manner. It is no light matter to stand here, in conflict with these people, and if we are in a fair way to get the upperhand, it should be remembered, that upon the least opportunity they will spring at our throats again.

I trust that the President will not consider me officious in offering these suggestions; but placed as I have been by the order of Genl Curtis at the head of a most responsible, and powerful office, I am convinced of the necessity of maintaining the ascendency of the Federal Government in Missouri by force.

To remove military supremacy, will be to let loose these evil doers again, upon true Union men.

There is on other point that I beg leave to present to the President.

I find that a considerable number of the Southern Sympathisers, desire to go South—

Genl Curtis has evinced decided willingness to allow them to go, but he is of the impression that ~~such is~~ to do so is not favored by the Government.

If permission can be given, to allow such persons to go, we will be rid of many unchangeable enemies, who will do us less injury there than here. I applied to Genl Curtis to day, to allow me to permit a Wife, Daughter— four small Boys of a Rebel Preacher in the South to go— and I understood from Him that he doubted if it would meet with favor at Washington.

There are several prominent Rebels in St. Louis, who ought to be sent South— There are many female spies, in good society, who ought to be sent— They are efficient aiders of the rebellion.

I urgently ask, that such Persons, of both sexes, I may be permitted, with the approval of Genl Curtis, to send to their Southern Friends. If the lines were opened, and Southern Sympathisers, with their slaves, were permitted to go, it would

work a most wonderful good effect upon Missouri, and in a
short time, its result would be permanent peace and tranquil-
lity to the State.

> I have the Honor to be
> Your Excellency's most obt. servt.
> F. A. Dick
> Lt. Col. Provost Marshal Genl
> Dept. of the Mo.[15]

In a memorandum of December 22, Dick spelled out regulations for
the office of the provost marshal regarding recordkeeping, gathering and
examining evidence, treatment of prisoners, and punishment. His
description gives valuable information about the types of offenses prisoners have committed.

> In determining the punishment of prisoners great weight will
> be given to the opinion of the officers who examine the cases,
> and especially where they personally examine the prisoner. In
> every such case the appearance and manner of the prisoner
> should be noted, and in my own examinations that not unfre-
> quently determines my judgment.
> Prisoners will be held for the war when having taken up
> arms they have returned home, taken the oath and again taken
> up arms.... The most difficult class is where men have taken
> the oath and afterwards taken up arms. The circumstances and
> motives which have induced men to take the oath are so vari-
> ous, its influence so various, and then the circumstances of vio-
> lating it so various and difficult to appreciate that each case
> will have its peculiarities. If practicable this class should have a
> personal examination and be attended to by the same officer,
> whose decision will be final.
> The class who during the last year have taken up arms for
> the first time is distinct. My impression of them is unfavorable,
> and as a general rule they should be imprisoned for the war.
> Men who have withstood the effect of the early heat and zeal of
> the rebels and who have seen the evil effects of the war upon

[15]Franklin A. Dick to Abraham Lincoln, December 19, 1862. Abraham Lincoln
Papers at the Library of Congress. Transcribed and annotated by the Lincoln Studies
Center, Knox College, Galesburg, Illinois (also in *OR* 2.5.99–100).

this State, and who at last went off when by the effect of enroll-
ing orders they considered themselves forced to take one side,
have proven themselves rebels. Many such pretend that they
acted under sudden influences; but that is not so, for the influences have been operating daily since the war began. Yet there
are some of this class who were so weak as to blindly follow
others. Theirs, however, is a permanent blindness. My opinion
therefore is that this class should be either imprisoned for the
war or be banished to the free States.

There is a troublesome class, being those who are traitors
at heart, but who not having committed any palpable acts yet
have so encouraged the rebellion that they have been put under
bonds, and after that have after an interval recommenced their
first conduct. The difficulty with these is in getting at the
proof. If such conduct is proven they should be imprisoned for
the war and they should be noticed as proper subjects to be
sent South.

Those concerned in marauding and going to Union men's
houses and taking their arms, pressing horses, &c., expelling
Union men, supplying provisions to rebel bands, especially
those concerned in small bands who have infested neighbor-
hoods, and such other crimes as make them triable by a military
commission, should be sentenced to imprisonment for the war
and sent to Alton. But they should be noted on the rolls as triable, to be tried by a military commission. And all such cases
should be entered on a list to be reported to headquarters for
trial by a military commission....

It is absolutely necessary that the prisoners' book be
made complete every day. It must be written up each night....

Prisoners who have been longest confined should be first
disposed of.

There are some cases where there is neither charge nor
evidence against the prisoner. It is important to hunt up such
cases that their release may be ordered. Prisoners are being
released every day because the evidence does not prove any act
of disloyalty; but if it shows the prisoner to be in active sympa-
thy with the rebellion it is proper to release such men in case
they consent to leave the State for the war.

Persons released to remain in Missouri will be required to
enroll in the Enrolled Missouri Militia, take the oath and give

bond of $1,000 or more. Most releases are accompanied by oath or bond.[16]

The regulations discussed in this letter were formalized in General Orders No. 35, issued by the Headquarters, Department of the Missouri, on December 24, 1862. The document ends by stating "The foregoing rules and regulations are made by command of Major-General Curtis," and is signed by "F. A. Dick, Lieut. Col. and Provost-Marshal-General, Dept. of the Missouri."[17]

Later that month, Dick wrote again to Montgomery Blair, asking him to arrange a meeting with the president.

> Office of the Provost Marshal General
> Department of the Missouri
> St. Louis, Mo., Decr. 29th, 1862
> Hon M. Blair: Post Master Genl
> Dear Sir:
> This will be handed you by George P. Strong, Esq. Member of the Bar. As a lawyer, Mr. Strong is one of the ablest & I personally know him in practice. He is one of our foremost men. I have full confidence in him in every respect. I mean just what I say. Urged on by many of our Union men, Mr. Strong goes to Washington to lay before the President a statement of the real condition of things here. I will vouch for every fact that he states. Will you do our Union people the justice of obtaining for Mr. Strong an early interview with the President.
> > I remain yours
> > very truly
> > F. A. Dick[18]

Franklin Dick and his fellow provost marshals throughout the state continued to work against rebel activities, but in Washington, Lincoln's cabinet feuded with each other and there were doubts about the provost marshal system. On January 14, 1863, General Curtis received a telegram from the secretary of war regarding General Order No. 35.

[16]Franklin A. Dick, Regulations, December 22, 1862, *OR* 2.5.110–12.
[17]Franklin A. Dick, General Orders No. 35, December 24, 1862, *OR* 1.22.1.868–71.
[18]Franklin A. Dick to Montgomery Blair, December 29, 1862, Abraham Lincoln Papers at the Library of Congress.

War Department
Washington, January 14, 1863
Major-General Curtis, Saint Louis, Mo.:

The President's attention having been called to the recent order of your provost-marshal in Saint Louis, published in the newspapers, it is disapproved by him, and he directs:

1st. That the order be suspended.

2nd. That all orders of provost-marshals in the State of Missouri respecting trade, commerce, or anything but the discipline and government of the troops in the United States service be also suspended, and the provost-marshals be relieved from service in such capacity, excepting Saint Louis.

Further instructions on this subject will be transmitted by mail.

You will please acknowledge the receipt of this telegram.

Edwin M. Stanton,
Secretary of War.[19]

General Curtis responded at once, asking Stanton to reconsider.

Headquarters
Saint Louis, Mo., January 15, 1863
Hon. E. M. Stanton:

Provost-Marshal's Orders, No. 35, is mainly a compilation of old orders. Where we have no troops, provost-marshals guard public property, arrest spies, and give immediate notice of guerrilla forces. The system was inaugurated over a year ago, and is the only way of keeping the peace in Northern Missouri, especially in border counties. I have no serious complaints coming to my knowledge. The rebels that attempted to capture Springfield are retreating, hotly pursued. Things every day grow more quiet. I am constantly curtailing restrictions regarding trade as safety seems to permit, and I fear the change required by your dispatch of the 14th will give new trouble. May I suspend action until I can confer by letter?

Saml. R. Curtis,
Major-General[20]

[19]Edwin M. Stanton to Samuel R. Curtis, January 14, 1863. *OR* 1.22.2.41.
[20]Samuel R. Curtis to E. M. Stanton, January 15, 1863. *OR* 1.22.2.42.

On the same day, General Curtis sent a letter to Secretary Stanton in which he said, "The provost-marshal system is not of my planting or growth, but is now so old, deep-rooted, and wide-spread it cannot be summarily disposed of without danger of losses and disasters." He described the duties of the office:

> ...provost-marshals took charge of prisoners, watched contraband trade, discovered and arrested spies, found out rebel camps, and pursued and arrested the rebels in the neighborhoods. They operate with volunteers, militia, and police force, just as circumstances require, and in Southern Iowa and large districts of Missouri, where recruiting guerrilla agents strive to organize their bands, they are the only stationary, permanent official sentinels, who keep me advised and guard public safety. Public arms, prisoners, contraband property, and forfeited bonds are held by them and properly disposed of, and immediate discharge would create loss and confusion where everything is now quiet and secure....
>
> I send you the letter of Colonel Dick, my provost-marshal-general, to show other duties devolved on these men. Soon after my assuming command, I presented to the General-in-Chief the importance of more exact and uniform rules in regard to the system, and desired the matter might be taken up at Washington, but, in the absence of any instructions, I directed the provost-marshal-general to compile and construct some general and uniform rule of action. This he did in Orders, No. 35, which I suppose is the order disapproved by his Excellency the President. It contains the gist of a great many old orders and some new ones, but in the main it conforms to the current business of the system. No paper or person here has made complaints against the order, and I am surprised that such apprehension and immediate necessity should be presented at headquarters....
>
> If they [provost marshals] are to have no supervision of trade, commerce, or anything but the discipline and government of the troops in the United States service, how am I to prevent contraband of war, guns, ammunition, and other supplies going into the hands of the guerrillas, and how am I to know what is doing or to be done in various parts of my district when I have no other command, and what am I to do

with the prisoners and other rebels that are held either in fact or fear by these provost-marshals?...

When a nation is at war, war exists everywhere, and we must have some sort of military representatives wherever military offenses are committed. It costs too much to keep stationary troops everywhere, but without such officers as I may trust and constantly employ in every county of this State and in various parts of my department, I must have many more troops in actual service in Missouri. While, therefore, there is no apparent necessity of a sudden radical change, I most respectfully request that some substitute may be allowed me for a system of military power which now serves a most important purpose throughout my command, or so order the matter that we may perfect what now seems to be a useful military expedient.[21]

Franklin Dick's letter, which General Curtis enclosed, describes some of the duties of the provost-marshals.

[Saint Louis, Mo.,] January 15, 1863.
Maj. Gen. Samuel R. Curtis, Commanding:
General:
    The telegram of the Secretary of War, of the 14th, to the major-general commanding this department, contemplating a change in the system of provost-marshals in the interior of the State, requires of me that I should present to you some of the duties performed by them.
    Commanding officers in the field turn over prisoners captured by them to provost-marshals, who take the evidence against the prisoners and forward it and them to Saint Louis. With guerrillas and marauding bands operating in the State, whenever opportunity occurs, appearing at first one place and then another, our troops are kept moving, and the officers in the field do not furnish the evidence against the men they capture. Were these prisoners considered prisoners of war, and to be sent forward for exchange, but little evidence would be needed, but they are many of them lawless men, known in certain localities. After their capture their friends constantly make efforts to have them released, and it is through the provost-marshals that the facts relating to them are ascertained,

---

[21]Samuel R. Curtis to E. M. Stanton, January 15, 1863. *OR* 1.22.2.43–45.

and upon which the proper action can be based, as to holding or releasing them. These provost-marshals are made by your orders conservators of the peace. They know and report the state of the country, and can and do determine better than any one else which men can safely be enlarged and which not. Remove them, and to whom shall we apply for the information constantly needed at your headquarters, and to whom will commanders in the field send their prisoners to be examined and forwarded? Again, it is well known that rebel recruiting officers and spies are constantly coming into this State. It is the business of provost-marshals to keep on the watch for them, and to break up their practices; and, but for their efforts, in many counties recruiting for the rebel army would be carried on without danger. There are many disloyal farmers who would constantly aid the rebellion with supplies of different kinds, but for the provost-marshal system. Remove the danger of detection, and the State would furnish (to the rebs) considerable amounts of supplies, and the stream of rebel soldiers southward would be largely increased.

I have released, all the time, men in whose promises reliance could not be placed, but I have felt justified in doing it by placing them under the surveillance of the provost-marshals of their counties. If, however, they have no local officer to care for, they either cannot be released or would soon again be led off into aiding the rebellion. Provost-marshals, too, give confidence to the Union men through the State; they stand as the representatives of the United States Government, and if a neighborhood becomes so rebellious as to endanger Union men, they feel that the report of the provost-marshals will call the attention of the military authorities to the condition of things. To relieve the provost-marshals will be a shock to the Union cause in this State, and will have a most depressing effect upon those who require the support of the Government. They acquire a local knowledge which is valuable and reliable. The men who have been disloyal in Missouri, most of them, remain so; and it will prove a costly mistake to act upon a contrary hypothesis. They are Southern sympathizers who have taken up arms, and they are none the less sympathizers because for the time disarmed; and I feel safe in making the assertion that, if they believe it not too perilous to do it, they will again take up arms, or by other means aid the rebellion. My belief is that these people have got to be kept down while the war rages, and my every day's experience confirms that belief. After the rebellion becomes powerless, then the Missouri rebels will give up their plans of co-operation, and not until then. So far as they have ceased hostilities, it has been from force, and not voluntary submission, and to consider these people no longer enemies of the Union is to fall into a practical error. They have had pretty hard experience in this war, and I believe, by vigilance, can easily be kept down; but a show of military power is necessary, and the presence of some military force, too, accompanied by the continuation of the military system sufficient to keep them sensible of this, that renewed hostilities on their part will be promptly met by force. If my hypothesis is correct, then the system of military law cannot be dispensed with in Missouri, while disloyal men believe that the Union will be dissolved, and they very generally do believe it. If my judgment and opinions are incorrect, then let the capture and detection of guerrillas and marauders be turned over to the civil authorities, and let military action be confined only to regular movements in the field; and it may be that it will be found that the State is * * *

I consider it my duty as an officer to make this statement relating to the disloyal men in Missouri, believing that the reliable supporters of the Union cause in this State are the men who feel that the safety of this State lies in the control of it by the military power of the United States, so long as this rebellion continues defiant; and these men who alone constitute the strength of the Government in this State will have bitter sufferings to endure, if the protection of the Government is withdrawn.

I have the honor to remain, most respectfully, your obedient servant,

F. A. Dick,
Lieut. Col. and Provost-Marshal-
General, Dept. of the Missouri.[22]

On January 26, 1863, Dick wrote a letter to Montgomery Blair about his problems acting as provost marshal general. He began by describing how he had been commissioned a lieutenant colonel in the Missouri State

[22]Franklin Dick to Samuel R. Curtis, January 15, 1863, *OR* 1.22.2.45–46.

Militia, on the staff of Major General Curtis, and was appointed as provost marshal general on November 5. His orders read: "Lieut. Col. F. A. Dick, M.S.M. is hereby assigned to duty as Provost Marshal General of the Department of the Missouri, and will be obeyed and respected accordingly." Dick tells what happened when he submitted an account to Major Johnson to be paid.

On that day Nov. 5 I entered upon such duty — Early in January I made out my pay a/c from 5 Novr. to 1st Jany. 63 and asked Major Johnson to pay it —He refused, upon the ground, that it had been lately decided by Genl. Halleck that, Lt. Col. Charlot, of the Staff of Genl. Curtis as Major Genl. of the M.S.M. was not entitled to pay — because not mentioned expressly in said agreement, as one of the Officers authorized to be appointed by the Governor....

If I am not entitled to pay, it must be, because Genl. Curtis is not entitled to a State Staff, and consequently my commission is void— That being so, I stand just as Col. Gantt stood, as volunteer Aide — & having been appointed Pro. Mar. Gen. by Genl. Curtis, after the order of Genl Halleck, prohibiting such appointment, may not my appointment be considered as void, because contrary to orders—

I have been acting as a Staff officer, & my orders of Pro. Mar. Genl. run in the name of Genl Curtis.

An other point— The said agreement provides that when the U.S. Major Genl ceases to command this Dpt. his Comn as State Major Genl ceases—

I have seen Broadhead to day, & he told me in confidence, that a few days ago, that under the influences exerted in Washn, it was decided to remove Genl Curtis from this Department—

Now to me, it is an important thing to know, what would become of my commission, and office in that event. When Genl C. ceases to be Major Genl of the M.S.M. I cease to be a Lt. Col. & Aide— Does that dispose of my office— I think so— Take away a Cols. Comn.— he can not command his Regt.

Having stated these matters, I now enter upon an other. By numerous, and unmistakable indications there is one, if not two parties of men in this State, who are preparing for a dispute of the authority of the U.S. in Missouri. When we had a large force of troops, U.S. Volunteers, & M.S.M. all commanded by U.S. officers, in the State, it was desperate and futile to question the power of the U.S. Gov't. in Mo— but of late I believe all the U.S. volunteer Regts. have been withdrawn, & the M.S.M. forces have I believe been most of them taken into Arks, by Blunt & Herron. There is only one Regt. that of Merrill, north of the Mo. River, & it too was ordered South, but Genl Curtis heard so much of dangers threatening, that he has not yet moved it.

What is called the Enrolled Mo. Militia, is expected to take care of this State. That is exclusively under the control of the Governor. Already ugly questions begin to arise, under this change, as to jurisdiction— the authority of the Governor,— of U.S. officers. Some time since, a Provost Marshal arrested a man who is a Col. of the E.M.M. on alleged grounds of disloyalty, & at once the Governor called upon me for an explanation of the act. The Gov. and I agreed upon the principles governing the case,— no trouble grew out of it, & the man was discharged; but I foresee that with the constant disturbances in this State, that serious difficulties will spring up— & the way further is prepared by the withdrawal of the U.S. troops— If no military force was needed to keep the state quiet, then the troops should be withdrawn; but such force is needed, and soon you will see the State in full control of the E.M.M. under command of exclusively State officers.

By an order issued a few weeks ago, the President has conceded or given to the Governor the Power to remove the Officers of the M.S.M, that is the special 10000. troops raised by that agreement; and under it, the Gov— has already removed Col. Jackson, (the Judge Jackson impeached in Claib. Jackson's time)— Thus every officer of his 10000 men, hold their commissions by the tenure of the Governor's consent.

I do not question the Governor's loyalty; nor his integrity.

Last fall or summer Genl Schofield made an order, to take away arms from disloyal men— under it, in many Counties, these guns were collected, and placed in custody of the Provost Marshals, and held subject to the orders of the U.S. Officers— That order of Schofield still stands in force, & is a necessary & proper order.

On the 20th inst. Lieut. J. A. Mayhall, of the M.S.M. one of the best officers in the U.S. Service, of his rank, writes to Genl Curtis, that when he arrived at New London, Ralls County, some 6 weeks ago, (where he is Pro— Marshal) he found the guns that had been taken from the Citizens, under Schofields order, 150 in all, had been returned by Col. Tinker & Major Johnston, (Col. & Major of Ralls Co. E.M.M. & subject to the order of the Governor) to their owners, particularly those belonging to disloyal men. Mayhall issued an order, to have them all returned to him. The loyal men obeyed— the disloyal did not. Major Johnston now states that he has an order from Genl Bartholow (a M Brig. Genl of the E.M.M. appointed by the Governor) to call in all the guns in the County, & also those now in the Provost Marshals possession. Mayhall says that Major Johnston is disloyal— also Col. Tinker (and I believe so too)— and Mayhall says that he will not surrender the guns unless ordered so to do by Genl Curtis— That Tinker & Johnston have obtained an order for all the enrolled militia of the County, who are loyal, except 60, to retire from active service, & say they intend to arm 2 Companies of conscripts— that is disloyal men, who refused to enrol. The Pro. Mar. says he believes these Militia officers are preparing to resist the laws & orders of the U.S.—

I regard Mayhall as a safe, reliable, discreet man. On the 24th the letter was referred by Order of Genl Curtis to me, without instructions.

If I direct the Pro. Mar. to give up the arms, it is conceding every thing to the State officers—

Why does not the Governor issue an order, to collect all the arms, if it is his purpose to do so. It is improper— irregular for a subordinate State officer to demand arms from an U.S. officer, taken in pursuance to a Gen. Order, issued by a Genl Commanding the State, as Genl Schofield did. You will see how difficult it is for me to direct the Provost Marshal, how to act, in the absence of any policy indicated by the Admin in such a matter: and you see how difficult is the position of the Pro. Mar. who if he refuses, may have his commission in the M.S.M. taken from him by he Governor; and if I sustain him, the Governor may revoke my Comm.

It may be asked why Genl. Curtis gave no instructions, how to answer the letter. I can not tell, but he may feel at a loss to know what answer the President would have him give. Col. Farrar is now engaged in collecting forfeited bonds, taken by orders of U.S. Officers, of disloyal men— who violated their bonds & a second time took up arms— The Provost Marshals write me that a military force is absolutely necessary to collect those bonds— The U.S. forces are withdrawn, & Gov. Gamble has issued an order, No. 50 which I enclose, declaring that the E.M.M. shall not aid in collecting assessments, & are exclusively under his control— These were assessments made under Schofields order 3, and U.S. troops being withdrawn, the assessments were necessarily stopped, because of this order of the Governor. Here then is practical defeat of orders of U.S. Officers, by State authority— It is necessary that these forfeited bonds be collected, otherwise, the farce will be played of the U.S. releasing men, & allowing them again & again to defy its power, without penalty— The men were released without being punished, because they gave promise in shape of oath & bond to be thereafter loyal— without provocation, they have again taken up arms— and now the Gov't. must collect the bonds, or acknowledge its inability to do so— The bonds, provide for enforcement by a military tribunal, & Genl Curtis months ago made the orders for such enforcement. Col. Farrar went out to start the work of collecting the bonds, and came back & reported to Genl Curtis, it could not be done, without military force. Lieut. Mayhall says Tinker & Johnston want the guns he holds, to put in the hands of disloyal men to resist, amongst other things, the enforcement of these bonds.

I could give you other examples of the way in which collisions are threatened— but it is too much labor for you to read & me to write of all these matters in detail. You can judge from these facts, how matters are going in this State; & of whether or not, it is expedient to allow the control of it to slip from the hands of the President.

To go back now to the point at which I started— The only semblance of the U.S. authority in a large part of the State, is the Provost Marshal system— it is an important matter to determine whether or not it shall be preserved In a long letter forwarded by Genl Curtis to Washn some days ago, I gave some facts to show its operation.

I took charge of it, in this State pretty well understanding its operations. What I want at this time, is to understand what is required of it. It should be known, that in this State, we arrest few or no State Prisoners as they are called— The men under

my charge are active aiders of the rebellion, by open deeds—
Marauders— Guerillas— Men taken in arms— in rebel
Camps— who rob & murder Union men— Talk of executing
the law against such men, in a Rebel community, where the
office holders & Juries are Southern Sympathisers, & worse— I
tell you it is a cruel farce— and a fearful injustice to the supporters of the Gov't. The Courts may sit in many Counties, but
witnesses, jurors &c. are disloyal— Arbitrary arrests made in
the free states are very different from the military arrests made
in this disloyal State— Missouri is disloyal, deeply so from end
to end, and the arm of military power alone has kept up a show
of quiet. In view of this, I believe that some military system of
Government, is absolutely necessary to be kept up— Gov.
Gamble sees this,— and is providing for it by his E.M.M.—
and it has at once to be determined whether the State or U.S.
Military force will have the occupancy & possession.

If the Pro. Mar. system is to be kept up, I am willing so
long as I can render service to remain in my present position.
But from the facts I have first stated, my position ought somewhat to be changed. Although the pay is small, yet, it is necessary for me to have it, to aid in paying my expences, for it takes
all my time, and I work at it from 8½ A.M. til bed time, every
day— The business of my office is enormous, & consumes all
my waking hours— The President should pass on the question
of my pay— and that I may not be turned out of the place, by a
change of commander of the State I should be appointed Provost Marshal of the Department by order of the War Department, with the pay of Lt. Col. so that a succeeding Major
Genl. could not appoint someone else to the place. I do not ask
this to be done— for I never asked for the place, and have no
desire to retain it. But I think it is due to me if the President
chooses to continue the office & me in it, that both as to pay
and tenure the uncertainty may be at an end.

When I took charge of this office, I found 1500 Prisoners
to take charge of— they had been captured in skirmishes, & as
bands of Guerillas— being the worst men in the State— I have
been hard at work all the time investigating & disposing of
their cases. In Missouri hundreds of singular questions arise, &
are disposed of by me— …There have been large numbers of
horses taken from the Guerilla and marauding bands in this
State— these horses have been turned over to the Provost

Marshals, and sold— under orders of Military officers— Some days ago the Provost Marshal at St. Joseph advertised such stock for sale— An agent of the U.S. Quarter Master wrote to Genl. Allen, Chief Qr. Master at St. Louis stating that the Qr. Master Genl of the State claimed that such stock belonged to the State— Genl. Allen referred the question to Genl Curtis; and finally the matter was dropped,— the claim of the State Qr. Master admitted Now if that is correct, it is beyond my comprehension That gives the State authorities the purse— they are getting hold of the sword— then, the next step depends upon what they choose to do— As I consider these matters of importance, I make them known to you, and hope that you will present them to the President.

I am very truly Your's
F. A. Dick

One more matter it is important for me to speak of— & that is, that St. Louis is the seat and centre of the rebel plots & schemes, and spies revel here. The women, & several of them of the better class act as mail carriers— at no time have the rebel sympathizers & secret workers been so active and bold as now— their course, of that of treason— These People ought to be sent South— Our Union People here know this, & urge it constantly upon Genl Curtis— I assure you that the authority of the Govt. here, before our face is despised & set at naught. The traitors seem to believe implicitly that there is no danger to them – for even if discovered, they will lie out of it: or beg off. What I mean here to state is, that the Representatives of the Government here, should be invested with discretionary power, and where it is complained that they are in error, explanation should be asked of them. Those who cry loudest when hurt, are always the worst offenders. The President can not be well served, if he unjustly listens to the Traitors who are selected by Officers of the Government for examples. It, deadens the energy & discourages the heart, to see wicked lying Traitors gain the confidence of the President, and succeed in over coming the efforts of union men in the service of the Government.

[Endorsed by Francis P. Blair, Sr.:]

There are some matters explained in this enclosure which it seems necessary the President should act on promptly to prevent [collision?] between National & state authority— Mr. Dick thinks the leading Rebels are contriving to create within the State new revolutionary movements by stirring up the [members?] of the old parties.

F. P. B.[23]

On January 1, 1863, President Lincoln issued the Emancipation Proclamation, and in the spring of 1863 the Union army began to enlist black troops. In addition, Congress passed a conscription act in March 1863, making all men between the ages of 20 and 45 eligible to be called for military service unless they could find a substitute or pay $300. This was seen as unfair to the poor and melées broke out in some working-class areas. Anti-conscription riots erupted in Boston; Portsmouth, New Hampshire; Rutland, Vermont; Wooster, Ohio; and Troy, New York. The largest was in New York City on July 13 to 14; 500 people were killed and much of the violence was directed against free blacks. The rioting was put down by Union troops rushed in from Gettysburg; in some cases they fired volleys directly into rioting mobs.[24]

Union Major General John A. McClernand took Fort Hindman on the Arkansas River from Confederate Colonel John W. Dunnington and Brigadier General Thomas J. Churchill in January, 1863. Union General Ulysses S. Grant advanced south on the Mississippi River with Rear Admiral David D. Porter's gunboat fleet.

In April, the War Department issued instructions dealing with martial law, prisoners of war, rebel property, Southern sympathizers, spies, and other issues. The orders directed commanders to "throw the burden of the war, as much as was within his power, on the disloyal citizens," and gave them authority to "expel, transfer, imprison, or fine the revolted citizens who refuse to pledge themselves anew as citizens obedient to the law and

[23]Franklin A. Dick to Montgomery Blair, January 26, 1863. Abraham Lincoln Papers at the Library of Congress. Transcribed and annotated by the Lincoln Studies Center, Knox College, Galesburg, Illinois.

[24]Katcher, *Civil War Source Book*, 19–45, 48–52; Faust, *Historical Times*, 160–61, 225–26, 369–70, 391–92, 429–31, 482–83, 583, 593, 727–28; Denny, *Civil War Years*, 251–355.

loyal to the government."[25]

With federal policy toward treatment of disloyal citizens shifting to banishment, Franklin Dick supervised the banishment of thirteen men and five wives of Confederate officers on May 14, 1863.[26] Banishments continued throughout the spring and included influential citizens like relatives of Clairborne Jackson's mother-in-law, the Reverend David R. McNally, the family of Confederate Surgeon William McPheters (who was earlier assessed by Dick), Mary Rowen, (wife of Confederate general John Rowen), Eliza Frost, (wife of Confederate general Daniel Frost), and physician Simon Gratz Moses. Banishing Southern sympathizers helped to reduce their influence and their ability to convince others to join the rebellion, but it also made Dick fairly unpopular in St. Louis.

Earlier that year, Dick had to deal with the bodies of two dead men, for which he was vilified by people and the press. Emmet McDonald, the man who had refused to take a parole after his capture at Camp Jackson, had fought as a colonel for the confederate army and was killed January 11, 1863, in Missouri. John Wimer, former St. Louis mayor, also died with McDonald. Since he was afraid that public funerals would cause violence, Dick had the bodies taken from their houses in St. Louis and secretly buried in the Wesleyan cemetery.[27] Another account says that Colonel McDonald's body was taken from his sister's house on St. Charles Rock Road and buried in a potter's field. Later, the family moved the body to the Wesleyan Cemetery and then Bellefontaine Cemetery.[28] This was a huge affront to the grieving families, as burials were especially important in the mid nineteenth century. People kept mementoes, locks of hair, and continued to mourn at graves of the dead. One classic example is Abraham Lincoln's having his son's coffin exhumed and opened twice after the burial, so he could see Tad's face again. Franklin Dick's actions took away important parts of death rituals for two families, and he was hated for his

[25]War Department, Adjt. General's Office, General Orders No. 100, April 24, 1863. *OR* 3.3.148–64, quoted in Gerteis, *Civil War St. Louis*, 177–78.

[26]Gerteis, *Civil War St. Louis*, 177–82, 357.

[27]Gerteis, *Civil War St. Louis*, 182.

[28]Dressel, *Self Guided Tour of Confederate Graves at Bellefontaine Cemetery*, quoted in "Biography of Col. Emmett MacDonald."

act. He was already disliked by many of the Southern-sympathizing old society in St. Louis for serving on the assessment board years before. Dick followed his conscience and sense of what was right and honest, without thought at times of what the future consequences would be for his own life and that of his family. Unfortunately, he served as provost marshal when situations that had been fomenting for years suddenly erupted.

Another problem Dick had to deal with was the prominent St. Louis McPheeters family who were close friends with Attorney General Edward Bates. William M. McPheeters was a doctor and professor at the St. Louis Medical College. His brother, Samuel P. McPheeters, who had been Frank Blair's roommate at the University of North Carolina, followed his father's profession and became a Presbyterian minister in St. Louis. William sided with the South and refused to take the oath of allegiance, which was required to practice medicine. He was assessed $800 in January 1862 by General Halleck's assessment board, on which Dick served. McPheeters refused to pay. Provost Marshal General Bernard Farrar, Dick's friend and predecessor, had to order that McPheeters' possessions be seized and auctioned. A McPheeters child was ill and dying in the house as the furniture was taken. Later, William McPheeters was assessed a second fine; he left St. Louis and joined the Confederate army as a surgeon for General Sterling Price.[29]

Samuel McPheeters tried to stay free of the political divisions in St. Louis to best serve his parishioners at the Pine Street Presbyterian Church. He was suspected of disloyalty (because of his brother), and his congregation confronted him to declare his political views publicly. He refused to make any public statements on his political views. On December 19, 1862, Franklin Dick was ordered by Samuel Curtis to send the Reverend McPheeters and his wife to a place of their choosing west of Pennsylvania and north of Indianapolis, where they were to be banished for the rest of the war. A military commission would govern the Pine Street Church. McPheeters traveled to Washington to object. Attorney General Edward Bates met with McPheeters and President Lincoln, who told General Curtis not to banish them. Then James E. Yeatman and Giles F. Filley, who attended the Unitarian Church, went to advise

[29]Gerteis, *Civil War St. Louis*, 174–76, 183.

the president to keep the banishment in effect. Lincoln, trying to offend no one, said that the military should never run churches, and the final decision on the McPheeters was left to Curtis. Parishioners continued to undermine McPheeters after Dick, as ordered by Curtis, had removed the "disloyal" parts of the church. It is unclear exactly what was removed or how it was done. Finally McPheeters left for a church in Kentucky. After the war, the congregation asked him to return, but he was ill and only visited.[30]

Franklin Dick had to walk a tightrope in St. Louis. There was a fine line between martial and civil law, and the tendency was to be severe to weed out the secessionists in the divided state. These disagreeable duties would create even more resentment toward Dick, which was extended to his wife and children. He was constantly concerned about their safety and well-being.

Office Provost-Marshal-General
Saint Louis, Mo., March 5, 1863
Col. W. Hoffman,
Third Infty., Commissary General of Prisoners, Washington.
Colonel:

Yesterday as you may have already been informed by telegram and letter I sent in obedience to you orders 150 citizen prisoners for exchange to Washington City.

There remain of the guerilla and irregular prisoners, many of them captured last fall and others along with them in prison, a large number of similar cases.

For the release of many of these prisoners a great influence and pressure is brought to bear. Many of them fall into bad health, the circumstances of the families of others excite the sympathies of their neighbors and other circumstances combine to induce great efforts to release these prisoners.

I believe that some of them ought to be released, but a large proportion of them are as obstinate rebels as they ever were and it will not be safe to enlarge such characters while the war lasts. I respectfully suggest that such prisoners be passed through the lines to be exchanged.

A considerable number of such irregular prisoners who

---

[30]Gerteis, *Civil War St. Louis*, 182–86; and Laas, *Wartime Washington*, 354–55.

are being captured continuously are determined rebels whose purposes no length of imprisonment will change.

Would it not be advisable upon capture of such men to exchange them at once? To detain them fills our prisons at heavy expense to the Government.

Several rebel mails have been taken in the last few weeks and I find that a large number of women have been actively concerned in both secret correspondence and in carrying on the business of collecting and distributing rebel letters. I have now the evidence upon which these women can be convicted. I have for some time past been thinking of arresting and trying them but the embarrassment is to know what to do with them. Many of them are the wives and daughters of officers in the rebel service; for example, Mrs. Frost, a wealthy, influential woman, wife of the rebel general D. M. Frost; Mrs. McPheeters, wife of a rebel surgeon at Richmond; Mrs. Cook, the wife of a rebel Senator [Representative] from Missouri; Mrs. Polk (and daughters), wife of Trusten Polk, lately of the U.S. Senate, and now in the rebel service as a judge I believe; Mrs. Bredell, mother of Captain Bredell, on the staff of rebel General Bowen, and very many others.

These women are wealthy and wield a great influence; the are avowed and abusive enemies of the Government; they incite our young men to join the rebellion; their letters are full of encouragement to their husbands and sons to continue the war; they convey information to them and by every possible contrivance they forward clothing and other support to the rebels. These disloyal women, too, seek out every opportunity to keep disloyalty alive amongst rebel prisoners. I have been appealed to very many times by our loyal people to know why these disloyal women were not sent through the lines to join their husbands and sons. I respectfully suggest that such an order be issued by the Secretary of War.

Again there is a large number of active, intelligent, wealthy, disloyal men in Saint Louis who keep up a constant intercourse with the rebels in arms and by every means that they dare they urge them on in the rebellion. These men exercise a telling influence upon the rebels in arms and upon the disloyal masses in this State. Open, notorious disloyalty is preferred by these men to even a reputation for neutrality. They abstain from open acts, such as giving money, arms and other supplies, but their secret acts, words, associations and sympathies are unmistakably hostile to the Government and they openly rejoice at our reverses and lament at our victories. Forbearance toward this class of people was first adopted because it was thought that leniency would reform them, but that forbearance has settled into a usage which has produced evil consequences and has led these people to believe that it is their "constitutional" right to speak and conspire together as they may choose. The quiet, secret influence of this class is injurious and greatly so. I suggest that they be sent to join their Southern friends if such a course should be approved by the Secretary of War.

I have at last accomplished the work of examining all the old cases of prisoners excepting only those who were too sick to be brought out.

I have the honor, colonel, to be our obedient servant,
F. A. Dick,
Lieutenant-Colonel and Provost-
Marshal-General.[31]

Franklin Dick's letter of April 7 shows how complicated some cases could be and how he constantly strived to do the just thing for each person.

Saint Louis, April 7, 1863.
Lieut. J. Guylee, Fourth Iowa Cavalry, Aide-de-Camp.

Lieutenant: On the 31st ultimo Mrs. General Jeff. Thompson, her friend Mrs. Colhoun (wife of a rebel officer), a nurse and two children arrived in Saint Louis from Helena, claiming to be here on honest business and to have been properly passed through our lines at Helena. They are now in close custody in their rooms at the Everett House under the charge of the U.S. police, having been arrested as being improper persons within our lines and under suspicious circumstances. You will take charge of the entire party and conduct them to Helena under close guard, to be passed through the lines in the direction they came from unless the commanding officer of the district may decide that the circumstances of their getting through there will justify their detention and trial. George Smizer, of Helena, is reported as having been instrumental in procuring

[31]Franklin A. Dick to Col. W. Hoffman, March 5, 1863. OR 2.5.319–21.

the passes for these women and to have changed money for them. You will inquire particularly into this and report all facts proper for his information and action to the commanding officer at Helena. You receive herewith the pass by which they left their lines, the pass by which they came into ours and the one by which they left Helena and went toward Memphis. The circumstances attending the reaching Saint Louis by these rebel women are so suspicious that General Curtis desires particular information in regard to it. A W. Paul Bently was arrested at the same time and is now in Gratiot [Street] Prison. You will take him also through the lines as a suspicious person. He admits having run the blockade from the South. On your return you will make full report to this office.

> By command of Major-General
> Curtis:
> F. A. Dick,
> Lieutenant-Colonel and Provost-
> Marshal-General.[32]

On April 25, Mary Louden, the wife of Confederate spy Robert Louden, was arrested in St. Louis for her part in a mail smuggling operation run by her husband. Other women who were also involved were arrested over the next month. There were often disagreements about how to handle specific cases, but in an April 29 letter to Dick, Hoffman reported that Dick's recommendations had been approved.

> Your letter of the 5th of March has been submitted to the Secretary of War and the suggestions made by you therein have been approved and I have to-day communicated to Major-General Curtis, commanding the Department of the Missouri, with a copy of your letter, the instructions of the Secretary of War that your recommendations in regard to disloyal men and women in Missouri be fully carried out....[33]

In mid-May, a number of Southern sympathizers, mostly women, were banished from St. Louis and sent South. The group included Mary Louden.

---

[32]Franklin A. Dick to Lieut. J. Guylee, April 7, 1863. *OR* 2.5.447.
[33]W. Hoffman to F. A. Dick, April 29, 1863. *OR* 2.5.539.

Office Provost-Marshal-General
St. Louis, Mo., May 12, 1863.
Maj. T. I. McKenny, Aide-de-Camp:

In pursuance to the order and instructions of the Secretary of War of the 24th of April, 1863, a cpy of which is herewith inclosed, and under instructions from Maj. Gen. S. R. Curtis, commanding the department, I commit to your charghe the persons whose names are upon the rolls herewith handed you as those of the class of disloyal citizens who are in rebellion against the Governement, and for that cause are to be conducted under goard South and passed through the lines of the U.S. Army and within the military lines of the enemy in rebellion, with instructions not to return within our military lines without the permission of the Secretary of War. You will proceed hence by steamboat or cars to Memphis, and thence either to Vicksburg or such other point as may be most proper for the delivery of these persons within the lines of the enemy. You will cause the baggage of these persons to be carefully examined; but as there are some families who voluntarily accompany their husbands permission has been given them to take an ample supply of clothing and those necessities required for their use which they otherwise might be without. Every regard and humane indulgence should on the way and in the delivery of the women and children within the lines be given to them consistent with their being safely conducted. It has been left to the option of the husbands to take their wives and children, excepting in the case of Charles Clark. As to the proper point of passing the lines you should consult with the officer commanding the U.S. forces, exhibiting to him the annexed order of the Secretary of War that the same may be duly obeyed in a manner not to interfere with the existing military plans of such commanding officer. In view of this it must be left to your discretion as to the plan of passing these persons through and within the lines of the enemy. You will return the rolls of the prisoners in duplicate to this office, with indorsement thereon of the time, place and manner of executing this order.

Very respectfully, your obedient servant,
F. A. Dick,
Lieut. Col. and Provost-Marshal-General Dept. of the Missouri.[34]

---

[34]Franklin A. Dick to T. I. McKenny, May 2, 1863. *OR* 2.5.599–600.

Special Order No. 74
Office of the Provost-Marshal-General
Saint Louis, Mo., May 12, 1863
    The persons herewith delivered to you to be conducted through the lines are ordered not to return during the war within the lines of the U.S. Army upon pain of imprisonment for the war, and in addition thereto such other punishment as may be imposed upon them by military authority. You will communicate this order to said persons.
        By command of Major-General Curtis:
                F. A. Dick,
                Lieutenant-Colonel and Provost-
                Marshal-General[35]

Franklin Dick must have felt he finally achieved something in his difficult position as provost marshal general, but he returned to civilian life shortly after this time. After the death of his son Otis on May 27, 1863, he moved his family back to be with his relatives in the safety of Philadelphia, taking Otis's coffin back to rebury in Philadelphia. In the summer, Dick took his family to Newport where Frank Blair and his family stayed with them, as Apo was not well after the St. Louis winter.[36] In Philadelphia, Dick practiced law, continued with his investments and debated privately in his journals about returning to St. Louis.

In May 1863, Confederate forces won the Battle of Chancellorsville, but General Stonewall Jackson was mortally wounded by mistaken fire from his own troops and replaced by Major General James Earl Brown Stuart. General Grant besieged and captured Vicksburg, Mississippi, on July 4, the day after Pickett's Charge at Gettysburg. General Robert E. Lee and his Army of Northern Virginia invaded Pennsylvania in June, where they were narrowly defeated at Gettysburg (July 1–3) and retreated to Virginia. The Union captured Chattanooga and Knoxville, the Confederates won the Battle of Chickamauga (September 18–20), only to be defeated at Chattanooga and retreat to Georgia.

Missouri continued to be troubled by conflicts between pro-Union and pro-Southern residents and by violence along the Missouri-Kansas

---

[35]Special Order No. 74, May 12, 1863. *OR* 2.5.600.
[36]McPherson, *Frank Blair: Lincoln's Conservative*, 176.

border. Women who aided Quantrill's raiders were detained and a number of female relatives of the guerillas were imprisoned in a temporary jail in Kansas City. The jail collapsed, killing four women and injuring several others. In retaliation, on August 21, Quantrill and his men raided the anti-slavery town of Lawrence, Kansas, not far from the Missouri border, and murdered about 150 men and boys.[37]

Brigadier General Thomas Ewing Jr. responded by issuing General Order No. 11, an attempt to eliminate any support the bushwackers might be getting from Confederate sympathizers living near the Missouri-Kansas border. Under Order No. 11, all residents were expelled from four counties along the border; those who could prove their loyalty to the Union were permitted to resettle near a military outpost, while all others were ordered out of the region. Union troops burned the abandoned buildings and crops, thus the area came to be called the Burnt District or Burned-Over District.[38]

In September, Robert Louden was arrested in St. Louis for spying and sabotage in the burning of Union boats and was sentenced to death. Over the next month, saboteurs in St. Louis burned more steamers and a barge. Louden's colleague, Absalom Grimes, was arrested in November; he too was tried and sentenced to death.[39] But the conflicts in Missouri were not limited to parties on opposing sides of the war. Charles Drake, a leader of the Radical Union party, wrote to President Lincoln outlining his concerns about disagreements among Union loyalists in Missouri. Lincoln wrote a long letter in response, in which he commented that "it is easy to conceive that all these shades of opinion, and even more, may be sincerely entertained by honest and truthful men, yet all being for the Union."

Washington, October 3, 1863.
Abraham Lincoln,
President of the United States:
SIR:
    ...There are in Missouri two bodies of soldiery known as Missouri Militia, the Missouri State Militia and the Enrolled

[37]Monaghan, *Civil War on the Western Border*, 280–89; and Faust, *Historical Times*, 427.

[38]Monaghan, *Civil War on the Western Border*, 289.

[39]Gerteis, *Civil War St. Louis*, 187–89.

Missouri Militia. The former and volunteer troops, enlisted into the service of the United States, and supported by the national Government. They are the "peculiar military force" referred to in Special Orders, No. 416, of the War Department, issued December 28, 1862. Its peculiarity consists in the fact that it is intended exclusively for the protection of Missouri, and in the further fact that under said Orders No. 416, "Governor Gamble may in his discretion remove from office all officers" thereof, and "may accept resignations tendered by such officers." Ten regiments of this force are kept afoot, and are wholly under the control of the commanding general of the Department of the Missouri, without being placed under his control by order of the Governor of Missouri. The Enrolled Missouri Militia are an entirely different force, organized by order of the Governor, controlled by him, and at no time subject to the orders of any U.S. officer, except as the Governor sees proper to make them so. The creation of this force was unauthorized by any law of our State. As it was called into existence by the Governor's order, so its existence may be terminated at any moment by his command. This force was enrolled in the summer of 1862. For some time it was entirely a State force, and kept up at the expense of the State when in active service. On the 30th of December, 1862, Governor Gamble issued his General Orders, No. 50, in the following words:

The Enrolled Militia are under the exclusive command of their own officers except when they are by express orders placed under the command of U.S. officers, and they will be governed only by such orders as may be issued from these headquarters. If, therefore, any officers of the Enrolled Militia are engaged in making assessments in pursuance of orders from U.S. commanders, they will immediately suspend all action under said orders.

This order indicates with precision the character of the force which Governor Gamble by his own mere will, without authority of law, embodied in Missouri. It was not only independent of the U.S. military commander there, but was ordered to co-operate with him in the measure therein designated, and which had been adopted by him against disloyal persons. In consequence of this order, Col. F. A. Dick, provost-marshal-general of Missouri, and his assistant provost-marshals, were denied the aid of the Enrolled Militia in enforcing certain of his orders against traitors and their abettors, whereby his efforts in that direction were greatly impeded.... We earnestly assure you, Mr. President, that as long as Governor Gamble can, through his military organizations, dictate his policy to the commanding general of the Department of Missouri, our State will be, as it has been, a source of anxiety to you. In times like these no such autocratic power as he has wielded for the last eighteen months should be intrusted to any State Governor, and least of all to one who has pledged himself to use his executive power to the utmost extent to protect the institution of slavery. It is in your power to settle the whole difficulty. Only three things are necessary to this end: First the cessation of all support from the Treasury of the United States to the Enrolled Missouri Militia; second the occupation of Missouri by U.S. troops; and third, the appointment of a department commander in Missouri who will not make himself a party to Governor Gamble's pro-slavery policy. This is the sum of our requests in regard to military affairs If they are granted, we can assure you of permanent peace in Missouri.

One other subject demands attention in connection with Missouri affairs On the 3rd of next month an election is to be held in that State for judges of the supreme and circuit courts. We have good reason to believe, and so assert, that a strenuous effort will be made to carry that election against the Radical party by the votes of returned rebels, guerillas, bushwackers, and others who have given aid and comfort to the rebellion. By an ordinance of our State convention, passed June 10, 1862, every voter is required in order to vote to take a prescribed oath. Unless the military authorities interpose we believe that thousands of the above-named class of persons will be permitted to vote without taking that oath. We ask that you will be pleased to direct the department commander to issue such an order as General Burnside issued in reference to the Kentucky election, holding the judges of election responsible to the military authorities if they allow votes to be given by parties who do not take that oath. This will tend to exclude such parties from the polls, and thereby secure a fair election We transmit herewith certain statements concerning the condition of things in Missouri, prepared by members of our delegation, which we earnestly commend to your attentive perusal.

By order of the executive committee:
Chas. D. Drake,
Chairman[40]

Executive Mansion,
Washington, D.C., October 5, 1863.
Hon. Charles D. Drake and others, Committee:
...We are in civil war. In such cases there always is a main question; but in this case that question is a perplexing compound, Union and slavery. It thus becomes a question not of two sides merely, but at least four sides, even among those who are for the Union, saying nothing of those who are against it. Thus, those who are for the Union with, but not without, slavery; those for it without but not with; those for it with or without, but prefer it with; and those for it with or without, but prefer it without. Among these, again, is a subdivision of those who are for gradual, but not for immediate, and those who are for immediate, but not for gradual, extinction of slavery. It is easy to conceive that all these shades of opinion, and even more, may be sincerely entertained by honest and truthful men, yet all being for the Union, by reason of these differences each will prefer a different way of sustaining the Union. At once sincerity is questioned and motives are assailed. Actual war coming, blood grows hot and blood is spilled; thought is forced from old channels into confusion; deception breeds and thrives, confidence dies, and universal suspicion reigns. Each man feels an impulse to kill his neighbor, lest he be first killed by him; revenge and retaliation follow, and all this, as before said, may be among honest men only. But this is not all. Every foul bird comes abroad and every dirty reptile rises up. These add crime to confusion. Strong measures, deemed indispensable, but harsh at best, such men make worse by maladministration. Murders for old grudges and murders for pelf proceed under any cloak that will best cover for the occasion.

These causes amply account for what has occurred in Missouri, without ascribing it to the weakness or wickedness of any general The newspaper files, those chronicles of current events, will show that the evils now complained of were quite as prevalent under Fremont, Hunter, Halleck and Curtis as

[40]Charles D. Drake to Abraham Lincoln, October 3, 1863. *OR* 1.53.573–77.

under Schofield. If the former had greater force opposed to them, they also had greater forces with which to meet it. When the organized rebel army left the State, the main Federal force had to go also, leaving the department commander at home relatively no stronger than before. Without disparaging any, I affirm with confidence that no commander of that department has, in proportion to his means, done better than General Schofield....

You charge that, upon General Curtis being superseded by General Schofield, Franklin A. Dick was superseded by James O. Broadhead as provost-marshal-general. No very specified showing is made as to how this did or could injure the Union cause. It recalls, however, the condition of things, as presented to me, which led to a change of commanders for the department.

To restrain contraband intelligence and trade, a system of searches, seizures, permits and passes had been introduced by General Fremont. When General Halleck came, he found and continued the system, and added an order, applicable to some parts of the State, to levy and collect contributions from noted rebels to compensate losses and relieve destitution caused by the rebellion. The action of General Fremont and General Halleck, as stated, constituted a sort of system, which General Curtis found in full operation when he took command of the department. That there was a necessity for something of the sort was clear, but that it could only be justified by stern necessity, and that it was liable to great abuse in administration was equally clear. Agents to execute it, contrary to the great prayer, were led into temptation. Some might, while others would not, resist that temptation. It was not possible to hold any to a very strict accountability, and those yielding to the temptation would sell permits and passes to those who would pay most and most readily for them, and would seize property and collect levies in the aptest way to fill their own pockets. Money being the object, the man having money, whether loyal or disloyal, would be a victim. This practice doubtless existed to some extent, and it was a real additional evil that it could be and was plausibly charged to exist in greater extent than it did.

When General Curtis took command of the department, Mr. Dick, against whom I never knew anything to be alleged, had general charge of this system. A controversy in regard to it rapidly grew into almost unmanageable proportions. One side ignored the necessity and magnified evils of the system, while the other ignored the evils and magnified the necessity, and each bitterly assailed the motives of the other. I could not fail to see that the controversy enlarged in the same proportion as the professed Union men there distinctly took sides in the opposing political parties. I exhausted my wits, and very nearly my patience also, in efforts to convince both that the evils they charged on each other were inherent in the case, and could not be cured by giving either party a victory over the other.

Plainly the initiatory system was not to be perpetual, and it was plausibly urged that it could be modified at once with advantage. The cause could hardly be worse, and whether it could be made better could only be determined by a trial. In this view, and not to ban or brand General Curtis, or to give a victory to any party, I made the change of commander for the department....

I concur in the propriety of your request in regard to elections, and have, as you see, directed General Schofield accordingly. I do not feel justified to enter upon the broad field you present in regard to the political defenses between radicals and conservatives. From time to time I have done and said what appeared to me proper to do and say. The public knows it all. It obliges nobody to follow me, and I trust it obliges me to follow nobody. The radicals and conservatives each agree with me in some things and disagree in others. I could wish both to agree with me in all things, for then they would agree with each other, and would be too strong for any foe from any quarter. They, however, choose to do otherwise, and I do not question their right. I, too, shall do what seems to be my duty. I hold whoever commands in Missouri or elsewhere responsible to me, and not to either radicals or conservatives. It is my duty to hear all, but at last I must within my sphere judge what to do and what to forbear.

Your obedient servant,
A. Lincoln.[41]

Although some people were displeased with his actions as provost marshal, Franklin Dick was still respected by many in the community and

[41]Abraham Lincoln to Charles D. Drake and others, October 5, 1863. *OR* 2.5.604–7.

Envelope to Hon. F. P. Blair, 1858. Photo by R. L. Geyer © 2007.

his opinion on affairs in Missouri was valued in Washington. In November and December, Dick was interviewed in St. Louis, along with Frank Blair's cousin B. Gratz Brown, by the American Freedman's Inquiry Commission. Secretary of War Stanton had appointed three abolitionists—Dr. Samuel Gridley Howe, Robert Dale Owen and James McKay—to the commission to interview people on the condition of the freed slaves. Brown told the commisison the Missouri blacks could manage for themselves with temporary supervision of Southern black refugees and that total emancipation could be achieved soon. Dick said that black troops enlisted under General Schofield's orders should be under the administration of strong antislavery advocates. He felt that blacks would enlist in the army if they were safe from retaliation from slave owners. He disagreed with Schofield's use of provost marshals for recruiting troops as being against Missouri's interests. He felt that Governor Gamble was honest, but not able to be fair about antislavery issues, and that General Schofield worked hand-in-hand together with the governor, instead of separately. He was against compensation for slave owners. "I have lived in this state twenty-one years," he concluded, "I regard it as absolutely indispensable that we should eradicate [slavery], in order that we may have a country such as we should have." Dick saw immediate emancipation as necessary for public justice.[42]

On December 12, 1863, sixty prisoners escaped from the Gratiot Street Prison through a tunnel. In January 1864, Major-General William S. Rosencrans replaced John Schofield, taking command of the Department of Missouri. Governor Gamble died on January 31, and Lieutenant Governor Williard P. Hall became head of the provisional state government. In February, Confederate boat-burner Arthur McCoy, a founder of the secessionist Minute Men and brother-in-law of Robert Loudon, was captured, but escaped several months later while being transferred to Alton Prison. Another escape attempt in June resulted in several prisoners being shot and several escaping. And in July, Confederate saboteurs burned four more Union steamboats in St. Louis.[43]

Despite the Union successes at Gettysburg and Vicksburg in 1863, the task facing the federal forces at the beginning of 1864 was daunting. Since Meade had not pursued Lee after Gettysburg, the Army of Northern Virginia had had time to regroup. The Army of the Potomac had yet to win a victory on Confederate soil. In the West, the Union controlled the Mississippi River, but the short-term effects of cutting the Confederacy off from the far West seemed negligible. Grant was having difficulty advancing through Tennessee due to Confederate resistance.

In March 1864, President Lincoln named General Ulysses S. Grant commander of all Union armies. By May, Grant had marched his troops south, where he fought Lee's forces in a large-scale, confused, and savage battle at the Wilderness. Though the battle was a tactical defeat for Grant, he kept marching south down to the North Anna River, forcing Lee to remain engaged in battle. The battle of Cold Harbor was a savage defeat for the Union Army, but Grant hung on grimly to besiege Petersburg, a major rail hub for the South. Grant's calculation, harsh but correct, was

[42]Gerteis, *Civil War St. Louis*, 284–86; and Civil War St. Louis timeline.
[43]Gerteis, *Civil War St. Louis*, 188.

that the Union could more readily afford the appalling casualty lists than could the Confederates. The fighting around Petersburg and Spotsylvania began to foreshadow the trench warfare of the First World War.

Meanwhile, Union Major General Benjamin Butler attacked Confederate Brigadier General Pierre Beauregard south of Richmond and was repulsed. Union Major General Franz Siegel attacked VMI cadets at New Market in the Shenandoah Valley, retreated, and was replaced by Major General David Hunter, who then retreated into West Virginia. Confederate General Robert E. Lee sent Lieutenant General Jubal Early across the Potomac to Frederick, Maryland. President Lincoln observed the skirmishing at the Washington forts before Early fell back to Virginia. Union Major General Phillip Henry pursued Early and destroyed farms in Virginia. In New England, exiled Confederates darted out of Canada to rob a bank at St. Albans, Vermont, and Confederate agents burned eleven hotels and Barnum's Museum in New York City.[44]

In the West, Union forces under Major General William T. Sherman moved slowly forward, using the weight of numbers to gradually push General Joseph Johnston backwards towards the crucial railroad hub at Atlanta, destroying railroad tracks behind them. While Johnston's line bent, his skillful defense showed no sign of breaking. Union attempts to use their strategic mobility to open other fronts mostly ended in failure, mixed with some flashy but inconsequential cavalry raids. Union Major General Nathaniel Banks was sent up the Red River to capture Shreveport, Louisiana, with Commander David Dixon Porter's naval force, but retreated in defeat. Confederate Major General Nathan B. Forrest's cavalry captured Fort Pillow, Tennessee. In May, Sherman fought Confederate General Joseph E. Johnston at Resaca and New Hope Church as Johnston retreated close to Marietta, Georgia.

Time was beginning to work against the Union. With presidential elections coming up, Democrats were split between War Democrats and anti-war Copperheads. In a compromise move, they nominated General George McClellan with an anti-war platform, appealing to many who wanted the war to end. The Republican Party changed its name temporarily to the National Union Party, urging voters not to "change horses in

---

[44]Faust, *Historical Times*, 98–99, 190, 233–34, 264, 320, 651, 679–81, 825–27.

the middle of a stream."[45] With Grant stalemated and Sherman's progress slowed to a crawl by summer, Lincoln was anticipating defeat at the polls in November. Crucially, President Jefferson Davis picked this moment to replace the abrasive but highly capable Johnston with the dashing but rash General John Bell Hood. Aggressive to a fault, Hood attacked Sherman in July, and was defeated at the Battle of Atlanta, abandoning the city.

Realizing the weakness of Hood's position, and knowing that Lee, under constant pressure from Grant, would be unable to spare any reinforcements, Sherman stayed in Atlanta to rebuild his army. He made the decision to cast off from his supply lines and begin the epic March to the Sea, his vast army using "Sherman's Bummers" to live off the land. This dramatic development restored Lincoln's political fortunes and spelled the beginning of the end of the Confederacy.

As Sherman neared the coast, Confederate Major General William Hardee retreated from Savannah, and Sherman offered the victory over the city as a Christmas present to Lincoln, who was re-elected in the fall. Confederate Lieutenant General Hood continued north against U.S. Major General George Henry Thomas at Nashville, where he set siege to the city. Thomas attacked and chased Hood to Tupelo, Mississippi, where Hood's Army of the Tennessee separated. In mid-September, General Sterling Price and his Confederate forces began their invasion of Missouri, marauding through the state. They reached St. Louis in September and Lexington by October. Union forces then pushed them back along the Missouri-Kansas line.[46]

By the fall of 1864, Franklin Dick had returned with his family to Philadelphia, where he carefully monitored events in Missouri, was interested in all the war news, and debated returning to St. Louis. His notes from the missing journals list his struggles to remain in the city that he felt had made him prematurely old. Dick writes of the dirt, mud, and dreary climate, meeting more disloyal than loyal lawyers in the courthouse, the coldness of the Union men, the selfishness of the people, and the discordant society. He felt isolated and worried about supporting his family on

[45]Faust, *Historical Times*, 564, 772–73.
[46]Faust, *Historical Times*, 38, 269–71, 285–86, 368–69, 594, 624, 681–83, 754; and Denney, *Civil War Years*, 357–461.

income alone if he left Missouri. He acknowledged that he had the power to develop a good law practice in St. Louis, but wanted to move his family away from the negative aspects of the city and to live in peace. He felt guilty at not helping his country in its time of crisis, and was torn between returning to St. Louis and remaining safe in Philadelphia.

JOURNAL No. 10

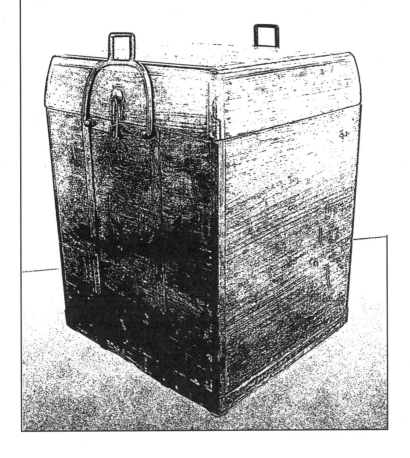

PHILADELPHIA SCHOOL

Note Book.

OF DESIGN FOR WOMEN.

Alexander, Printer and Stationer, 52 South Fourth St. Phila'a

Franklin Dick's journal, notebook #10. Photo by R. L. Geyer © 2007.

September 1864

"In fact the State seems to be in perilous condition, and certainly needs every man to defend its soil."

Philadelphia, No. 715 Locust Street.   Friday, Sep. 23, 1864

I have just finished reading the speech of Wm. D. Kelley M.C.[1] of Phil'a. made last night at the Union League Hall & have just written him a note of encouragement, & wish I had kept a copy of it— But it was about as follows:

"Phil'a. Sep. 23, 1864.

Hon. Wm. D. Kelley. Sir: I have just finished reading your speech reported in the "Press" of this morning— It is clear, forcible, effective, convincing— If such speeches were generally read by the common people, prejudice & darkness will be replaced by truth & the light that truth produces. Its convincing truth leads me to hope that the mass of the Democratic voters may be reached and rescued from the charnel of destruction made & controlled by the Leaders of the Party called Democratic. Nothing

[1]William Darrah Kelley (1814–90) was elected to the U.S. Congress fifteen times (1861–90) and served as the chairman of the Coinage, Weights and Measures Committee.

is lost by offering encouragement to anyone: therefore these words are thrown across your path. Respectfully etc. F.A.D."

I have felt badly this morning at thinking that I am doing nothing at this time of the country's crisis to help & save it. I am out of the current completely, and although I read with deep interest the history of the day, I cannot say that I am aiding the cause forward. My dislike to public life has very much to do with my present position— I have felt disposed to make brief analyses of the effective speeches, for the press, some to give the hasty readers the substance & pith of them. Now the destiny of the nation is in the hands of the People. Should they vote to give control to Northern traitors, it w'd have been far better, had the war never been accepted— My heart & mind long for peace— I will now go on & finish what I was writing yesterday morning.

Contd. from p. 114 Book[2]
"For everything which is not of God, is soon brought to naught.
Observe this short, but certain aphorism.
Forsake all, & thou shalt find all.
Let go desire & thou shalt lay hold on peace.
Consider this rule diligently, & transcribe it into thy practice, for practice will explain & prove it to thee.
++ Buy therefore of me the pure refined gold, of a heavenly & refined disposition, for that shall make thee rich above all the Treasures of this world.

Cast off the wisdom of this generation, and do not sooth thyself with their foolish assignations: for they pursue shadows, & take delight in vanity & nothing"

And read all of this Chapter, to give the thoughts which should follow.

And when I have read such thoughts, and look about & see People dying in every movement of the pendulum— dropping with their half finished enterprises on hand— & then look at my own condition, I wonder that I am so easily led off in heart to earthly things.

---

[2]Dick is quoting from *Imitation of Christ* by Thomas à Kempis, a fifteenth-century monk.

Last night I awoke & got up a few moments: and at once the thought of <u>death is near & pressing</u> towards me, came so forcibly into my mind— & so it is, every time I awake at night. Oh that God could take me by the hand and lead me in the path of useful duty: for I am helpless of myself. Yesterday I felt much worse & thought w'd remain in Phila.

Sat. Sep. 24, 1864. 8:40 P.M.—

I have just come from Walnut below 8th looking at a magnificent Union procession— I never saw finer looking men in any mall before. I feel considerably bright about the Country to-day. The news from Sheridan[3] continues that he has a succession of victories over Early—[4] he is constantly in pursuit of him— Under the late successes <u>gold</u> has descended rapidly of late—

On the 22nd it was 220
   "   23rd   "   210
   "   24th   "   197

It went down from 220 to 197 today & there is a panic of prices— This morning I felt almost desperate, not to be doing anything active to help the Country, at such a time, impressed with the consciousness that if the Chicago men carry the election, that the Country will be ruined— Today is published another great letter of Genl. Sherman's to the Mayor of Atlanta— I regard Sherman as the foremost man in the nation— the papers he has put out are unequalled by those of any other man.[5]

This P.M., E. R. [Evans Rogers] stepped in a short time, & expressed solicitude to have been doing something in the way of business. He is my warm friend.

---

[3]Philip Henry Sheridan (1831–88) was a captain when the Civil War began, but rose to the rank of major general and commander. He was known for his aggressive cavalry raids and victories in the Shenandoah Valley.

[4]Jubal Anderson Early (1816–94) opposed secession, but when Virginia decided to secede, stayed loyal to his state and entered the Confederate army, where he rose to the rank of lieutenant general. From the Shenandoah Valley, he raided into Maryland and Pennsylvania, burning Chambersburg, Pennsylvania, in return for the devastation of the Shenandoah Valley by Union forces.

[5]The campaign around Atlanta lasted from May 1 through September 2, 1864, when Atlanta was finally captured by Union troops under General Sherman.

Tuesday, Sep. 27, 1864 12:15 P.M., noon

Genl. Sheridan continues vigorously the pursuit of the defeated
Early— Genl. Grant still continues quiet. Sherman is putting things in
order in Atlanta, & the miserable copperheads in the north press the People to elect McClellan—[6] Reverdy Johnson[7] has come out for McC— In
Missouri, matters are greatly agitated— the draft has been going on for
several days— & is focused in the 4th & 6th wards— I do not know
whether I am enrolled in the 4th or 6th but I may be drafted in the 6th—[8]
The Bushwhackers[9] continue their murders in the State at a fearful rate—
and Shelby[10] has invaded the State, along with Old Price again in large
forces— the enrolled militia is again called out— Rosecrans[11] has called
the People to arms. It looks as if they would have bloody times there—[12]

Yesterday I went to see Rev. Wilbur F. Paddock at his request about
taking up work in the church— and agreed to start a class at 2 o'c. Sunday

[6]George B. McClellan was the Democratic candidate in the 1864 presidential election. The Republican Party (calling itself the National Union Party) nominated Lincoln,
but many delegates voted for Ulysses S. Grant, who was not a candidate.

[7]Reverdy Johnson (1796–1876) was sympathetic to the South, but devoted to the
Union. He was a delegate to the Peace Convention. Johnson served in the Maryland
House of Representatives (1860–61), in the U.S. Senate (1863–68), and as minister to
England (1868–69).

[8]The Union Draft Act conscripted men between the ages of 18 and 35 in July 1863,
and March, July, and December 1864.

[9]Dick is referring to Confederate guerillas who made raids into Missouri.

[10]Joseph Orville Shelby (1830–97), a member of the Missouri State Guard, enlisted
in the Confederate army, where he was known as an effective cavalry leader and for always
wearing a black plume in his hat. He led a cavalry division for Price's invasion of Missouri
in 1864.

[11]William Starke Rosecrans (1819–98) enlisted in the Union army and became
drillmaster of the Marion Rifles. He was made brigadier general after the Union victory at
Rich Mountain, Virginia (West Virginia) against Confederate General Robert E. Lee.
Rosecrans commanded the Department of Missouri. He was loved by his enlisted men,
but noted for his harsh dealing with officers.

[12]On September 19, Confederate forces led by Major General Sterling Price, Major
General James F. Fagan, Brigadier General John S. Marmaduke, and Colonel Joseph O.
Shelby crossed into Missouri with twelve thousand soldiers. Union General William S.
Rosecrans, commander of the Department of Missouri, was afraid that the longtime
Southern organization, the Knights of the Golden Circle, would reorganize itself, join
Price, and conquer the state. Rosecrans stepped up enlistments to increase his forces. On
September 27, Marmaduke attacked Union General Thomas Ewing at Fort Davidson at
Pilot Knob, south of St. Louis. Ewing fought delaying skirmishes with Confederates until
Price retreated from Missouri at the end of October.

P.M.s. My uncertainty about staying here seems to be paralyzing my acts. I wish so much that I c'd decide to remain here, for I fear that some event will carry me back there.

Yesterday I saw the death of Judge Wells, & went to the law library to see if I c'd take the appointment without residing in the district— & if I c'd have done so, my impression is that I w'd have tried to get it. After reading the papers, I often read Law; & generally of late The Reports— but yesterday Evng. Blackstone—[13]

Thursday, Sep. 29, 1864, 9:35 P.M.

Genl. Sheridan has continued his pursuit of Early & is today by rebel papers reported to have reached Staunton last Monday—[14] & it is believed that Lee has reinforced Early— this Evng. It is s'd that Grant has commenced moving on Richmond on the W. side of the James, & that his troops are about 6 miles distant from Richmond. I suppose it is necessary for Grant to move to keep Lee from sending large numbers to fall upon Sheridan— but for the ability of Sheridan & Grant. I w'd feel uneasy about Sheridan, as he is so far now from our lines. The Rebels have begun working actively on the Rail Roads, to destroy them in Sherman's rear.

The Rebels in Missouri have come within 70 to 80 miles of St. Lewis, & then advance nearer. All the militia are called out & no doubt they will have hot times there.

Gold is about 200 & rather below it.

Camden & Amboy bonds are down to 100 to 101 & now that I can sell my U.S. bonds at 5 to 6 per.c. more & convert the money into C&A, I do not do it— Some time ago, I felt very much like doing it.

---

[13]Sir William Blackstone's, *Commentaries on the Laws of England,* an easily readable four-volume treatise on English common law, was originally published in 1765–69, and covered the rights of persons, property rights, private wrongs, and public wrongs. It played an important role in the development of the American legal system, and had long been considered a standard reference for lawyers.

[14]Union Major General Philip Henry Sheridan, commander of the Army of the Shenandoah, had defeated Confederate Lieutenant General Jubal A. Early at Third Winchester and Fisher's Hill, Virginia. Sheridan was then made brigadier general and continued to pursue Early.

Friday, Sep. 30, 1864 11:10 A.M.

I feel anxious and tired in spirit this morning. The news from St. Louis is that Genl. A. J. Smith,[15] in command of the troops below St. Louis, who was some days ago down on the Iron Mt. R.R,[16] has continued falling back, & is now at Jefferson Barracks with his troops. That Gen'l. Ewing,[17] who was isolated at Pilot Knob, has blown up the Fort there & moved across to the S.W. branch of the Pacific R.R. Thus the country to the South is evacuated and our force is concentrating in & around St. Louis.

There the militia are all called out & every man is needed for duty. In this state of things, I feel as if my decision cannot be postponed with credit to myself. If I have quit St. Louis, it c'd not be expected of me now to go there to join in the defense: but unless that is my position, how can I stay here at such a time? And aside from my thoughts about myself, there would I not be of much advantage in encouraging others by my presence and example? If Phila. was attacked, being unknown, I could count only as one common soldier; but in St. Louis, where I am universally known, I count very differently. The Rebels on the North Mo. R.R. at Centralia have committed horrid cruelties: massacring the prisoners they have taken. In fact the State seems to be in a perilous condition, and certainly needs every man to defend its soil. In this condition of things, here am I in Phila. doing absolutely nothing, and remaining undecided, & of no weight, value or influence.

5 m. to 1 o'c. P.M.

I stopped writing & made out a statement of my affairs to be left with Myra, in case I decide to go to St. Louis. It begins thus—

[15]Andrew Jackson Smith (1815–97) was made a colonel and chief of cavalry in Missouri, and then brigadier general and major general. He spent most of the war on important detached service. He served at Corinth, and was sent to chase Price out of Missouri.

[16]The Iron Mountain Railroad went from Pilot Knob to St. Louis and was captured by Confederate Brigadier General Marmaduke, but he had no car or locomotive to travel anywhere.

[17]Thomas Ewing Jr. (1829–96) was chief justice of the Kansas state supreme court (1861–62). Ewing tried to keep Kansas anti-slavery. He recruited the Eleventh Kansas Volunteers, serving as their colonel.

"Phila. Sept. 30, 1864

"Being about to start to St. Louis to take part in the defense of the loyal men against the invasion of the Rebels, I make this memorandum of property belonging to me— as follows:"

And now the question & matter that fills my thoughts is, what will I do? God alone knows what I ought to do. If I cherished any feeling of ambition, I would have remained in St. Louis; and the thought yesterday & the last few days back in my mind has been, what are all the things that make Phila. desirable to me, when placed against those which make it undesirable— namely that I am <u>as a man</u> nothing here. I am simply out of place; for there is nothing here for me to do. The disagreeable matters of St. Louis are set on the one hand, and the completion of life in Phila. on the other. I here care nothing for the amusements of the place, & do not participate in them. This is the time for me to go back, if I am going— While thus doubting, undecided, & doing nothing. My days, weeks & months are passing over my head, & drawing me nearer to the grave, & that awful event, the close of my life.

October 1864

*"The truth is I know not what I will
do nor where all this will end."*

Saturday, October 1, 1864, 10:50 P.M.

The army of Grant is said to be in motion— part of it. The 10th &
18th Corps, or part of them, have crossed the James & moved towards
Richmond & met with some success; but we have not enough from there
to know much about it. Sheridan is now out of reach & we have not heard
from him for days. The rebel scouts are in his rear & capture his couriers.
From Missouri the news comes bad— Our forces keep close. Genl.

144

McNeil,[18] I think, is isolated at Rolla & is certainly in danger there of being cut off. The scoundrels will hang or burn him if they capture him, which I hope he will not permit alive.

Today I have felt like remaining here— the fragment of my life left, I had better spend here, rather than go where I detest everything— Rev. F. Marshall died on 22 Sep. at Versailles, Ky.

Gold is down to 93 per oz.

Sunday Oct 2, 1864, 4:13 P.M.

I went to the church at 2 P.M. today to teach a bible lesson— I prepared the 2nd Chapter of Luke— but no one came & after waiting till about ½ past 2, I came back. Today I took the Holy Communion & I prayed, as I always do, that it might be with faith & profit—

I have just read No. 17 of the *Rambler* (Vol. 1, p. 110) on the shortness of life &c. and am struck by the similarity of the views in the *Imitation of Christ*.[19]

At p. 111, it says— xx "When we reflect, how that vehemence of eagerness after the common objects of pursuit, is kindled in our minds.

We represent to ourselves the pleasures of some future possession, & suffer our thoughts to dwell attentively upon it, til it has wholly engrossed the imagination & permits us not to conceive any happiness but its attainment, or any misery but its loss, & every other satisfaction which the bounty of providence has scattered over life, is neglected as inconsiderable in comparison of the great object which we have placed before us, & is thrown from us as encumbering our activity, or trampled under foot, as standing in our way."

---

[18]John H. McNeil (1813–91) served as a colonel in the Missouri Volunteers at Camp Jackson; he also captured Fulton, Missouri, and defeated General Harris. He was provost marshall of St. Louis until August 1861. He commanded the District of Northeast Missouri in Palmyra, where he campaigned against guerillas and was blamed for killing some prisoners by the Confederates, who said they would shoot him if he were captured.

[19]*The Rambler*, by Samuel Johnson, was published in England twice a week from 1750 to 1752. Johnson wrote in a roundabout but serious vein about his thoughts on morality, religion, politics, literature, and society. Franklin Dick quotes from #169 (October 29, 1751) and #185 (December 24, 1751).

Then adding how vain this would appear to us on the approach of death, it adds, "We should then find the absurdity of stretching out our arms <u>incessantly to grasp</u> that <u>which we can not keep</u> & wearing out our lives in endeavors to add new tenets to the <u>fabrik</u> of <u>ambition</u>, when the foundation itself is shaking, & the ground on which it stands, is moldering away."

How true do I find this, as to myself. How in my thoughts of what of professional elevation is within my reach at St. Louis, have I found myself for hours <u>absorbed vehemently</u> by the thought of it, until it seemed to exclude all other considerations— and such feeling has been apt to continue until something would occur to present to my mind the shortness of life.

Yesterday thinking of the death of Judge Wells rather tended to end the previously existing feeling that I must go to St. Louis.

I am 41 years of age, & the remaining <u>active</u> years of my life are few— Why shall I not forego what supposed advantages <u>connected with ambition</u> I may have in St. Louis, & yield to the quieter, more peaceful considerations, which would keep me here.

Last winter in St. Louis, I deliberately decided not to stay there & devote myself to my profession. Since then, I have acquired a house here, & settled my income and Myra has fully settled down in her mind to staying here & <u>certainly is much happier</u> in it.

Two or three times last week I was on the point of telling her that I must go back to St. Louis— & I am so glad I did not do so, as it would have unsettled her mind & heart.

Oct. 3, '64 wrote a short letter as follows:

No. 715 Locust St., Phila. Penna. Oct 3, '64
To the Sheriff of Dane County, Ms.[20]

Sir: I have owned for several yrs. a house & lot in Mad. which I have wanted to sell for a long time. By looking on the Town plat you will see

---

[20]Franklin Dick's note may refer to Dane County, Wisconsin, and the town of Madison, which was made the capital of the Wisconsin territory in 1836 and became county seat in 1846. Since he notes Dane County, Ms., in his journal, it is not possible to be sure.

the property designated as lots 8.9.10 & 11 in Block 179. If you can sell
the property for me, I will pay you a liberal comm. Please let me know yr.
opinion of what you can get for the property & if sale can be effected. I
will go up to Mad. on my way to St. Louis, next month. Jas. R. & Co.
have had charge of the property for me, & still have & as they do not succeed in selling it, although they have been authorized to do so for years, I
write to you in hope that I may be able to sell it for near its value. By
looking to the records you will see the deed to me recorded about the year
1855 & can get a precise description of the property from that.
Your obt. Servt.
F. A. D.

Saturday, Oct. 8, 1864, 11:45 P.M.

I have just come in from seeing a great Union procession. It passed
for 2 hours & then I left, not knowing how much more there is of it.

The last few days, I have felt to be rather dull— I have seen no one &
been with no one— I do not go out to try to make acquaintances, nor to
start doing anything here, because I keep uncertain as to what I will do. Yesterday & today I have been reading Blackstone. On Tuesday comes the election in Penna., Ohio, Indiana & Iowa, which are the pre-runners of the
momentous Presidential Election. Will be a strong indication of the result.[21]

In Missouri, the Rebels seem to be unchecked & to have their own
way. Grant has been tightening his lines around Lee— The Rebels have
gotten in Sherman's rear, to break up the R.R. The Rebel invasion caused
new bonds to the P.R.R. [Pennsylvania Rail Road] to sell yesterday in
N.Y. at 65 & 66 & this A.M. I telegraphed Riggs & Co to buy me
$15,000 of them at not over 70=.

This evng., I felt as though I had better go back to St. Louis for the
winter to have occupation, & make some money. As carefully & moder-
ately as we live, I find that our expenses are very large each month. Much

[21]Ohio, Indiana, and Pennsylvania held congressional elections on October 10,
1864; the results of these elections were generally regarded as indicators of how those
states would vote in November presidential elections. Iowa held elections for state offices,
Congress, and president on the same day in November. Apparently Dick was mistaken
about when Iowa's elections would occur.

larger than I thought they w'd be.

Sunday, Oct. 9, 1864, 10:10 A.M.

On reading just now no. 71 of the *Rambler* (vol. 2, p. 1) the thought comes into my mind, that I am not destined to be a prominent man in life—

The feeling is constantly present to me, that I am here not only doing nothing, but not asked, nor expected to do anything by the community here, because not known. But in St. Louis, I always shrank back from prominence, & why? Was it not because I despised prominent men; finding them activated by mean motives & carrying their selfishness into all their public actions.

It may well be believed, that that Society most exclusively amongst the Selfish, the conceited, the vain, the overbearing & the unscrupulous, is that amongst prominent men— & to be prominent, a man merely to accomplish his own advancement must give up his time to those who can promote that end.

Monday, Oct. 13, 1864. 11:32 A.M.

Just returned from Cumberland Hotel to call on S. T. Glover— Ans'd. a letter from J. T. Swerinton, saying I c'd soon be in St. Louis— The last day or two have been thinking of taking my family back there for the winter—

On Monday, Sam Simmons came in from Jersey Shore— He left yesterday for St. Louis— told him to enquire about Hitchcock's house— I went into Court on Tuesday & sat a little while, & felt that I c'd. not begin practice here— My work here is <u>ready made occupation of a kind congenial to me</u> and therefore I keep thinking all the time of going back to St. Louis. Things there are in an excited state on a/c of the Rebel Invasion. Price passed by Jefferson City a few days ago, skirmishing there. Our forces are after him; but he destroys the Pacific R. R. after him—

Riggs & Co. on Sat. 8th bought for me $10,000 Mo. State bonds issued to the P.R.R. Co. at 68 costing $6,800 & 25$ com. = $6,825. On the 11th, they bought for me from E.R. $2,000 of same at $66—

The most of my time here is spent in the House— After breakfast I read the papers— write &c.— & some days about 10 o'c. go to the exchange, or elsewhere— After dinner, read the Papers— & walk— & in the evng. often read some law— But my thoughts daily & all the time are on What will I do.

I hate the thought of giving up to going back to St. Louis— but here, the thought & feeling of being nothing & doing nothing make me undecided and uncomfortable—

On Tuesday, the Elections came off— Ohio & Indiana went largely for the loyal Party— but Penna. is in some doubt yet on the home vote— it is believed the Soldiers' vote will carry the State by about 10,000 majority—

Genl. Sherman has gone back to fight Hard in his rear— Grant is very close to Richmond & seems to be tightening his hold on it. Sheridan, after devastating the upper part of the valley & falling back to near Strasburg—

Friday, Oct. 14, 1864 — 17 to 11 P.M.

No special war news from any quarter— the election in Penna. is so close that the result will be known only by the count. Yesterday evng. I felt like writing to Simmons to see Col. Callender about our going to the arsenal— & feeling like it this A.M., I did write, saying we w'd probably go out if Callender was to have no one there.

I have not spoken of it to Myra, not wanting to do so until I determine. I do not want to go, except that I am without occupation here—

Read Mo. law all this A.M. & Blackstone this evng. I have not yet decided to go out, but it looks as if I w'd go, that I may have some business to do. I might study here, but I can not ask anyone to give me business, nor occupy the attitude of one wanting patronage. Nor do I feel contented to stay here week after week doing nothing & out of employment.

I pray daily to God to guide, aid & keep me.

Thursday, Oct. 20, 1864, 12:40 Noon

On Saturday last, I changed & felt as if I w'd prefer to stay here & so continued to feel four or five days— Today I feel nearly balanced— My idea being to study & practice law— & if in Mo., I c'd do it to much advantage— On Monday, Edward Rogers came to ask me if I would serve with him as one of the Trustees of his Father's estate. I s'd I did not see any reason why I should not & implied that I would. Since then, I have been examining the Statute law of Penna. applying to the subject— viz— Decedents— Trustees— Wills— Married Women's Estate— Orphans Court— Register of Wills— Auditors— and it has kept me pretty hard at work—

Uncle E. did not seem to favor my acting as Trustee. A question as to my eligibility on grounds of Domicile may prevent— It is undecided in my mind.

In Missouri, Price has not been at all molested by Rosecrans, whose energy I suppose is wasted away by liv'g. & hard drinking. The State has been horribly ravaged by the Rebels. Sherman has followed Hood[22] back to Dalton & thereabouts— Hood, I believe, is on the retreat back-ward. Matters around Richmond remain about the same. Maryland, by a close vote, has adopted the free State Constitution— Thank God for that— May Missouri soon do the same.

Saturday, Oct. 22, 1864, 10 P.M.

Another great battle has been fought near Strasburg at Cedar Creek in the Shenandoah Valley by Sheridan, who turned impending defeat into a great victory, by his timely arrival pending the battle—[23]

In Missouri, Rosecrans is not molesting Price. The Rebels seem to have it all their own way & are devastating the country generally— The Rebels seriously discussing putting their slaves into their army— I hope they will do it.

[22]John Bell Hood (1831–79) served in the U.S. Army (1855–61), then transferred to the Confederate army (1861), rising to the rank of brigadier general commanding Hood's Texas Brigade, then rose to a division commander in the Army of Northern Virginia. Hood's success in battle was due to being in the right place at the right time; he was also popular with his men, who followed him when he seized the initiative. He was wounded in the left arm at Gettysburg and lost his right leg at Chickamauga, but returned to duty as a lieutenant general, leading the Army of the Tennessee.

[23]The Battle of Cedar Creek occurred on October 19, 1864. Sheridan left his troops camped at Cedar Creek and went to Washington, DC for a strategy conference. Early made a surprise attack, forcing the Union troops to retreat. Sheridan heard the battle's noise, returned, and counterattacked, crushing Early's troops, who retreated to the south.

The last 2 days, I have been thinking very seriously of starting to St. Louis soon. I may go any day, & yet it is untimely to go now— unless I want to get involved in the strife there. I pray that God will guide me in this matter.

Alexander Kayser died on the 17th of this month at 6 A.M. after a short illness, aged 49 years & 3 months. A miserable man he has been ever since he entered public life—

Sunday, Oct. 23, 1864, 4½ P.M.

I have been thinking today of how I may try to satisfy myself to remain here; & I have thought that it was strange that men should continue to live in such severe countries as the artic regions— & wondered during this rebellion that the occupiers of the disputed territory did not leave it— The Rebels are now in Missouri ravaging a country where many Union men are found. Why have they not left—

Might I not here equally ask myself, why I have not left St. Louis— i.e. given up all idea of returning to it. The answer is difficult and complicated; for there is a strong drawing of one to a place where there are many associations with it. These associations inhabit the mind & lead it to dwell upon & linger around its former scenes. The want of associations in a new place, make it empty & almost void. This matter of association is perhaps an animal instinct— for we see Dogs & other animals frequenting & remaining in the same localities— may not the disposition of men be of the same nature, only mine intelligently developed.

Certain it is, that one of the most difficult operations in life is the change of the place of abode. Life to me here, is as yet unattractive, & almost forbidding— & when I come to meet face to face the obstacles of beginning here in the realities of a Resident, I turn away from them with more than distaste. And yet, what do I encounter on the other hand in going back to St. Louis— The notes of many a writing set out what I so detest.

The difficulties are so real & practical, that again & again I feel that to God alone can I turn to guide me. The consideration of the shortness of life and uncertainty of all worldly things makes me feel that to go back & encounter what must be met in St. Louis for the hope of living through it to the enjoyment of peace & prosperity in the future is almost unworthy of the attempt & effort.

Monday, Oct. 24, 1864, 10:5 P.M.

Yesterday I got a letter from Simmons, advising me not to take my family to St. Louis this winter— that all is in disorder there & the very air "murky"— it made a considerable impression on me— Today I got a letter from Apo. saying "it is a final fact" & that in the spring they will go to California to live— that she supposed we'd remain in Phila.— & she was happy at the prospect of leaving St. Louis—

This has made me feel during the day more <u>practically</u> like remaining here, than I have of late & I began to look around in my mind for what I can do for a business— Now, should a business offer, I suppose it w'd determine me. I wrote to Simmons today to move into a cheap office & that I might never again practice law in Mo. If I can only get occupation here, I believe I would easily settle down to staying here.

There is no war news today— It seems that in Genl. Sheridan's victory on the 19th at Cedar Creek, we took over 50 guns &c—

Thursday, Oct. 27, 1864, 7½ P.M.

Phil. Lee came yesterday & leaves at 10½ this Evng. en route to Cairo, where he takes command of the Mississippi Squadron—[24] I have been with him nearly all day & tonight I am tired—

But I am also weary in mind. I ought to be contented & happy, when I contrast my condition, during these dreadful days of Civil War with that of the thousands of suffering ones. But this Evng., I feel dull & weary for the want of occupation & employment & have been thinking of the Farrar's & St. Louis occupation. And yet I can not make up my mind to take my loved ones back there; & I can not endure going without them— There is so much there that is hateful & forbidding, that it repels

---

[24]Phillips Lee's wife, Lizzie Blair Lee, followed her husband to Philadelphia at the start of his trip to Cairo, Illinois, for command of the Mississippi squadron.

me— & then, here is the emptiness of my life without the kind of occupation I have been accustomed to.

Having no house there to take my Family to also operates strongly upon me to deter me from such change. The hard climate there, with constant dirt & mud to keep people in-doors— the many cloudy, chilly, clammy, damp days are sickening to look back upon— the truth is I know not what I will do— nor where all this will end—

The Rebels seem now to be seriously debating putting their slaves into the army.[25]

Saturday, Oct. 29, 1864, 11 A.M.

On Thursday Evng. I wrote to Ben. Farrar to enquire at the Lindell [Hotel] for rooms & board— On Friday, I wrote Simmons again about the arsenal. Yesterday, I studied Mo. Law & especially the cases on practice & pleadings.

In relation to going back, I simply feel that here I am without occupation & I can not go to work to study law here & try to get position— I have no place or standing as a man of business here & it is not in me to work for it, because I am obstructed by my independent means & the feeling that I have all that in St. Louis ready made & am now there higher that I would ever get here. I appreciate the cleanliness & sweetness of everything here, but it is with a kind of holiday or idle feeling— I am in the place, but not of it & no part of it. There seems to be a compulsion upon me to leave, simply because I have nothing to do here and much to do there.

I hate the thought of living in such a community as bloody Missouri, but when ever I give up thought of going there, the emptiness of my position here strongly stares me in the face. Yesterday I told Myra to get Evans ready to go to St. Louis, so that I can take him with me next week, should I conclude to go—

[25]Confederate President Jefferson Davis stated in his November 7, 1864, presidential message that if slaves served as soldiers, it could lead to their emancipation. The heated debate on both sides of the issue continued. Finally, on March 13, 1865, the Confederate Congress passed an act to enlist blacks in order to provide Lee with more troops, but it was too late to change events.

Sunday, Oct. 30, 1864, 9:05 P.M.

I had pretty much made up my mind to start to St. Louis on next Thursday, & after dinner talked to Myra, & said if the elections on the 8 Nov. go right, that perhaps I w'd buy a house in St. Louis & go to practicing law & the last several days I have been reading Mo. Law. After coming to this point this P.M., I started out to walk & think about it, when the feeling came over me, that I dread to do it. I felt that it was to live over again the struggles of the past, in such striking contrast with life here.

I must recognize the fact, that I <u>fear</u> life in Missouri— were I not a Christian, & did I not strive to live by Christian principles, I might nerve myself to the brutal & beastly & cruel contest that w'd enable me to bear down all hostility & opposition there. But with such hatred as I have of pro-slavery traitors, to cope with them and preserve a Christian action & spirit, is to be in the contest at disadvantage. And then too, the thought of my children being fated to live there, weighs in my mind.

It was in my mind that I w'd buy a house— to cost say $25,000.— which w'd reduce my money at interest to $80,000— and then to practice w'd require me to remain in St. Louis a part of the hot weather— & it w'd probably run into my getting a country place there. Well all that might answer if Missouri was settled & purged of its violent elements.

If peace is restored to the country, & slavery is eradicated, & the population becomes a settled & temperate one, I might then go back & enjoy life there. But to go out now & settle down there while the storm is still raging— it does not seem to be in me to do so— Not being compelled to remain there to make a living, I feel at liberty to stay away, while it is so horrible to my mind to be there.

So that now, I think I will not go out until after the election— after that, my action can be determined by the existing state of things. Last Evng. I went and had a talk with Aunt H. P. R. [Harriet P. Rogers] about their business affairs; & while I was gone, E. R. [Evans Rogers] left deed for me to draft one for the house 717—

Later. 20 M. to 12

Since writing the above, I looked over my journals & noted down the memo read at the back of this book <u>of this date</u>, to fortify me against going back by seeing how I had struggled against it & how on going back to St. L. last fall "to practice law & have occupation," I soon fell into disgust & discontent & w'd not practice— if I w'd not <u>then</u>, when I had not sold my property, can I think I w'd now when I am really independent.

Oh no, I hope I will not go back & may it continue in my mind that I dread & fear to go back; & may I make my breast & mind contented here— where my precious wife is beginning to make herself happy & useful.

November 1864

"Oh, it is today an honor to be an American. Our strength is re-established our permanency assured; for the ability of the nation now to suppress the rebellion cannot be doubted."

Wed., Nov. 2, 1864, 8:20 P.M.

Today I have been busy preparing to go to St. Louis, & have my trunks nearly packed; and now I am almost sorry I have done this— and at this moment I am hanging almost in doubt whether or not to start, in view of the uncertainties of the election—

Phila., Friday, Nov 4th, 1864, ¼ to 1 P.M.

I almost hate to put my pen to paper, so distressing has been my experience the last 2 or 3 days. Yesterday at 11:40 A.M., I started for St. Louis with a heavy heart & most unwilling feeling. All the way I rode, I felt that I wanted to be going the opposite direction. By 6 to 7 o'c., I became so unhappy & desperate, I determined to turn back from Altoona, & did so, getting here at 7 this A.M.

And from the time I changed my mind, I felt the intense pressure off of me. I could not bear the separation from my Family— I knew my experience in former separations that all the time until we came together, I

156

would be unhappy & suffer. And I feared too, that being in St. Louis, I w'd be a long time in determining whether to return, or to send for my Family— which time w'd be one protracted struggle & term of intense suffering— for I suffer all the time I am separated from those I love so tenderly— My precious little Frank showed the greatest regret at my going away, & joy at my return— He is tender hearted like his Brother Otis.

I felt when I made up my mind last night to return— that I never would go to St. Louis again— but w'd live East. It was horrible to me to face the reality of living again in St. Louis. May God have mercy upon me. I was a dreadful sufferer & almost ready to become insane last night, as I was whirled along in the cars until I determined to turn back.

Sunday, Nov. 6, 1864, 10:08 A.M.

I have felt satisfied every moment since my return. In starting, I acted upon the restless principle that makes men desire what they have not, & seek what others indicate as desirable. In coming back, I acted by my own internal disposition— of enjoying quiet domestic comforts which are around me, & not sacrificing them even for a few weeks or days, for other things which, looking through my own eyes, I do not value— & they only seem desirable, in looking through others' eyes; or from a standpoint different from my own.

All men & women are somewhat mean— we all have the same qualities, though not in the same proportions. Envy is common to all— some cherish it— others try to suppress it; yet all are subject to its operation; just as all feel the sun & wind & elements. So with ambition— desire for distinction— worldly praise, or admiration— fondness for riches— or for luminaries— or for display &c— &c. And then by combinations, artificial or secondary principles grow up as influencing elements or principles, & produce such elements of character as cruelty— deceit or falsehood— treason.

Now all are liable to the influence of such passions or impelling currents. Is it strange then, that a man feels that he can not control him-self; which means that he can not keep uppermost certain principles; which he decides ought to govern his life; when new circumstances force into action other principles.

There they are, made by God— & for a purpose, or they would not have been made. They may lie dormant, until they are played upon by a cause; but when principles, usually inert, because not exposed to common action, are subjected to excitement, which brings them into action, then they become literally <u>motives</u>; that is, they move the man ahead, & in the direction of that operating cause.

These principles are aroused & made active, just as digestion is aroused, or the ear is aroused to hearing, or the eye to sight, or the exposed nerve of a tooth to pain. It is a new combination of circumstances that arouses the elements of our nature to action. This is illustrated every day— Bad actions of others, such as ingratitude— oppression of the poor— &c— produce their effects on us; & we feel the effect of music to be an illustration of the same general fact.

The general treason in action in this Rebellion, subjects all loyal People to the operation of certain aroused principles— Our loyalty is aroused by their disloyalty— the quality produced being the same as its opposite, according to circumstances. Thus some loyal People are aroused to active resistance, while others, influenced by qualifying motives, are operated upon differently— e.g., not so much attached to the past Government, as disposed to acquiesce & tacitly support the existing Government upon a formidable attempt to overthrow the Govt. They quietly await events, their loyalty turning them to the support of the new Govt., just as the compass of a ship ever drawn by the magnet, yet may by intervening magnets, be drawn aside from the pole of the earth.

How shall a man then govern him-self; how shall he acquire self-control. It happens that most men are forced by circumstances to labor for their living, and as their labor must be constant to yield the necessary support, then their surrounding circumstances continue about the same, & so their conduct day after day continues about the same. Industry, reliability & honesty are requisite to enable a man to secure employment, & therefore so do principles become habits, & by their force operate as steady causes, or continuing motives.

But when the necessity for continuous daily effort on the same beaten track ceases, new principles of action come into play. The man can do what he chooses, because his circumstances are "independent." What then will he do (Stopped here at 11¼ to go to church)

4:23 P.M.

The *Rambler* Vol. 2, p. 260, No. 185 says,

"Every one wishes for the distinctions for which thousands are wishing at the same time, in their own opinion, with better claims." And further on P. 263—

"To be driven by external motives from the path which our own heart approves, to give way to anything but conviction, to suffer the opinion of others to rule our choice, or overpower our resolves, is to submit tamely to the lowest & most ignominious slavery & to resign the right of directing our own lives." This I read this P.M.

See what I wrote this A.M. on p. 22— as showing how I acted in conformity with it.[26]

10 P.M.

See the *Rambler*, Vol 2, p. 302, No 118 as to the little extent of <u>Fame</u>.

"The numbers to whom any real or perceptible good or evil can be derived by the greatest power, or most active diligence are inconsiderable xxx and the only motive to the mention or remembrance of others is curiosity."

He then shows the masses are considerably with necessities xx

The truth is that very few have leisure form in dispensable business to employ their thoughts upon narrative, or characters; & among those to whom fortune has given the liberty of living more by their own choice, many create to themselves engagements by the indulgences of some <u>petty ambition</u>, the admission of some <u>insatiable desire,</u> or the toleration of some <u>predominant passion</u>. xx

Even of those who have dedicated themselves to knowledge, the far greater part have confined their curiosity to a few objects, & have very little inclination to <u>promote any fame</u>, but that which their own studies entitle them to partake. xxx

No man can be venerable or formidable, but to a small part of his fellow creatures."

Rambler 3rd Vol., p. 366, No. 203 says,

[26]Franklin Dick wrote, "I have felt satisfied every moment since my return."

"Whether to be remembered in remote times, be worthy of a wise man's wish, has not yet been satisfactorily decided; & indeed to be long remembered, can happen to so small a number, that the bulk of mankind has very little interest in the question. There is never room in the world for more that a certain quantity or measure of renown. The necessary businesses of life, the immediate pleasures or pains of every condition, leave us not leisure beyond a fixed proportion for contemplations, which do not forcibly influence our present welfare.

When this vacuity is filled, no characters can be admitted into the circulation of fame, but by occupying the place of some that must be thrust into oblivion. xx Reputation therefore is a meteor, which blazes a while & disappears forever; & if we except a few transcendent & invincible names which no revolutions of opinion or length of time is able to suffice; All those that engage our thoughts or diversify our conversation, are every moment hastening to obscurity, as new favorites are adopted by fashion."

See Vol. 3, p. 322, No 196— for the changes which time produces on life—

On p. 324–5 is an admirable picture of what the man, as he advances in life, proposes as his career.

Phila., Wed. Nov. 9, 1864, 10 m. to 2 P.M.

The Presidential Election is over & the Country has decided to carry on the war without halting or stint.

On Monday Evng. & yesterday & this A.M. before the paper came, I felt perfectly free from excitement or uneasiness as to the result. In this City yesterday, there was no excitement, noise or sign of anything going on. In New York everything was quiet. There were troops sent there & a Brigade of Regulars to New York, & Genl. Ben. Butler to command them.

The nation has passed the vital point— the dreaded days— the event on which its future rested & wonderful has been its success, & Glory in it. I thank God deeply & from my heart for this evidence, of the steadiness and majesty of the Nation.

It proves to the world & all times the ability of the People for self government— Oh, it is today an honor to be an American. Our strength is re-established— our permanency assured; for the ability of the nation now to suppress the rebellion cannot be doubted. It rained Monday & Tuesday & again today, but not much on any one day. The returns in are only partial, but clearly show the result.

December 1864

"I cannot determine what course of life I will adopt; I want to decide, but I cannot."

715 Locust Street   Phila. Thursday, 29th December, 1864,   ¼ to 7 P.M.

I have allowed all this interval from the 9th of Nov. to pass without writing, because I was dissatisfied with recording my vacillations & indecisions— I had kept a record of my feelings as to leaving Mo. for the purpose of strengthening my intentions, but my experience was that it did not work effectually.

Great military events have passed since I wrote. The great March of Genl. Sherman from Atlanta to Savannah— leaving Atlanta the 14th Nov. & entering Savannah about the 23rd of Dec. For a long time we had no news from him except through the Rebel Papers. He is now at Savannah & we are just getting the full details of his march. There have been but 2 or 3 arrivals from Savannah since he took the place. Genl. Bragg[27]

[27]Franklin Dick says Bragg in error. Confederate Lieutenant General William J.

with about 15,000 men escaped from the City across the Savannah River.

Genl. Thomas has also had a great victory over Hood's army at Nashville— This was about 10 to 14 days ago, since when Thomas' army has been pursuing Hood's— & we have news today that Hood has reached the Tenn. River at Florence & may be crossing there.

Hood got in Sherman's rear back of Atlanta— followed the Rail Road up to Dalton, Sherman followed Hood, who crossed the Pigeon Mountains too fast for Sherman to catch him— Went S.W. into Alabama— When Sherman started back to Atlanta & thence on his wonderful march leaving Hood to go North & to be cared for by Genl. Thomas— Hood crossed the Tenn. River near Decatur— Thomas with about 20,000 men fell back from Pulaski & to Franklin on the Harpath River, where Hood came up with an army under Schofield, attacked & was heavily repulsed— Thence our army fell back rapidly to Nashville, closely followed by Hood, who threatened the City for several days—

Thomas was reinforced by A. J. Smith's Corps, lately from Missouri, & by other troops & then attacked Hood & defeated him terribly— Gen'l. Stoneman & Custer have just beaten Breckenridge & other Rebels near the Tenn. & Va. Line— destroying Saltville & other valuable places.

At this time an attack upon Fort Fisher, N.C., under Admiral Porter with land forces under Butler is going on— The attack began on the 24th— & as yet we have no decisive results. The fleet sailed from Hampton Roads about 2 weeks ago, & met with severe storms & much bad weather. Gen'l. Davidson with 5,000 cavalry has been marching from Baton Rouge towards and threatening Mobile— In the last few days, Gen'l. Sheridan has moved with his cavalry towards Gordonsville— but I have not been able to read the a/c of it yet. The papers are so filled with these various matters, it is almost impossible to read them all—

And yet, I have the last 4 weeks been reading a great deal of law— On 30th Nov. I took a ticket $10 for the Law Lectures of P. P. Morris, & on 1 Dec, Law Lectures of E. Spencer Miller, on 12 Dec, bought Sergeants' Land Laws of Penna. & Corkling's treatise on Practice in the U.S.

Hardee and his troops escaped on a pontoon bridge of rice flats across the Savannah River the night of December 20. Sherman occupied Savannah, offering it to Lincoln as a Christmas present.

Courts— & began reading to be able to argue Uncle E's Iowa cases in the Supreme Court of the U.S.

On 14 Decr. Bought myself a pair of skates for $4.50.

On the 16th, Ben. Farrar arrived here from St. Louis— On 18th, Sunday night, I went to Washington with Ben— On Monday, 19th, Tuesday 20th & Wed. 21st was much of the time in Supreme Court of the U. S., looking at the proceedings & examining the Records— On 20th called with Ben. to see Chief Justice Chase— & on Wed. to see Mr. Fessenden, Secy. of the Treasury— left Wash. On Wed. 21st at 3 P.M. & went to Balto. & stayed one night with Evans Rogers & on Thursday 22nd at 8½ A.M., started for Phila. Ben. Farrar came up on Sat. night the 24th & stayed Sunday the 25th with me & left for St. Louis the 25th at 10 P.M.

In Wash'n. I saw Gratz Brown, Hy. T. Blow, McClung & Boyd & Hendersons. Ben. trying to get a Resident Ministership to Europe & has a good chance for it. Ben. brought me on in his trunk my a/c books & law books— viz:

Strong's Equity— 2 vols
Tidd's Practice— 2 vols
Gould's Pleading— 1 vol
Clancy on Rights— 1 vol
These books to prepare myself for practicing here.

Up to the time Ben. came, I was well set to read law here. But going to Wash'n. & seeing our Mo. men there & how my contemporaries are the men in power now & hearing them talk of Mo. matters &c. has somewhat dashed me.

So on Monday, Gratz Brown having sent me his card from the Continental, I went there & to the N.Y. Kensington Depot to see him & spoke about getting the U.S. Judgeship for Mo., as he said Congress w'd change the Court & put Treat out.

The long cont'd. bad, wet, cloudy weather depressed me & made me feel unsettled & dissatisfied. Today is clear & I have felt in much better spirits— The Mo. Legislature met on last Monday the 26th & Tom. Fletcher will be inaugurated in a few days. What could I not now be in Mo. if I choose to go there & strike out for myself. But my ambition is dead— I have none. I feel a dull aversion to Missouri, as yet, I have acquired no interests here at all, but with everything within my reach in

Mo., I feel that I cannot go there. I have tried to cultivate a quiet feeling of contentment; dwelling upon the emptiness of worldly pursuits— & occupying my energies in reading law.

Today the paper says Sam Gardner is lying at the point of death— so goes the world. Charles D. Drake dined with us on Fri. the 23rd. On Monday, 26th, we ate our Christmas dinner at Uncle E's. Emma came in on Friday & stayed till Tuesday—[28] This evng. at 7, Myra went over to the Church Children's Festival. She is greatly interested there & enjoys life in Phila. very much.

Today I made out the a/c of Ed. & Cornelia & Harriett P. Rogers & took them up to their House with checks for the amounts due them. Yesterday I copied in a/c my Bank a/c from last April— I am kept busy all the time & have no time at all hanging on my hands. I w'd go into an office with someone if I c'd find a suitable person; but I am in no hurry for it.

On the _____ I wrote to Simmons to send me U.S. Reports, Brinney & Eng. & R., & other law books— which are now on their way here. I also at the same time wrote him to give up the office & sell my parlor furniture— and I am very glad I did, for I want to make a real sincere trial to stay here.

On Sunday 25th, had a good talk with Ben. Farrar as to my staying here, that I c'd not be satisfied to go back to St. Louis, until I had in good faith made the trial to stay here— if not successful, then I w'd be satisfied to remain in St. Louis.

Gen'l. Grant still lies in front of Richmond holding Lee in a vice, while our armies elsewhere ruin the Rebels.

I want to write a good deal more now, but must close & go over to join Myra at the Church Festival. We all feel certain (next thing to it) about the result of the war. The Rebel cause never was nearly so low down & ours so high up. Thank God that light comes apace through the past trials and gloom.

---

[28]Emma was Franklin Dick's third sister, married to Professor E. Otis Kendall

January 1865

"I shrink back from the thought of going to Missouri, where there is so much of brutality. I hate these disloyal People more than ever, & never want to see them again."

January 1st, 1865 Philadelphia   Sunday — 18 m. to 10 A.M.

Yesterday closed another year of my serious life & of the sad life of a headlong world, and today begins a new year of the same. Since the 1st of Jany., 1864, how many men, active in the parts they were bearing in this Civil Strife, have passed away— their hands fallen by their side— their faces silent— their place, unfilled.

How the world rushes on in the pursuit of an excess of the share of its fruits— the rich seeking to gather in from the many poor— & holding with a hard hand, what they thus obtain— & looking across their wealth into the masses of men, feel an artificial antagonism to rise up, surround & cut them off from the Common People.

Thus the Rich man transfers his interest from his fellow Man to his treasures of gold; the envy of the many between whom & himself there is neither love nor admiration. His hoarded money turns him into a slave— a watchman of it. His every thought & effort is for it. His earlier natural impulses, sometimes raise within him a sigh at the things that he once longed to do, but could not because driven by the necessity of his daily labors— and now would enjoy to do, but that he can not, because his passion for gain admits of no division of his affections, & no diminution of his time & efforts.

Thus grows the man distorted, & more distorted still, until the very condition of departure from the platform of truth, & developed nature, becomes itself a secondary, but the controlling principle. The balance between the centripetal & centrifugal forces being lost, all the momentum that should belong to the combined movement is thrown into the one direction— & the misguided man rushes forward unchecked to his distorted end.

Our beloved Otis has been dead a year & a half, & although time has enabled us to feel that he has gained by not extending his life here, yet we miss him sadly & sorely all the time. Yesterday came a beautiful frame for his portrait that hangs in our room— For Christmas, Myra got a bouquet basket & filled it for him. We think & talk of the blessed child constantly & at times my grief for him is keen to anguish. I feel as if I lost the noblest thing in life in him.

Phila.   Sunday, Jany. 8, 1865, 9 A.M. 1865

The last few days the Rebel papers have been very wild in their discussions of their cause— Whether they should become dependent upon England & France, rather than be conquered by the Yankees— and denunciatory of Jeff. Davis & his management. Arming the slaves has not been much said about— for they seem to be divided on that. Lately South Carolina places itself opposed— They cannot work out on the slavery question— Lee's army is very close cooped up at Richmond & must begin to feel want approaching—

The People of Savannah at Pub. Meeting have passed resolutions accepting the pardon offered them as repentant & claim the protection of the U.S. clemency— What Sherman's next movement from Savannah will be, is not yet indicated— The failure to reduce Fort Fisher after the terrific bombardment of the 24 & 25 Dec. by Admiral Porter, is a wretched blunder of Gen'l. Butler's & ought to cause Butler's supersedure— There is a great deal of dissatisfaction at such a result at this time— but it is said by officers in that army, that Gen'l. Grant sustains Butler— it is not believed that Grant approves & likes Butler— but the Admn. keeps Butler in his command & so Gen'l. Grant is unapproachable to effect anything adverse to Butler.

There is much bad feeling against Butler on the part of all officers of the Regular Service, both Army & Navy— He is an ambitious & able man, and a power in the past political campaign. He was backed by Mass. & most of New England, & was therefore a great power in the election— to secure him as a support, as he had his own strong political pretensions, the Pres't. had to give him large military power & scope. Thus, Gen'l. Grant has not attempted to cross his path, or stand in his way— although he feels it a burden & clog to have Butler where he is, as a Military Man, yet to have him politically opposing the Adm'n. might be more injurious— or so it was before the Election. Good faith of course requires that no early change sh'd. take place after the Election.

In Missouri, the Legislature met the last Monday of Decr., the 26th & a few days after Thom. Fletcher[1] sent in his message. It is very crudely written, but of course is all right so far as it goes. The Constitutional Convention met on Friday the 5th at St. Louis & will no doubt in a few days abolish Slavery, & make many of the fundamental changes in the law of the State.

Phila. Jany. 12, 1865— 18 m. to 12 Noon

Yesterday the 11th, the Convention made Missouri a <u>Free State</u>— Thank God for that consummation.

Yesterday I sent to Ben. Farrar a letter saying if Governor Fletcher wished from his judgment & from a sense of public duty, to make me Chief Justice of the Supreme Court to be re-organized, I would feel it to be my duty to accept— That I want no office— & he w'd not <u>personally</u> do me an act of kindness, or benefit by it— I did not want the office from favor nor friendship— but only in case the Gov. thought it his duty to

---

[1]Thomas C. Fletcher (1827–99) was elected governor of Missouri in 1864, in the first election since the state was placed under martial law at the beginning of the war; he issued an emancipation proclamation on January 14, 1865, and returned the state to civil law.

apt. me on a/c of my qualifications for the duties of the place & that he must not bring it before Fletcher, unless he showed him the letter— This was caused by a letter of the 3rd from Ben, suggesting my taking a place on the Sup. Bench—

I s'd, "Gov. F. w'd do me no act of kindness personally, nor any benefit by aptg. me to the office. Feeling thus, I c'd accept the office only from the belief that I am called for by the man upon whom rests the responsibility of the Govt. Unless he needs me for the place, I sh'ld not be willing to accept it."

Today I wrote to Simmons to keep my name up in his office, I said— "I told Ben to ask you to put my sign up at your door— Please do so, so as to keep people in knowledge of where my business matters can be attended to, & so that when I go back to resume practice, the people will be familiar with my name as a continued thing & not feel that it reappears. If you get an office in one of these large buildings, you had better have my name alongside of yours, on the outside pillar & also on the office door."

Gen'l. Butler has been relieved of his military command of the army of the James at City Point & ordered to report at Lowell— of which I am very glad. I think the rebellious power is getting rotten.

I wrote also to Simmons to sell my gold in St. Louis, which I have kept through the war up to this time, $298, for I now regard the rebellion as a broken power. I wrote, "On receipt of this please sell my gold at the Bratmans. I regard the rebellion as a broken & wasting power, and emphasize my belief by parting with this small plank."

Jany. 14, 1865, 10½ P.M., Saturday night

There has been for 6 weeks & more almost continuous inclement weather & the last few days, I have been really sick— I write tonight merely to say— that I wish that Fletcher will not appoint me— I prefer quietly to remain here & take my chances for enjoyment. I shrink back from the thought of going to Missouri, where there is so much of brutality. I hate these disloyal People more than ever, & never want to see them again—

Wed., Jany. 18, 1865, 10½ P.M.

Fort Fisher, N.C.[2] was captured by the Army & Navy on the 15th inst— The Army led by Gen'l. Terry. This is a great victory & a stunning blow to the Rebel cause—

This evn'g. I got a letter from Ben. Farrar in reply to mine of 11th in relation to Sup. Ct. of Mo. I hope & wish that Fletcher will not appoint me & break up for the present my Phila. plans. On Monday & today, went to Eastwick Skating Park. I have been out of sorts for ten days past from overwork on the Iowa cases in Sup. Ct. of the U.S.

Monday, Jany. 23, 1865 Noon

I copy a letter just written as follows:
My dear Ben: This morning I have yours of 19 & 20th (also vol. with legal opinions). I hope you will not have gone to Jefferson. You say you wish I had written you privately as to my wishes &c. How could you be at a loss as to knowing my wishes, when the whole communication was confined to a letter placing the matter in the light of <u>duty</u>— simple, bare duty. I do not want the office— nor at this time any office. For you to press my appointment & show such a letter as I wrote certainly w'd appear strange to the Governor. I believe that my health, physical & mental, will be greatly benefited by my remaining for the present out of the turmoil of public matters. It is my wish to do so. During the conflict now enacting in Mo., feeling is bitter & flows in deep channels. Excitement is so strong that coolness & calmness are impaired, or thrust to one side. The struggle to obtain power & the resistance to yielding it up— the efforts of ambitious & selfish men to profit by the distributions now being made of offices & advantages, make the strife & conflict the more heated & exciting. I turned away from the prizes being distributed, when perhaps my share w'd have been worth having, in a worldly view. But although not drawn by a desire for reward, yet I wrote you that if I was needed for real work, I w'd not refuse to do that. Can you not understand me. I think the office, no matter what, not worth the price & suffering it costs to fill it.

[2]Fort Fisher, called the Gibralter of the South, was outside Wilmington, and was the last Confederate port to be captured by the Union on January 15, 1865.

My enjoyment lies in other things. But if defense of the rights of the
Common People needed me to fill a position of power & difficulty, &
such was the unprompted judgment of the man whose only duty should
be to promote the general welfare, I felt that I ought to yield to the call. It
was in that spirit that I wrote you. I did not write you privately, because if
you understood my letter in the spirit that prompted it, you could see that
I had no desire to be placed in public position. I do not want to go back to
Missouri now. I greatly prefer to remain here while the conflict I speak of,
is being enacted— Madness, fury, ambition, hate, jealousies, the desire
for gain, the grief & frenzy at losing all worldly advantages by a large por-
tion of the People, who heretofore have possessed them— the vast radical
& sudden changes to take place in the relations of men in different conditions of society in the State— the rich becoming poor— the landholders
becoming poor & outcasts— the ignorant slaves becoming free & placed
in new attitude to all around them— this great upheaval coming on, in
which one Party will attempt to drag to the bar of justice those who have
been actors in the late outrages— while those accused will, in turn,
believe themselves to be entitled to power, property, control of the Govt.
&c— all those things have to be gone through. Do you wonder that I
shrink from taking a part in the work? You are not at liberty to ask anything of the Governor for me & if you have done so, I want you at once to
recall what you have said. I am to be pitied if called to office in Missouri
in the days to come,
       Your friend
       F. A. Dick

Ben. Farrar, Esq.
St. Louis
       I will be relieved to hear from you that this whole matter has been
dropped and is at an end—

Sunday Evng. Jany. 29, 1865 — 13 m. to 9—

       I have been extremely busy the last several weeks— So much so as to
be all the while pressed for time— Preparing for the cases in Sup. Ct. of
the U.S.— in which I have taken a wide and thorough range of law, with

other things have kept all my time filled— I have bought a number of law books. Viz:

21ˢᵗ, 22, 23, 24 How. Sup. Ct. U.S. Rep.

1 & 2ⁿᵈ Black

1ˢᵗ Wallace

Conkling's Treatise—

Sedwick on Laws—

Kent's Coms. Ed. of 1858

Parsons' Maritime Law—

Brightly's Prudence

Sergeant's Land Laws

On Friday, I had a letter from Adml. Lee to look after some cotton salvage cases of his & was very busy yesterday reading up the law in the matter— I have been so busy in reading other law, that I have not at all had time to read Penna. law.

My time passes pleasantly, & very swiftly & not only do I have no time hanging on my hands, I am always pressed for time. I studied so hard for about 2 weeks after Ben. Farrar left, I had to let a week pass without looking at a law book— & now I have to limit my hours of study, for I want to do it all the time.

On Friday, read the papers till about 10. Then studied law till 2— Law lecture at 4½ to 6½— Evng. to F. Rogers—

Sat. Papers till 10— Law Library till 1— studying salvage— Then in carriage to Eastwick Skating Park till 4. Then went out & bought Kent & Parsons Mercantile Law, which last I studied till the clock struck 12 midnight, reading on salvage & admiralty practice—

To see Gratz Brown at 10 to 11 A.M. today— read papers— to see Gratz Brown, then to church— also in P.M. to church— Evng. read Chalmers' *Sermons*—3

This evng., Myra said she was so homesick to see her Mother & Sister, & if they stay in St. Louis, she wanted to go back— but the climate there is so bad, I hate the thought— & yet at times, I think of it seriously—

3The Rev. Thomas Chalmers (1780–1847) was a Scottish preacher and lecturer in mathematics and science. After the deaths of his brother and sister, and ill himself, his interests shifted from mathematics to theology. He was one of the originators of the Free Church of Scotland. Franklin Dick was reading Chalmers' *Sermons for Public Occasions*.

The war still jogs along slowly— the certainty of its end has become acquiesced in, but the work is immense & seems far from an end yet. Since Fort Fisher fell, the Rebels have become most restive & bitter with each other, but yet they are obstinate & defiant. Sherman is preparing for some other movement & I believe troops from Thomas have been of late going to him— & the time for the new draft is approaching— & I hope it will be made without stint— the war debt goes on increasing— finances continue high— though of late gold has been down to 202 to 208—

Grant still lies near Richmond & of late no military movements are being made. It seems to me that Sherman will soon be able to move up & join Grant, when they will so confine Lee that he must try an aggressive movement. This is the End I suppose Grant has in view, but it takes much time to work it out. Old Mr. Blair has of late been twice to Richmond to see Jeff. Davis— what he did & said has not been made public— he returned 2 or 3 days ago.

February 1865

*"I detest and despise human nature & have
very little of kindness of charity for it."*

Sunday, Feby. 5, 1865, 3½ P.M.

On Thursday night, I went to Washington— arrived there at 7½ A.M. & left there Friday at 3½— upon the business of S. P. Lee, with the Navy Department.

On Saturday about 10½ to market— then to see Spencer Miller about Lee's cases— which took till 2 o'c.— Uncle E. here to tea & till 9— at 9¼ to 1 at night, read admiralty law. All my time since Friday, 27 Jany., has been occupied by Admiral Lee's business— I must take up & finish the Iowa cases for Sup. Court of the U.S.

Saw Mr. Blair in Wash'n. & he told me that Jeff. Davis is so broken & old that he did not know him when he saw him, & he took him to be an old clerk.

Last week— Judge John Archibald Campbell,[4] R. M. T. Hunter[5] &

---

[4]John Archibald Campbell (1811–89), known as conservative and able to compromise, ruled on the Dred Scott case, which was argued by Montgomery Blair. Confederate president Jefferson Davis appointed him assistant secretary of war in 1862.

[5]Robert Mercer Taliaferro Hunter (1809–87) served in the state legislature and the U.S. House (1837–43, 1845–47) and Senate (1847–61) as a leading Southern conservative. He resigned in 1861 and was named Confederate secretary of state, then became a senator; he was sent to meet with Lincoln and Seward at the Hampton Roads Peace Conference in 1865. He was imprisoned at Fort Pulaski with Campbell after the war. After being freed, Hunter served as Virginia's treasurer and as port collector for Rappahannock, Virginia.

Vice Pres't. Stephens,[6] Rebels, came through our lines & were taken to Fortress Monroe, where Mr. Seward met them— and Mr. Lincoln went down to meet them— after about 4 hours conference, the President returned, & it is believed that the conference was ineffectual.[7]

Some days ago, Gen'l. Sherman commenced marching on Charleston or Branchville & his army now is working its way through South Carolina— This is the first time in the war, that our troops have penetrated that vile State. I hope they will create devastation there. Gen'l Blair is with Sherman.[8]

The Rebel papers are very confident of achieving their independence, but I believe firmly in their subjugation. The Rebel Congress has lately passed a law to create the office of Gen'l. in Chief, intended that Robert E. Lee shall command & control military movements, & take away that power from Davis. The attacks upon Davis have been persistent and severe. Large numbers of troops have lately come from Thomas' Army to the East, either to Grant or Sherman— I saw Gen'l. Schofield in Wash'n., whose corps has lately come in.

Hood has been superseded by Beauregard. A few days ago the House of Reps. by over ⅔rds passed the Senate joint resolution to amend the Constitution to abolish Slavery in the U.S. — ¾ of the State Legislatures must ratify this— Several have already done so — viz: Ills., Michigan, Maryland, Rhode Island, &c.[9]

[6]Alexander Hamilton Stephens (1812–83), a longtime friend of Abraham Lincoln, was opposed to secession, but remained loyal to his state when it voted to secede. As Confederate vice president, he constantly disagreed with President Jefferson Davis.

[7]Francis P. Blair Sr. had a creative idea to make peace and end the Civil War. He decided to ask Confederate President Jefferson Davis to join with the Union to fight the French in Mexico, since the Emperor Maximilian was a threat to both the North and the South. Davis was interested and appointed two peace commissioners to go with vice president Alexander H. Stephens to discuss Blair's idea at Fort Monroe. President Lincoln, Secretary of State Seward, and the Confederates met for four hours on a ship in Hampton Roads. The meeting failed over wording. For the agreement, Lincoln insisted on the words, "one common country," and the Confederate representatives' instructions were "between two countries."

[8]Blair led the XVII Corps under Sherman in the March to the Sea, and was praised as one of the most competent military leaders.

[9]On January 31, 1865, the U.S. House passed the Thirteenth Amendment abolishing slavery, but it did not become law until December 18, 1865, when two thirds of the states had approved it.

Sunday, Feby. 12, 1865, 20 m. to 3 P.M.

Today is the heaviest snowstorm of this very snowy winter. It has rained & snowed oftener this winter I believe than any I ever noticed. Now the snow is falling so fast, you cannot see through it & the roofs are covered & it is knee high on the pavement— Nearly all the Pews were empty at Church this A.M.

Yesterday & today, I have been thinking a good deal about St. Louis. Yesterday, I had a letter from Apo., saying she thought Frank could not leave there— to which I answered saying I thought they ought to stay— The climate there is a bad thing to encounter— and the hatefulness & dreariness of the place— but there I have, or would have business with strength of position. This last I cannot have here for a long time to come, & then only as the result of much labor & application.

Military movements are now going on by Sherman in South Carolina & Thomas in Ala., but we know no facts yet. Our lines below Petersburg were extended 4 miles westward accompanied by a battle, a few days ago in which we lost 1,100 men— 4,000 being engaged in the movement. But in these days no one ever makes mention of such an event, so accustomed are we to heavy losses.

Gen'l Grant says that he has arranged for a general exchange of Prisoners — I trust that it will go on & that our poor soldiers may speedily be released. The last 2 days or so, I have felt loss of confidence as to our subjugating these People— on a/c of the failing of credit of our Gov't. Not that its credit is yet going away— for it is not— Its loan is high— but there must come some limit to it. Sherman seems to think that the war will last for many years— I do not know what to think about it. It seems to me that the Rebels are in worse condition than ever before— but I have at all times thought they could not or would not hold out much longer— Of late I have felt discouraged at not seeing any Union feeling manifested around them; but yet I ought not to look for that— for no man could live there if he showed such feeling— but the long continuance of the war will at times cause doubts as to the result to arise in my mind. It is all with God and I try to keep contented & rely upon his providence. This life is a poor one for me at least, and far worse for the majority of the People.

It is to me all a mystery— death comes so suddenly, and cuts off People in the midst of things; so that no one can feel any assurance of another hour. With me, this operates to check my desires & acts & to confine me to narrow limits— It stops my ambition & keeps me from anticipating— This is my natural tendency & this war, having broken off my business relations, I feel it the more. If I could only content myself, I would do so. Though of late generally I have managed to keep myself pretty well contented— This life is a poor, meager thing— & a mystery—

Sunday, Feb'y. 19, 1865 10 A.M.

As usual the past week has gone very swiftly— I have read law all the time— On Monday, I got my brief in the case of Evans Rogers v. Burlington City in hands of King & Baird, the Printers, & got it home yesterday— It is 24 pages— $48, & $3 for the cover cost— $51 to print it. I also got the other 2 cases— & Lee County & Keokuk all ready & tomorrow will hand them to the Printer— This was all done by last Wed. when I took up Kent to read regularly, & intend going on with it— reading about 30 p. a day, I could finish it in about 3 months— say the 15th to 20th of May— but as I will read a good deal of other law with it; & have interruptions of various kinds, if I get it done by 1st of July (when we will be going out of town) I will be well satisfied, in a fact even by 1st of Septr.

Sherman is in South Carolina, & a few days ago attacked Branchville & took it— but we have no particulars up to this time. Gen'l. Schofield, in command in N. Carolina, is moving on Wilmington— We have lately sent 20,000 troops to New Berne, N. C., so the Rebel papers say— We are threatening Mobile, & marching a large Cavalry Army South from Tennessee— Grant is ever ready to push his lines further around the S. W. of Richmond. Sherman's position has cut off the Rail Roads in So. Car.— so that altogether we are keeping the Rebels very busy & gaining great ground upon them all the time. Their papers still discuss arming the Negroes— & they debate it in Congress; & vote on the thing in various ways; but yet stand upon it. It looks as though the Negro question is to divide every country & section that treats it as a practical one. While it was National, it divided the nation. Now that it has become Southern, it divides the South. Some fear the Negroes will not fight well & many that they will not fight for <u>them</u>— then it is such a direct blow at slavery— & then the Army is a National motley, while the Negroes belong to state rights &c.— &c.— & every kind of trouble is on them with it.

Benjamin[10] a few days ago said in a speech at Richmond, if they did not put Negroes in the Army, Richmond would be abandoned— that they have not sufficient white troops; & that Virginia <u>as a State</u>, must lead off in the matter—

(9:18 P.M.) I cannot keep from thinking nearly every day about going to St. Louis— & some days feeling as if I w'd go; & then the reverse. And it is all in connection with the thought of my taking an active part in the reality of life— Here, I am like a tree planted in a moveable vessel— I may grow & improve, by studying law, & I study that I may grow; but to what purpose? It seems like uphill & fruitless work to localize here my law reading; & I have not read a word of Penna. law for 2 to 4 months— The truth is, I am rather drifting along; but improving myself as I drift.

I never see a list of St. Louis names, that my hatred & disgust are not excited— & I have not a thought connected with the place that is not hateful or revolting; but whether the necessity of taking an active part in the practical part of life may not carry me back, is more than I can say.

Sometimes I think of going to New York, to work into practice there; for here I have the feeling that the leaning is against <u>interveners</u>. Thoughts of going to San Francisco a few days ago came into my mind.

Tuesday, Feb'y. 21, 1865 10½ A.M.

Yesterday we got news that the Rebels have evacuated Charleston on the 18th— I rejoice that So. Car. is now feeling the war, & I want desolation to crown the work there. The enemy do not show any spirit there, but run away.[11]

---

[10]Judah Philip Benjamin (1811–84) became secretary of war, then secretary of state for Confederate president Davis. Franklin Dick here refers to Benjamin's proposal that any slave who served in the Confederate army would be emancipated. Benjamin hoped this would bring Great Britain to support the Confederacy, but it did not happen.

[11]Beginning on the night of Thursday, February 16, 1865, Confederate troops left

Yesterday A.M. I was all the A.M. writing business letters— P.M. read papers & walked & Evng. read Kent.

This A.M. have been writing to Sep. Levering about business, rents, taxes &c. & I stopped to write to:...[blank]

Note how bitter my feelings are usually against mankind in general. I detest & despise human nature & have very little of kindness or charity for it. It is base & mean, selfish & horrid almost everywhere & in all relations.

Yesterday the St. Louis papers presented to me a nice savory dish to contemplate with the idea of returning there—

1st Alex. J. P. Garesché,[12] as base a man as under the Roman Lobby has a large income— from disloyal & Garesché business I presume.

2nd Chris. Pallis has returned from the South— & St. Louis will be full of such vermin.

3rd The Germans are abusing the convention— I constantly see hateful names & things in the St. Louis papers & I pray to God that I may never go back to that detestable People to live.[13]

---

the Charleston forts (Moultrie, Sumter, Johnson, Beauregard and Castle Pinckney) after 567 days of Union attack. On Saturday, February 18, the mayor of Charleston surrendered. The Confederates scuttled boats, burned cotton, and blew up military supplies before retreating from the city.

[12]Alexander John Peter Garesché (1823–96) was a St. Louis attorney, sometimes called "Alphabet Garesche" in the newspaper. He participated in the state militia muster at Camp Jackson, and was arrested and paroled.

[13]The Missouri Constitutional Convention met January 6, 1864, and, in unity, quickly voted to amend the constitution to abolish slavery. Then the factions separated. The Germans, led by Isidor Bush, tried to end the convention, turning against Charles Drake, the Radical Republican leader. The Constitutional Convention adjourned April 10, 1865.

March 1865

"All through the war, I have felt, as though it must soon end; & yet it drags on, changing gradually from one phase to another; so that instead of being broken into parts, this is its character."

Thursday, March 2, 1865, 9:34 A.M.

On 22ⁿᵈ Feby., the Rebels evacuated Wilmington, N.C., being forced back by the skilful & impenetrable advance of our troops under command of Gen'l Schofield— which way they went we do not know;[14] Nor from Charleston of Sherman we have not heard for many days. The Richmond papers are not allowed to speak of military events now, so full of heavy disasters to them are the times. The events of late are too great for me to give any a/c of them in this mem[orandum] of events. The information of late in the northern mind is that the war will be over in a

[14]Wilmington, North Carolina, the Nassau and Bermuda blockade runners' best port, had two passages, guarded by Forts Fisher, Caswell, Campbell, Holmes, Johnston, and Anderson. The port received supplies for the Army of Northern Virginia, and easily distributed them on its road and rail connections. When Confederate General Braxton Bragg ordered his troops to evacuate Wilmington, most of the military equipment was sent to Richmond by train. They burned the rest before Mayor John Dawson surrendered the city to General Terry on February 23, 1865.

few weeks or months; for it is not seen how Lee can prolong the existence of his army under the losses they have had.

And although I feel as though the result can be only one way, yet the possibilities of the worst evil to the country is in my mind at times, and even if we gain, yet how much longer the thing may last is beyond knowledge. All through the war, I have felt, as though it must soon end; & yet it drags on, changing gradually from one phase to another; so that instead of being broken into parts, this is its character. This has been so only since Gen'l. Grant took command in Chief.

But the People of the North have become accustomed to the war— here in Phil'a. the People go on just as in ordinary times— They gay continue their giddy amusements— the errands go on with business as usual, & the war is an interesting exciting topic, which they keep more or less in mind.

But the rise & fall in prices, seems to be a nearer & more vital subject to most of the people— the mania for speculation in oil stocks is very great— All classes & descriptions of people here are in it, and large fortunes are lost & made rapidly in those gambling operations.

Ben. Farrar arrived here on Tuesday Evng, Feb'y. 21st. On 22nd, he & I went to the Navy Yard & that night he went down to Washington to look after his foreign mission. Today I had a letter from him, saying that he saw the President, who said he had determined to give him one of the places.

This morning I had a letter from Dr. James M. Martien, from St. Louis— in which he tells me of the continued suffering of the Union men in Missouri. I feel sorry for the good old Patriot. What he says, & what every other man tells me who comes from Missouri, proves to me that there could be nothing but sorrow & suffering for me, if living there.

On 1st March, yesterday, I made arrangement with John Hill Martin to have a desk in his office & to pay ½ the expenses, viz:

130 rent

24 hired man to clean &c.

<u>52 Office Boy</u>

$206— the ½ of which I pay = 103

I began to go to the office yesterday, 1st M'ch. The day before, Tuesday, I went before the Asize Commis, Flanders & Young, in matter of 90 bales of cotton in contest between the Connecticut & the Slave State— & I was engaged yesterday in reading admiralty cases on joint capture & association, so as to determine what is best to do for the interest of Admiral Phil. Lee in these matters.

At 5½ we went to dine at Aunt Harriett's to meet Mifs. Molly Meigs & her intended Husband, Dr. Hart.

Sunday, March 5, 1865 8m. to 5 p.m.

Yesterday about 2 to 3 o'c., Wilmer Lewis was shot in the right eye by a son of F. Carroll Brewster, accidentally, & Dr. _____ [blank] says that he will lose his eye. Poor Boy, I feel great sorrow for his misfortune, & we are all overwhelmed by it. We were in there all the P.M. and Evn'g., & a while this morning.

Yesterday Mr. Lincoln was inaugurated for his 2nd term of office. May God direct him in it, & give him wisdom & virtue.[15]

Of late it has rained so much that military operations have been checked— The Rebels are in great fear— Sherman's movements we do not yet know about since he left Columbia, S.C., nor do we know where Schofield is going. It is believed that they will unite & perhaps near Fayetteville, N.C. & move on Goldsborough, & thence up the Wilmington & Weldon R.R. I thought a few days ago that Lee is preparing to leave Richmond. Gov. Brown[16] of Ga. is out with a message, which in Richmond is said to be treason to the South & it looks to me much like it.

The past week I have felt contented, going to the office each day— my time passes pleasantly & usefully. Ben. Farrar on 1st wrote me that he was going to St. Louis, having been promised a post in Europe by the President.

[15]When Abraham Lincoln was inaugurated on Saturday, March 4, 1865, his vice president caused a stir. Andrew Johnson was ill, on medicine, and had taken a drink. His drunken, rambling acceptance speech shocked the audience. Lincoln's short speech was remembered: "With malice toward none...."

[16]Joseph Emerson Brown (1821–94) was elected governor (1855–65). He was known as intelligent and pro-Union, but strongly in favor of states' rights, especially the rights of his own state of Georgia. When Sherman invaded Georgia, Brown fled; he was arrested, but released at the end of the war.

The weather today is pleasant & clear, but we have had a great deal of rain of late.

Saturday, March 11, 1865 5½ p.m.

I have been busy the past week at the office in making up a/c's— writing letters about the investment & sale of Pacific R.R. 1st mgr. 7 pr. Ct. bonds, of which I have sold 31,000, viz:

12,000 to E. Rogers
13,000 to F. P. Blair
5,000 to F. A. Dick, all at 93

I yesterday authorized J. A. Biddle to sell my 5,000 City of Phil'a. loan which I bought at 106 at 94— & by turning it into the Pacific 7 pr. ct. at 93, I get a better investment & make up the loss on it, lacking 5 pr. ct.

I cannot help more or less of thinking of St. Louis, as hateful as it is. I am busy here all the time— My time passes rapidly & pleasantly too; but I feel the great difference in my standing here & there. I do not want to go back, & hope I will be able to remain here. We have no news yet of where Gen'l. Sherman is— The Rebels are in a great state of turmoil & growing very desperate.[17]

I invested $1,000 more for myself a few days ago in U.S. 7³⁄₁₀ bonds.

10½ P.M.

When I feel somewhat dissatisfied here, I wish I c'd content myself with what is reasonable & a quiet unobtrusive life. I am so sensible that the best part of my life is spent, & that in what remains of it, I will do nothing to distinguish myself, that I ought to quietly settle down, to make the best of it here. I enjoy very much historical reading, but a restless impatience as to falling into obscurity, keeps me at work at the law. I believe it w'd be an unhappy thing for me to go back to St. Louis, & therefore I am anxious to work into the business of life here.

[17]Sherman's troops entered North Carolina on March 6, 1865, occupying Fayetteville on March 11. They were careful to hurt no people, but burned most of the town in the next five days as they waited for supplies.

Sunday, Mch. 12, 1865 3 P.M.

This is a clear day, but cold in the morning. The weather has been severe & inclement all winter. Human nature is a mixed, incongruous & perverse thing. Crowds are dying every week— unknown & unnoted beyond a narrow circle; & even by them soon forgotten, & yet there is a feeling that makes one desire to be known & noticed.

I realize the truth of the saying that "the times change & we change with them." When the war began, I felt as if all I desired for myself, was a competence & quiet somewhere off from Mo. Now I find I have an ample competence, & I am situated here so as to have my time pass cheerfully by, with moderate occupation; & yet I am not satisfied. But it is not in Human Nature ever to be satisfied.

Sunday, March 19, 1865 10 A.M.

The past has been an exciting week in commercial circles, the gold gambling circles & the oil— stock circles. Gold has plunged down to 64 pr. oz., having fallen 5 to 10 pr. ct. a day for several days. Sherman's arrival safely at Fayetteville, bringing him & Schofield close together— The failure of the Rebels to hold Kinston, N.C., of which we have posn— The successful movements of Sheridan in destroying the Canal & other property of the Enemy west of Richmond— the closing in upon Lee, so evidently going on— these things have brought almost the certainty of a rapid downfall of the Scoundrels.[18] The U.S. 7³⁄₁₀ notes absent all the capital seeking investment— of late it has been selling at from 2½ to 5 millions a day; while other investments of first class have fallen immensely. Pa. Cen. R.R. 1ˢᵗ mge. bonds selling at 102, which last summer sold at 117— Camden & Amboy bonds that sold at 108 are now at 92.

Last fall, I thought seriously of selling out my U.S. bonds of 1881 & putting them into these bonds of C& A— the 81's then were at about 108, & the C & A's at 106. Now the 81's are 110 to the C & Amboy's 92—

---

[18]On their way to meet Grant in Richmond, Sheridan's cavalry troops skirmished, ripped up the Virginia Central Railroad, and destroyed the James River Canal. Starting on Monday, March 13, they advanced through Beaver Dam Station, South Anna Bridge, Hanover Court House, and White House.

A few days ago I sold my $5,000 City of Phil'a. 6 pr. ct. loan for which I p'd last July 106 at 94¾— but I put it in Pacific R.R. 7 pr. ct. 1st mge. Bonds at 93— thus making up my loss on them.

Of late, I have been investing all of my money falling due in the 7 $^3/_{10}$ notes now subscribed for. This I do from the feeling that the war is coming to a close, when the U.S. loans will be greatly in demand at a prm. See how it is ever from the effect of this belief— U.S. loans of 81 at 110 & 111, whilst 1st mge. Bonds of Penna. R.R. are at 102— & other 1st class securities sell from 90 up, and the U.S. Notes too pay 7$^3/_{00}$ interest & are free from all tax except the U.S. income tax, and too, they will be easily convertible into money if that is desired.

On Thursday last, Charles Hodgman, Cashier of the Boatman's Saving Institution, came here to sell the County of St. Louis 7 pr. ct. 20 yr. Loan, & left with me $70,000. of the bonds to be sold at 92½ & 93— paying me ½ prm.

On Wed., John F. Lee was here to see me about Phil. Lee's business.[19]

I think a great deal about getting a place permanent to live in, but until the war comes to an end, I hardly know where I will come out. I feel a little like getting a place in Germantown, on a/c of the children. But prices are too high yet, & altogether it is premature to do anything permanent.

For a day or two early in the past week, I felt rather restless about St. Louis— but the last several days I have not felt at all that way.

[19] John F. Lee was Admiral Samuel Phillips Lee's brother and handled financial matters for him during the war.

April 1865

"This is great & glorious and wonderful;
We feel safe & restored."

Phil'a., Tuesday, April 4, 1865 5:15 P.M.

Great & wonderful events have happened since I last wrote— the successful march of Sherman, coming out at Fayetteville & Goldsborough N.C.— his defeat of the Scoundrels under Jo. Johnston[20] near Bentonville

[20]Joseph Eggleston Johnston (1807–91) was named commander of the Department of the West, then the Army of Tennessee. He retreated to Atlanta pursued by Sherman's troops. President Davis replaced him with Lieutenant General John B. Hood, who then lost battles at Atlanta, Franklin, and Nashville. Johnston was reinstated at the end of the

& Averasboro, N.C.—²¹ Sheridan's magnificent movement & destruction of the James River Canal & the Rail Roads N & W of Richmond— and on last Wed. began Gen'l. Grant's great movement against the South Side & Danville R. Roads, in which he forced Lee to come out— Grant's general attack on Lee's fortifications, & on yesterday Monday, Apl. 3ʳᵈ His capture of Petersburg & Richmond.²²

I was in Washington when the news came, & the whole Country was ablaze with the glad tidings— The news now comes in of our capture of thousands of Lee's army & its rapid flight. Mr. Lincoln, for several days, has been at the front & yesterday he was in Petersburg— This makes us feel as if the war was near its close— Thanks & praise to God Almighty for our deliverance. The Nation will be preserved & we saved from ruin.

Two weeks ago Gold went rushing down till it reached 50 pr. oz., & the speculators & Rebel sympathizers stood aghast. It is now down to 45–47½.

This is great & glorious & wonderful— We feel safe & restored.

On the 23ʳᵈ Mch., Old Mr. Blair wrote to me, proposing that I should go to Washington to live & go into Partnership with Montgomery Blair. On the 25ᵗʰ, I wrote in reply— On the 31ˢᵗ, I went down to see the Judge about it— he is very anxious for it— I stayed there from Friday until Monday 4½ P.M.— I felt a good deal inclined to do it, but reluctant too.

Today a view, under this new idea & the effect of these victories, I feel a good deal like going back to St. Louis to live, on account of business. If I should go to Washington for business, why not go back to St. Louis, where I have a business ready made, & so much reputation & knowledge—

---

war to the command of the remnant of his troops for the Carolinas Campaign. He met Union Major General Sherman for the first time when they negotiated surrender terms.

²¹The Battle of Averasboro took place on March 16. Sherman had marched two sections of Union troops from Fayetteville—one toward Goldsborough and one toward Averasboro, where they fought with Hardee's troops, who then retreated toward Smithfield. The Union troops continued toward Bentonville, where they fought Confederate forces under Johnston on March 19 and 20. Johnston, aware of the Union superiority, soon opened negotiations for surrender.

²²The Petersburg campaign for control of the railroad center and the Confederate capitol of Richmond lasted from June 15, 1864 to April 13, 1865. As Union troops secured the cities, the Confederate government evacuated, setting fire to Richmond.

It is only today, that the thought of going to St. Louis has been strong in my mind— But I cannot tell yet what I will do— though I do not feel as if it w'd be best to go to Wash'n.— rather than St. Louis.

Thursday, Apl. 6, 1865 11 a.m.

I have been enjoying reading the few imperfect details we have from around Richmond. One from Grant[23] from Nottaway Ct. House, on his way to Burkeville Junction, says Sheridan is on Danville Road, west of Amelia C. H. & Meade[24] following— Lee & his Routed Men are at or near Amelia C. H.[25] From this, I hope that Lee will be headed off, & his army captured or dispersed— Into how many fragments it has split & how many prisoners we have is not yet known. The newspaper rumors yesterday were that we have from 18 to 25,000 prisoners—

Mrs. Gen'l. Lee remained in Richmond, which indicates that she would be safe nowhere else. Jeff Davis was at church on <u>Sunday the 2</u><u>nd</u>, when he learned from Lee that he must evacuate. A large fire destroyed many blocks in Richmond, started it is said, by the Rebel Gen'l. Ewell.[26] Gen'l. A. P. Hill[27] was killed— on the <u>3</u>rd, I believe.[28]

[23]Union General Ulysses S. Grant followed Meade and his troops to Appomattox.

[24]George Gordon Meade (1815–72), as commander of the Army of the Potomac in 1863, fought Lee at Gettysburg and received the Thanks of Congress. Grant left Meade in charge of the pursuit of Lee, but remained close by, to be ready to discuss surrender with Lee. Meade was promoted to major general at Appomattox.

[25]Confederate General Robert E. Lee set up Amelia Court House, west of Richmond, as his army's center point when the city was evacuated. Retreating in front of Sheridan, he found no supplies at Amelia Court House, and kept moving.

[26]Richard Stoddert Ewell (1817–72) was promoted to major general in the Confederate army in 1862. He lost a leg at Groveton. When he returned to duty with a wooden leg, he was promoted to lieutenant general to replace Stonewall Jackson. At the battle of Bloody Angle at Spotsylvania, he fell from his horse; as he was unable to command in the field afterwards, he was transferred to Richmond for defense supervision.

[27]Ambrose Powell Hill (1825–65) resigned from the U.S. Army to become a Confederate colonel and was quickly promoted to brigadier general, where he was known for his red battle shirt and his hard attacks. Hill fought at Williamsburg, and was promoted to major general, commanding Hill's Light Division. At Chancellorsville, while himself injured, he carried the wounded Jackson to the rear. He had returned from sick leave to rally his men when he was shot and killed.

[28]On Thursday, April 6, Confederate Lieutenant General Ewell's troops were captured at the battle of Saylor's Creek. On Saturday, April 8, Lee continued retreating, but Sheridan was to his south and west, and had already taken Lee's supplies at Appomatox

This news makes me feel a little like going back to St. Louis— though that does not bear as yet very close thought. After peace, and things have quieted down, I may feel decided to go there.

Yesterday, gold rose a little from 145 to 150–151— Well, the bottom is certainly knocked out of the rebellion now— I feel <u>certain</u> this hour that the Country & Government are saved. Thanks to God Almighty for this deliverance.

Sunday, Apl. 9, 1865 20 m. to 10 A.M.

On Friday came news that the powerful Gen'l. Sheridan had overtaken the Rebel Army, & that a large number of Generals, headed by Ewell & thousands of prisoners, had been captured— This was glorious news— about 1½ on that day it was telegraphed to Jay Cooke here, that Gen'l. Lee & his army had surrendered— This was felt to be the close of the war— 2 hours later, this was contradicted— the scoundrels who started this lie deserve universal contempt & hatred. I have not gotten over the effect of this revulsion yet, & it makes the former victories seem almost tame.

Yesterday we had no news, nor any since Friday— On Saturday, I felt very much like going back to St. Louis, that I might take part in the realities of life, in practicing law— so strongly did I think of it, that it brought me very close in mind to the reality, when I got to thinking of the hateful characters who live there— Garesché, Gibson, Mauro, Wood, Davis & the other disloyal lawyers who fill the Courts with large practice & the best clients— & it so disgusted me that I was turned from it. If the Union feeling was the only one left there, I w'd certainly go back; but the Rebel interests are individually so large, that I dread to encounter the feeling with my intolerant nature.

I went to the Opera last night & heard "Ernani"—[29] & after coming

---

and Lynchburg. On Sunday, April 9, Generals Grant and Lee met at Appomattox Court House in the McLean house for the official surrender of the Confederate forces. Word spread by mouth faster than the official news, and the Union celebrated.

[29]*Ernani*, an opera by Giuseppi Verdi, was based on the play *Hernani* by Victor Hugo. With its focus on honor and loyalty, the play and opera were popular with mid-nineteenth-century audiences.

back went ½ through 24 Hou. Sup. Ct. Rep. & I got to thinking & feeling quite favorable to Washington. Since the late victories, I feel as if I
must go somewhere where I can take part in leading law interests— here I
cannot do it at once— I used to think if I only had occupation here, I w'd
be contented; but I find an impetuous desire to take prominent part in
managing Real Interests— large & prominent interests.

Gold remains about the same, ranging from 46½ to 51½ pr. oz.
Dry goods & groceries have greatly fallen in price; but provisions in market are full as high & even higher than they were when gold was up to 190
pr. oz. (= to 290)— My poultry woman yesterday asked 35 c. for chick-
ens— I paid 70 for butter— 30 eggs— mutton was 25— Shad 75 a
piece— The Country People, or the Market People, defy the fall in
gold— though they went up with it.

GRANT captures Lee

Monday, Apl. 10, 1865 10:20 a.m.

Last night, Sunday at 10½ P.M., the steam whistles began blowing
& heavy guns firing, gave sign that a victory was known. Yesterday P.M.
Gen'l. Lee surrendered his army of "Northern Virginia" to Gen'l. Grant
at or near Appomattox Court House, Virginia.

This morning the correspondence of the 7th, 8th & 9th, Friday, Sat.
& Sunday, between Grant & Lee is published. And now, Praise the Lord,
the War Closes— the end draws near— Our Nation is preserved—
Slaughter & wounds will cease— peace & tranquility will be restored.

In this hour of assurance of victory, success & safety, I feel how
inadequate are the feelings of human nature to the occasion of joyfulness
& greatness. In this war I have found that we are much more capable of
suffering, than of joy— There is not enjoyment in encited good—

Gen'l. Grant now stands the greatest General of the World, & one
of its greatest men. I honor & love him—

Last night had a talk with Myra about going to Washington— I feel
inclining that way—

GRANT captures Lee

Monday, apl 10. 1865 10 20 a. m.

Last night, Sunday at 10 ½ P. M. the Steam whistle began blowing a heavy gun firing, gave Sign that a victory was known,

Yesterday at P.M. Genl. Lee surrendered his army of "Northern Virginia" to Genl. Grant. at or near Appomattox Court House, Virginia.

This morning the correspondence of the 7th. 8th & 9th. Friday, Sat. & Sunday, between Grant & Lee is published,

And now praise the Lord. the war closes - the end draws near - Our Nation is preserved - Slaughter & wounds will cease. peace & tranquility will be restored.

In this hour of assurance of victory, success & safety, I feel how inadequate are the feelings of human Nature to the occasion of joyfulness & greatness.

In this war I have found that we are much more capable of suffering, than of joy - There is not Enjoyment in Excited good -

Genl. Grant now stands the greatest General of the World, & one of its greatest men. I honor & love him -

Last night had a talk with Alyea about going to Washington - I feel inclining that way.

It was to-day word that there that we learned the great news of the

Franklin Dick's entry noting Grant's capture of Lee. Photo by R. L. Geyer © 2007.

It was today back there, that we learned the great news of the surrender or abandonment of Richmond, on the 3rd, Monday last— For some time past, a movement under Gen'l. Canby[30] has been going on against Mobile & fighting has begun there— hourly, I expect to hear of the capture & surrender of the place.

Gen'l. Sherman will soon now deal with Gen'l. Jo. Johnston, if necessary— but as Johnston is left alone to fight Sherman & Grant, he will not last much longer— As Johnston has the remains of Hood's army & the armies at the various seaports & Ports taken by Sherman, there is no Rebel Army this side of Mobile to deal with.[31] Forrest[32] has some thousands of loose troops, part cavalry, somewhere in Ga. or Alabama, but I suppose that Gen'l. Wilson will disperse them—

West of the Miss. River, we hear nothing of late— Kirby Smith[33] is in command there— but no movements have taken place for a long time. Gen'l. Price, we hear nothing of, & I do not even know that he has a command. So that the surrender of Lee leaves really nothing in the field against us. Such is Gen'l Grant's skill & power. The war in the field

[30]Edward Richard Sprigg Canby (1817–73) was a Union major general and commander of the Military Division of West Mississippi after 1864. He captured Mobile and accepted the surrender of Confederate Generals Richard Taylor and Edmund Kirby Smith. Mobile's Spanish Fort had been under siege by Union Major General Canby. On April 8, Fort Alexis and Spanish Fort surrendered, stripping Mobile of defenses. On April 9, Canby's troops took Fort Blakeley. The last two forts, Tracy and Huger, surrendered on April 11, and Confederate forces retreated to the north. The mayor of Mobile surrendered the city on April 12, 1865.

[31]Johnston was told by President Jefferson Davis and his cabinet that the Union would only accept a full surrender and was authorized to meet with General Sherman. On the same day that Lincoln was shot, Johnston wrote Sherman asking for a "temporary suspension of hostilities," to which Sherman agreed. They signed a conditional agreement on April 18, which President Johnson rejected. Johnson felt Sherman was too lenient, and insisted on the same terms as Lee and Grant had signed. Johnston signed the corrected terms on Wednesday, April 26, 1865.

[32]Nathan Bedford Forrest (1821–77) rose quickly in the Confederate Army to brigadier general in 1862, major general in 1863, and lieutenant general by 1865. Forrest, "The Wizard in the Saddle," finally surrendered at Selma, Alabama, on April 12, 1865.

[33]Edmund Kirby Smith (1824–93) was promoted to lieutenant general of the Confederate Army and put in charge of the Trans-Mississippi West. Smith remained in the army, though he wanted to become a minister. He defeated Banks's Red River Campaign, sent Price to invade Missouri, and concentrated on guerilla raids until Lieutenant General Simon B. Buckner surrendered the Department of the Trans-Mississippi in Smith's name to Union Brigadier General Canby on May 26, 1865. Smith escaped to Mexico.

ceases— the rebellion is broken— crushed— our national flag will float the country over.

And now this morning with my heart & mind full of this subject, & all else excluded, I feel about St. Louis no regrets at not being there— no affection for it— no longing to see it— I do not know how I might feel if I was thinking today of going back— but the last 2 days, not feeling like going back; but rather of going to Wash'n.— I therefore do not have my mind run on St. Louis—

In Missouri, I think there is more of hatred & discord amongst the People than in any other State or People. Except Myra's Family & the Farrars, I have no friends there (a few other exceptions)— but the hatreds & contempts are innumerable— Well, let me turn from this mean subject to better things; the salvation of our Government.

Saturday, April 15, 1865, 7 m. to 11 A.M.

Mr. Lincoln, the President, was assassinated last evng. in Washington, & died this morning at 7:22 A.M.— having been insensible at the time. He was shot at 9:30 P.M. An attempt to assassinate Secy. Seward was made at the same time.[34]

Here now is the life of the Nation struck at by this vile rebellion. Mr. Lincoln throughout has failed to appreciate the wickedness of these people— pardons & pardons have fallen from him into the hands of guilty doers— who have turned again from their pardoned crimes, to again slay & destroy the defenders of Nation.

He has now fallen, an early victim of his own leniency & errors. May vengeance now pursue these enemies of the laboring Man.

I thank God that Andrew Johnson knows & feels what these Traitors are— & in a speech a few days ago, he proclaimed that they ought to be hanged for their treason. Amen to that, say I.

[34]In a plot to assassinate top Union officials, John Wilkes Booth shot President Lincoln in Ford's Theater and slashed his guest, Major Henry Rathbone. At the same time, Lewis Payne wounded Secretary of State William H. Seward, his son, and secretary. Seward's life was saved by a heavy neck brace he was wearing. Both attackers escaped.

Saturday April 15th 1865   7 to 11 a.m.

Mr Lincoln, the President was assassinated last Eveng. in Washington, & died this morning at 7 22 am - having been insensible all the time. He was shot at 9 30 P.M.

An attempt to assassinate Secy. Seward was made at the same time.

Here now is the life of the nation struck at by this vile rebellion.

Mr Lincoln throughout has failed to appreciate the wickedness of these people - pardons & pardons have fallen from him, into the hands of guilty doers - who have turned again from their pardoned crimes, to again slay & destroy the defenders of [the] nation.

He has now fallen an early victim of his own lemency, & errors.

May vengeance now pursue these enemies of the laboring man.

I thank God that Andrew Johnson knows & feels what these Traitors are - & in a speech a few days ago, he proclaimed that they ought to be hanged for their treason. Amen to that, say I.

I left this min, because the President would not allow the defenders of

Franklin Dick's entry on the assassination of President Lincoln. Photo by R. L. Geyer © 2007.

I left Missouri because the President would not allow the defenders of the country to strike down their Enemies. As soon as we had disarmed the Enemy, the President stepped in & disarmed us. Thus he left the suffering, virtuous Union Man a victim & a prey to those bloody-minded Traitors.

In a Traitor, he saw not a man to be punished, & hardly restrained, if in his power & begging for indulgence— He was not fit to govern this Nation, when Mercy could ruin it—

Now I want Mr. Johnson to deal with these Rebels, as only the Border State Union Man knows how to do. Mr. Lincoln has played his part— & played it out too. He nauseated the Southern heart with his extremes of mawkish sensibility— they had no appreciation for him— & now have swept him aside as of no value to them. And yet, he was the very bulwark of safety to them.

Overwhelmed & stunned as I am at this shock— & this terrific crime— in which act has culminated into the perfection of fruit of this slaveholders movement, yet I feel as though Mr. Lincoln's mission was ended— The reign of mercy would prevent the destruction of the Nation— its safety required a victim— and now they summoned the spirit of justice of the whole Nation to arise & take vengeance for all the murders they have committed in this war— for every Union soldier killed has been a murder.

God's ways are not as man's ways— they are inscrutable, & past finding out. I feel now my old St. Louis longing for vengeance— for in that, lies justice & safety— Forgiveness here is disgusting inertness. Let these Murderers & every supporter of them be reduced into a state of neutrality, by being punished until their power is gone.

I fear not injury to the national welfare— on the contrary, the change from Lincoln to Johnson tends to increase our national safety.

Sunday, April 16, 1865, 3 m. to 10 A.M.

Yesterday the stores & business places (excepting the grog shops & tobacco stores & eating houses) were closed early in the day & the People thronged the streets— a great many looked horrified— a good many did not care what had or would happen. Indignation against disloyal people was faintly talked— & loose talk seemed the highest form of indignation that was developed— The Murderers have not yet been traced, though it was known abroad that John Wilkes Booth[35] was one of them.

Andrew Johnson was sworn in as President as soon as Mr. Lincoln died— & from his speech made on the fall of Richmond, it is evident that he retains his old spirit of vengeance against these People. It is a good thing now for the country that a man of his vigor & vim, and hatred of treason & experience with these pro-slavery wretches has the control of the natural power. What was called Mercy, but it was a strong desire to get back to trade & to take the shortcut by not stopping to punish these wretches, was getting the ascendancy— in a few months we would have had the old set of Traitors in control in the South— I know this would have been so, & under Mr. Lincoln's regime in Missouri to this day. Traitors are in the ascendancy in many ways. At all events, I left Missouri because Traitors had the same positions, social, business, political & in every way, as before the war.

My own personal feeling (aside from the sorrow I feel at the cruel murder of a good man & a thorough Patriot & a benevolent man) is that the country has gained much by this change; & under Mr. Lincoln, I doubt if we would have worked the necessary reform in the slave states to produce peace there.

Now Andrew Johnson, a brave & unflinching man, who knows the wickedness of these wretches, and will not fear to bring destruction upon them, will, I believe, commence the good work in the spirit that I want it done. Oh, I long for vengeance upon these monsters. I thank God that Johnson is the successor of the good man who has been so cruelly murdered. I believe that a large proportion of the People are inclined to feel as I do.

[35]John Wilkes Booth (1838–65) felt the South was an oppressed nation and became quite radical in his beliefs. He had planned to kidnap Lincoln before the 1864 inauguration, but failed. He plotted several times to capture the President and take him to Richmond for a prisoner exchange, but the fall of Richmond changed his plans. On April 14, 1865, at Ford's Theater, Booth shot Lincoln in the back of the head and slashed Lincoln's guest, Major Henry Rathbone, with a hunting knife. Despite breaking a leg as he jumped from the presidential box, he escaped with David Herold. That night, Dr. Samuel Mudd set his leg, and Booth fled to Virginia, but was trapped in a tobacco shed at the farm of Richard H. Garrett near Port Royal by detectives Everton J. Conger and Luther B. Baker. Herold surrendered, but Booth was shot as the shed burned.

I feel no concern for the result of the war, on account of the change in President. Mr. Johnson is wise enough not to make unnecessary changes— yesterday he directed the Cabinet to go on as before, as Governor of Tennessee, both Civil & Military, & Senator, he has had full experience in public matters— I feel full & unhesitating confidence in him.

Tuesday Apl. 18, 1865 10½ P.M.

Ben. Farrar has just left for St. Louis, having come Sat. night from Washington— just as I finished writing the above on Sunday, he came here. The last 3 days, the public mind has been engrossed with the President's death— & the feeling is very much what I expressed above— None of the murderers have been taken yet. Public indignation demands a severe policy towards the infernal Rebels & clemency & leniency are scouted.

Thursday, Apl. 27, 1865 10 A.M.

There was continued excitement & deep feeling about the President's murder— last Saturday his corpse was brought to Phil'a. & laid over Sunday in Independence Hall—

On Sunday morning, we were astounded at the armistice & terms made by Sherman with Gen'l. Jo. Johnston— Every day since, the papers have been full of it— the general opinion is of universal condemnation of Sherman, with hatred & contempt. Never has a man fallen so suddenly from the pinnacle of greatness in public eye, to the depth of shame & scorn. Many believe him base & untrue. At first I felt only that he had made a great mistake— but vindications began to carry me to attribute bad motives to him. Grant at once was down to attend to Sherman, & yesterday we had his dispatch of the 24th from Raleigh— He left Wash'n. on Friday night, I believe.

President Johnson has been making a great many speeches in Washington to persons & talks openly of the policy of severe punishment to Traitors.

May 1865

"Our armies are beginning to march north to be mustered out, as victors; & the Country feels that peace has been achieved; God be praised for the result."

Monday, May 1, 1865, 9:20 A.M.

I wish to note down as a very striking & weighty fact to prove how much more capable we are in this life of great suffering, than great enjoyment, that although the war is ended, yet a compending sense of enjoyment is not experienced by me.

Last Friday, the 28th, I read Grant's telegram of the 26th from Raleigh, saying that Johnston had surrendered his whole army to Sherman, on the terms of Lee's surrender. This, of course, was an end of the war. I felt it so myself relief & joy— but oh how inadequate was this relief & joy compared with the immensity of the fact. Of course, when the Rebels were defeated at Petersburg & Richmond, & Lee's surrender forced & his army broken up, that rendered the end of the war inevitable— but still Johnston's army remained which might possibly have kept up some protracted defense by flying— so that when it gave up on the 26th, the curtain fell on the great actions & the rebellion ceased. No man living [had] more hatred [of] the rebellion than did I & had less of compromise with it in me— & yet I am incapable of that degree of enjoyment which I supposed I would have— The ordinary cares of life, troubles come & go about

198

as usual. I keep thinking more or less of what I will do— I have not been able to decide about going to Washington— & keeping that in my mind, causes me at times to think of going to St. Louis— But it is uncertain yet, what will be the condition of society in St. Louis— & what political questions may arise can not be anticipated— nor whether these scoundrels who have survived the war are to be permitted to take a share in them. At this time, the People of Missouri are dividing over the new constitution to be voted on by them in a few weeks— So perverse are the union men there, that they split up on every question that arises.

If political power is to be struggled for, with these scoundrels who have aided the rebellion, certainly that state is not fit to live in. Yet 13 members of the convention are openly opposing the Constitution—

How could I live in peace in such a community? How could I enjoy life there? I pray that God will guide my mind & heart into the path of peace & contentment.

The last several weeks, operations have been going on against Mobile under Gen'l. Canby— & the place was taken about 2 weeks ago— but so small did this matter appear, coming with Lee's defeat & surrender, that I have not noticed it. So too, Gen'l. Wilson's Cavalry campaign through Alabama has been going on for 6 to 8 weeks, and he has had great successes, but more absorbing movements have drawn the mind completely from him.

No military movements have taken place west of the Mississippi for a long time. Kirby Smith has had a rebel army somewhere in Western La. or Texas, but no attention has been given to it— Now, of course, it will soon be disposed of, if he does not surrender— Excepting western La., Texas, & Southern & S.W. Arkansas, & Southern Mississippi, & the country along the Gulf, we hold all else. But the Rebels have no force anywhere that I know of except under Kirby Smith— Gen'l Dick Taylor has a straggling force in Ala. & Mississippi— but it is of no account.

The Rebel Ram *Stonewall*[36] has been in the public eye for some time past— She is still at large— but must now soon be sunk. This morning

---

[36]The CSS *Stonewall* arrived in Havana on May 11, 1865, and the crew learned of the Confederacy's surrender. Captain Thomas Page gave the ship to the governor general of Cuba for $16,000 to pay the officers and crew, who returned home.

comes the return news from England, of the evacuation of Richmond. The English secesh papers are very sick over it.

Gold of late has ranged from 145½ to 151⅞. Johnston's surrender put it down to 145½. Sherman's armistice put it up from 147 to 151⅞.

Jeff. Davis & his cabinet are in flight & not heard from for many days. Every effort is being made to overtake them— but Sherman's armistice left them a chance for escape— but as they took with them the gold from Richmond Banks, it may delay their flight— they are on horseback crossing the country around by Cheraw & Columbia, Macon &c.— the route not yet known.

Booth (John Wilkes), the murderer of the President was shot in a Barn, near Port Royal, Va. on the 26th & died in 3 or 4 hours— shot in the neck by Serg't. Corbett. Herold,[37] an accomplice, was captured with him. The War Dept. is carrying on investigations into the crime & its ramifications vigorously.

All these exciting events pass on & create very little excitement now. We read of them, but go on attending to business as if nothing unusual happened. I am busy all the time in reading law, & directing Simmons in St. Louis matters, so that my time passes very rapidly away— in truth I feel that I am growing older & older.

Today finishes my 41st year.

Tomorrow— May 2nd, 1865, I become **42 years of age— My father died at the age of 42— on 13 Aug. 1837**.

I do not feel that I have filled the measure in the public eye that I could have done had I had qualities of ambition, which make men seek distinction.

But this world is a transient place, & if I can only become contented, I can greatly enjoy life in a quiet way, earthly honors do not compensate, & practically, I have not desired them— but have turned my back upon the path leading to them.

---

[37]David E. Herold (1842–65) was to help Lewis Paine escape through Maryland after killing Secretary of State William H. Seward. Instead, he fled, met with Booth, and helped him escape. Herold was tried by a military court and hanged on July 7, 1865.

Sunday, May 7, 1865. ¼ to 4 p.m.

The past week has been comparatively quiet— Our armies are beginning to march north to be mustered out, as victors, & the Country feels that peace has been achieved— God be praised for the result. Jeff. Davis & his companions are in flight, & have not been heard from— A few days ago, the President offered $100,000 reward for Davis, as instigator of Mr. Lincoln's murder— I hope he has the proper proof to justify such a remarkable proclamation.

I have been busy for many days, in studying the law on Mrs. Frances Block— & in reading general law— all my time is passed reading law that I can give to it, so that I may be prepared to practice. I read hard & vigorously & with great profit too. Whether I will go to Washington, or what I will do, I cannot yet determine. Phil'a. is so inviting, I feel unwilling to leave it.

On Wednesday at ¼ to 6, Mrs. Alexander & Mrs. Blair & the children arrived from St. Louis— On Monday & Tuesday, Mr. Benson S. Lossing called to see me— The weather is now charming— I am going in a few minutes with Apo. to see Gen'l. Grant.

Gold the last few days from 141½ to 143½.

June 1865

*"Peace is sweet to the People and they leave the
various matters of getting rid of the army
& fixing the Rebel States to the Adm'n."*

Sunday, June 4, 1865, 5 P.M.

Since I last wrote, the Country has been quiet & free from much excitement. Our great armies marched through & around Richmond northward near Washington to be mustered out. Peace is sweet to the People and they leave the various matters of getting rid of the army & fixing the Rebel States to the Adm'n—

On Wed. the 17th May, I went to Washington & stayed at Silver Spring until Tuesday the 23rd, & on that day came home— On Tues. 23 day, the army of the Potomac passing in review— on the 24th Sherman's army passed, but I was impatient to get home & did not stay to see it— Quite a contest in the papers has been going on over Sherman's terms with Johnston— & Stanton's infamous order giving them to the public— Sherman's Report shows his reasons for what he did— which though not good, yet shows how outrageous was Stanton's dispatch.

When in Wash'n., I looked around to see about getting a house there, & felt discouraged about it & after coming back here pretty much concluded not longer to think about going to Wash'n.— & so continued to feel until Thursday Evng. when Gen'l. Blair & Apo. came up from Wash. en route for New Port— She says Johnston is thinking seriously of making Frank Secy. of War— If that is true, I may conclude, & probably would to go to Wash'n. for a while.

Gold has gone down from 131 & 138— & does not fluctuate much.

Jeff. Davis is now at Fortress Monroe & will soon be tried for treason, & I hope will be hung.[38] The military trial of the conspirators for the
assassination of Mr. Lincoln is yet unfinished.

I have been busy working on law business— St. Louis matters— &
studying law.

[38]Jefferson Davis was captured with his family as they fled from Richmond, accompanied by Captain Given Campbell and his cavalry from Missouri. Davis was put into
Fortress Monroe without trial for 720 days, under harsh conditions ordered by Stanton,
who hoped to implicate him in Lincoln's assassination and try him for treason. Grant
wrote in his memoirs that he believed President Lincoln was glad Davis had escaped, since
he did not want to deal with his punishment and wanted an end to the war. Grant was
concerned that Davis might rally Confederate soldiers and try again to conquer the
Union. At first at Fort Monroe, Davis was shackled in leg irons in a cold, damp, dungeon-
like cell with a light burning day and night. The guards were under orders not to speak to
him, and he was not allowed to leave his cell. Public opinion slowly turned, and Horace
Greely, editor of the New York Tribune, supported Davis's case. After two years, Davis
was released on $100,000 bail with a surety bond signed by many people, including Greely
and another abolitionist, Gerritt Smith.

July 1865

Sunday, July 30, 1865 11 A.M. Stonington, Connecticut[39]

Every day is in my mind tossed with anxious thoughts for the future (of this life). And this has been my condition for several years— I cannot determine what course of life I will adopt— I want to decide, but I cannot. This is a weakness, or defect in my constitution, that has caused me much suffering of mind— Again & again have I longed to be able to decide, & when I think I have done so, I find myself swinging off the opposite way. I now oscillate like a pendulum between St. Louis and the East— One day or hour, I almost fix myself to go to St. Louis in the fall— & then when I feel the realities of that I turn away from it with distaste, if not aversion & disgust.

I could much enjoy life, either in West Chester, or by having a small country place & my house in Phil'a. for the winter months, if I could only shut out from my mind what I fail to secure to myself by going back to St. Louis— But that tormenting thought comes into my mind & keeps me from closing out St. Louis from my mind & heart— And yet, do I not know this— that even if I stay in St. Louis— & there have success— influence— high professional position— & wealth, none of them will yield <u>contentment</u>— for they are all vanity, & vexation of spirit.

If I go to St. Louis I have certain discomforts— heat, dirt, climate &c., whereas in the East, I can be as contented as there— for I will have discontent, wherever I am, but without these discomforts. <u>Ambition</u> is

[39]This journal entry was written on an empty page in the front of the journal, but is clearly dated after the last entry in the back of the journal.

the rock in my path— dissatisfaction at being of no account— & yet the very struggle for it is the distinction in St. Louis, accompanied by bitterness, & disgust. By labor & effort, I can there have a fine establishment— along with a enviable position— But is this enviable position an off-set for the discomforts of life—

Notes at End of Journal No. 10

"Receipt" for recipe no. 206 of Rambler, vol 3, p. 384
good thoughts for restlessness p. 8

(Sunday Evng. Oct. 30, '64)
Note my variableness while in St. Louis—
On 26 nov. '63,   I was busy— pleased & reading Mo. Law to stay there &
                practice—
On 8 Jan'y. '64 = felt that our stay was temporary—
" 12 "   " —felt I c'd succeed at the Bar, but felt unlike staying.
" 15 "   " —I noted my feelings & objections to St. Louis for future use
                on recurrence of doubts &c.
" 17 "   " —I again wrote in same way, noting the objections to St.
                Louis,& anticipating my very present trouble of doubts &
                uneasiness of <u>want of occupation</u>—
" 22 "   " —Same object—
" 23 "   "   "   " strong— hateful climate, dirt, mud, &c.—
                hateful society &c.— I say, "I put down these thoughts, so
                that when I look back from Phil'a. & see how when I have
                the opportunity to enter successfully here into business, I
                feel unwilling to do so— that outside of law business, I have
                not a solitary reason for staying here—
" 24 "   · " Wrote with same object— strongly thinking why I c'd not
                live in St. L.— I said, "I must beware acting under poignant,
                or excited feelings, & when I shall be in a position of <u>quiet
                obscurity</u>, I must bear in mind, that <u>now, I deliberately</u> con-
                clude that to the best xx here I can <u>not have a life of peace</u>."
"3 Feb'y. '64. "I do not feel any <u>interest</u> in St. Louis." See that— I do feel an
                <u>interest in Phil'a</u>. "I am not willing to go to labor at my pro-

206

fession."

Note, I said that <u>Every Day</u> above cited— almost. Yet on 26 Dec'r., I was studying to practice & on that <u>day</u> I doubted my staying & stated, "but the dirt, mud & dreary climate made the place horrible."

On 14 Feb'y. '64—I wrote again for the same purpose, approving what I had written 24 Jan'y. I spoke of the horrid things in St. L. & the "broils of life in this horrid society" & hoped I w'd bring myself to leave it—

On 28 Feb'y. Comes the 1st change of tone— when for 10 days I had been interested in business, the 5th N. R.R. &c.— but I noted how dusty & then muddy & disagreeable it had been—

On 3rd M'ch. Still on same subject— & note my pensiveness & the difficulty of overcoming myself—

" 13 " doubts, in consequence of my being busy & important— but add, I look to the time of going East with pleasure— Monday after this, I notified Wiegel to vacate our house & thought we might remain, & by what I wrote on (27th)

27th it appeared I felt we might remain indefinitely, as I might not be able to live on income without business— felt doubtful about the war—

Ap'l. 3rd Long cont'd bad weather— bad spirits about the war— all unsettled & uncertain—

" 8 —felt cheerful at hope of selling 5th St. lot to go to Phil'a "I have felt so strongly of late that excepting for business, I have no reason for remaining here." xx "And of late I have felt how hateful it is to be in the C.H. [Court House] where I meet more disloyal than loyal lawyers."

" 10 Dirt & other discomforts— "Sitting & looking out over the dirty smoky city, how entirely without congeniality here."— I set out the hatefulness of the place— & my struggle against insignificance— xx "Why should I hesitate when all the time I feel that I cannot be contented here." xx "Now I have it in my power to get into good practice x and yet I feel it to be a mistake to go back to it."— discordant society— no attachments &c. "Oh I do

not want longer to protract this struggle about remaining in St. Louis."

That cleared Book No. 8

Ap'l. 17	"I long to leave this discordant city— & go to Phil'a." xx "I do not think that I can become so perverse as to return to it— I raised the window & looked over the City & felt that I have no affection for it, and will break no ties in leaving it."
" 24	gloomy over the war— anxious to sell & lease— "I will choke down if I can the feeling of unimportance which I will encounter for here there is nothing to remain for."
1 May—	gloomy over the war— "I hope things may work so that we will never come back here again."
8 "	The war— not able to leave unless I sell my property—
10 "	About the war only } Grant's dreadful battles in Va.
12 "	" " " " } filled my mind
13 "	" " " " }
22 " 1864	had been sick— the war— archie's death— had been think-ing of taking a house for several days in St. Louis— all uncertain—

That was the last written in St. Louis

---

7 June 1864	In Phil'a.— hope to remain— I review my feelings while in St. Louis— & my sufferings there— becoming prematurely old.
9 " "	Reasons vs. St. Louis & in favor of Phil'a.— The climate, heat, dirt, selfishness of the People, "make life there <u>dreary</u>."
10 " 1864	the same thoughts—

---

8 Feb'y. 1862	My stay in St. Louis temporary
4 Ap'l. "	I wrote— "and now tonight, I feel here in St. Louis, almost separated & isolated from all around me x how sad & dreary— here have I lived nearly 20 years, & not a solitary person but Ben's family who warm my heart— can I wonder that I do not enjoy life in St. L. xx cold, sad & cheerless." I wrote but seldom then on that subject—

25 Dec. '61	"This city is disgusting to me as a place of residence." &c.—

2 Feb'y. '62	My disgust at the feeling from my acting as Comm. to assess disloyal People & the coldness of the Union men—
6 Ap'l. '62	am practicing again & like it & am doing well. After this I wrote nothing of going East until
28 Sep. '62	when I said, "I keep all the time thinking of removing from this troubled region to the free states— Either Davenport or Penn'a.
Oct 11 "	"Oh how I long to get out of this miserable place— I am tired & disgusted with it."
" 26/62	2 years ago I enter at <u>large</u> for the 1st time in writing into the subject, expressing strong reasons & anticipating the precise difficulties that I now experience.
Nov 2 "	Same thing— <u>no friends in St. L</u> "I wish so much that I had occupation in the East, for I long to leave here

Book No. 5 = see indexed at the end
Shows how constantly & urgently my thoughts were on the subject in
Feby., Mch., Apl., May '63

Phil'a, Nov. 15, '64 11:15 A.M.
In what does happiness consist.
Is it in the pursuit of worldly profit?
They who are immersed in such pursuit, are always hurrying on from one thing attained to the next, & never at <u>rest.</u>
Successful they are, but with much chafing & vexation each day.
The slowness, inefficiency, stupidity, inertness, ignorance, perverseness, dishonesty &c. of agents who must be employed—
The cross purposes & opposing efforts of Rivals—
The mis-calculations & miss-chances.

These & many other causes serve to mar the enjoyment of day by day; while still the man advances through them with success & overcomes all difficulties, just as the Boat propelled against the current moves ahead.
Occupation is necessary to happiness; and it should be useful

It serves to improve and advance the individual, while it makes him useful to society.
By it, he gains respect, and good treatment

On happiness, read the admirable number 68 of the Rambler, vol 1, p. 429
It says—
"Fame & wonder & applause, are not excited but by external & adventitious circumstances, often distinct & separate from virtue & heroism.
Eminence of station, greatness of effect, & all the favors of fortune, must concur to place excellence in public view. xx
The main part of life is in deed, composed of small incidents & petty occurrences; of wishes for objects, not remote, & grief for disappointments, of no fatal consequence. xx

So a few pains & a few pleasures are all the materials of human life: & of these, the proportions are partly allotted by Providence & partly left to the arrangement of reason & choice.
As these are well, or ill disposed, man is for most part, happy or miserable. xx
The great end of prudence, is to give cheerfulness to those hours, which splendor can not guild, & acclamation can not exhilarate. xx
To be happy at home is the ultimate result of all ambition: the end to which every enterprise & labor tends. Xx
It is indeed at home, that every man must be known by those who would make a just estimate of his virtue or felicity."

The article goes on to show that they who are happy at home diffuse enjoyment there: and that servants are the most correct witnesses as to a master's character. The purpose is to show how in every day & minor matter, lies enjoyment and real happiness. That few are concerned in large matters, & even they have most of their time given to home matters.
No 69 of the Rambler is upon the want of enjoyment of old age, showing that no kind of life will give such enjoyment but a Pious one. It shows that the expectations of youth must be disappointed—

P. 437, "To a young man, entering the world, with fullness of hope, & ardor of pursuit nothing is so unpleasing as the cold caution, the faint expectations x which experience and disappointments certainly infuse" xx

& further on speaks of the "Schemes and expectations, the pleasures & other sorrows, of those who have not yet been hardened by time & chilled by frustration."

Is this not my present thought upon the success of life with professional efforts and rewards?

To encounter an unfriendly People & an evil climate for the gain of such a career. Is there not present comfort & enjoyment here. Give that up, for what. How much of happiness would such success give? Can a good answer be given to that. If I am to make professional effort, why make it there rather than here? Success & profit attend it there— But will that produce happiness— It is there that should be the pause.

No 67 of the Rambler, vol 1, p. 423 is on "Hope" & is full of wisdom—

It says, p. 424. "Hope is indeed very fallacious & promises what it seldom gives." It then describes a dream in which the world is represented as pursuing the offers of Hope as a Goddess— She sits in a garden, having 2 gates by which to enter it— Most go in by the Gate of Fancy & they wander without getting near the throne— A few get in by the Gate "Reason"— & by the Straight of difficulty begin the ascent by which the throne of Hope may be reached— Many fail to attain the end— Of the few who do, it says—
"Of these few, the greater part, when they had obtained the gift which Hope had promised them, regretted the labor which it cost, & felt in their success the regret of disappointment: the rest returned with their prize, & were led by wisdom to the bowers of content."

This seems a good answer to the case I put— Let me be also led by wisdom, by the prize I have now— for if discontented with this, I certainly will not be satisfied with any future one.

No. 63 of the Rambler gives a fine account of the vascillation of the intelligent mind, as to public or private life determined by his contrary experience in the two, his dissatisfaction in each.

P. 402. "To take a view, at once distinct and comprehensive of human life, with all its intricacies of combination, & varieties of connection, is beyond the power of mortal intelligences.
Of the state with which practice has not acquainted us we snatch a glimpse, we discern a point & regulate the rest by passion & by fancy.
In this inquiry, every favorite prejudice, every innate desire is busy to deceive us.
We are unhappy, or at least, less happy, than our nature seems to admit: we desire the melioration of our lot. xx

Irresolution & mortality are often the faults of men whose views are wide, & whose inauguration is vigorous and exclusive, because they can not confine their thoughts within their own boundaries of action, but are continually ranging over all the scenes of human existence, & consequently are often apt to conceive that they fall upon new regions of pleasure, & start new possibilities of happiness."

It goes on to show how evenly balanced the good & ill of different modes of life appear to a guessing mind— & so it oscillates in conclusions; for as soon as it determines in favor of one mode, on careful examination then a counterbalancing advantage of an opposite mode seizes the mind.

"And the resolutions which are suggested by the nicest examination, are often repented as soon as they are taken."

It then goes on to give the sketch of life of a man of wealth, who went from private to public life, twice forward and back, from conflicting motives; & ends up by advising constancy. "because life allows us but a small time for inquiry & experiment, & he that steadily endeavors at excellence, in what ever employment, will more benefit mankind than he that hesitates in choosing his part till he is called to the performance."

The article also examines the discontent each man feels with his occupation, & the cause why he would give preference to another, knowing the evils of one, but not of the other.

FIN

Epilogue

THE GIFT OF FAMILY STORIES

As I deciphered Franklin Dick's journals, the entry that seemed most poignant to me was entered on May 1, 1865, when he wrote, "<u>Today finishes my 41st year</u>." His father had died at age forty-two, so Dick felt that he was near the end of his own life; he felt himself growing older and noticed time passing rapidly away. He was discouraged that he had not risen as far as he hoped to and felt he had not accomplished much in his life. Previously, on March 11, 1865, he had written that the best part of his life was spent and he would not distinguish himself in what remained of it. His only option was to quietly settle down and make the best of what was left.

Like Pip in Charles Dickens' *Great Expectations*, which he mentions reading, Franklin Dick was an idealist, at least at the beginning of the journals. There is an alpha to omega journey in *Great Expectations* and in these journals. Pip, Dickens' hero, and Dick, both had great expectations for their futures; they feel guilty about their mistakes and strive to improve themselves. Dick's reaction to the explosion of the cartridge factory shows his remorse about the people injured and his wanting to have nothing to do with anything that harmed people. By the end of the journals, Dick writes of being horrified by the disloyal lawyers in St. Louis and says his friends are few there; he is always concerned about doing the right and honest thing, and wants a simple, quiet life.

When the journals end, it had been over twenty years since Franklin Dick moved to St. Louis, where he practiced law and was involved in business and politics. He had arrived in Missouri full of plans for his future, which were interrupted by the war. Because of the path he chose, supporting the Union and Frank Blair's policies, Dick was hated by the

213

old St. Louisans, Southern sympathizers, and Conditional Unionists. However they exhibited their dislike obviously made a deep impression on him, for he wrote of various people as base men and that he hated everything about St. Louis. It was difficult for him to see his old friends from Missouri in Washington in late December 1864, and to realize that his contemporaries were in power in the state and he was not and never would be, despite all his years of hard work there.

When Benjamin Farrar suggested the possibility of Franklin Dick serving as chief justice of the Missouri Supreme Court, Dick found the idea enticing, since it offered a chance at recovering some of the status he lost through his service in unpopular positions. But he vacillated between returning to familiar St. Louis, staying in Philadelphia where he had grown up, moving to Washington DC as Francis P. Blair Sr. suggested, or even moving to San Francisco. He worried about the "thought of his children being fated to live in St. Louis" in an atmosphere of hatred and vengeance that repelled him. He did not want to subject his family to that sort of life, so he became what he described as "a tree in a moveable vessel."

It is assumed that soldiers suffer during a war, but these journals show what war can do to civilians. Dick had invested his youth in St. Louis, but all his efforts were swept away by the war. In Philadelphia, he was dislocated from the life he had built for himself; this depressed him and made it hard for him to decide what to do. At one point, he started back to St. Louis, then uncharacteristically became fearful, turned back and returned to Philadelphia. Before the war, he never would have been indecisive in this manner.

Franklin Dick wrote that before the war, "we felt as if we were forever safe." In 1865, he wrote "the People in the North have become accustomed to the war— here in Phil'a. the People go on just as in ordinary times— They gay continue their giddy amusements— the errands go on with business as usual, & the war is an interesting topic, which they keep more or less in mind." He tried to act that way too, but his constant anxiety about the present and future prevented him.

The American frontier had been a land of violence from the start. The Civil War brought the frontier destructiveness back into long peaceful settled areas. In battle areas, soldiers fought soldiers. Generals may have tried to keep private citizens from being harmed, but any property in the way was destroyed to terrorize the population, demolish supplies for the army, and economically ruin the other side. Both sides were led by officers trained in the same techniques. Many were classmates at West Point or had served together in the army before the war. They used the same strategies (based on Henry Halleck's *Elements of Military Art and Science*), seeing individual battles, but not an overall strategy for the entire campaign. In both Union and Confederate troops, foot soldiers from the middle and lower classes stood shoulder to shoulder in mass formations of long deep lines while officers, usually from the upper classes, watched from above the noise and clouds of smoke, and marched them toward the enemy muskets and cannon. This was the first war when these weapons were standard battle issue. The minie ball, a new invention, expanded on impact, shattering bones and resulting in more amputations. Injuries were more severe and larger numbers of men were killed than in any war in living memory.[1]

The American Civil War has been called the war of brother fighting brother; many families, towns, and states were divided. Some made peace after the war. Nathan Bedford Forrest expressed the national feeling eloquently when he said in his farewell address to his men,

> Civil war, such as you have just passed through naturally engenders feelings of animosity, hatred, and revenge. It is our duty to divest ourselves of all such feelings, and, as far as in our power to do so, to cultivate friendly feelings toward those with whom we have so long contended.... Neighborhood feuds, personal animosities, and private differences should be blotted out; and, when you return home, a manly, straightforward course of conduct will secure the respect even of your enemies. Whatever your responsibilities may be to the government, to society or to individuals, meet them like men.... You have been good soldiers; you can be good citizens. Obey the laws, preserve your honor, and the government to which you have surrendered can afford to be, and will be, magnanimous.[2]

For most of the war, Franklin Dick described himself as being anxious, tired of waiting and waiting, with the future uncertain. His heart

[1]Weigley, *A Great Civil War*, xiii–xxviii.
[2]Hurst, *Nathan Bedford Forrest*, 258.

and mind longed for peace. He wrote of the war dragging on from one phase to another, not divided into separate parts with beginnings and ends, as he thought it would be. He concluded that we were much more capable of suffering in war, and could not feel joy as easily under those conditions. In St. Louis, he wrote, he had suffered and become prematurely old from the climate, heat, dirt, and selfishness of the people. Today he would be diagnosed as having post-traumatic stress syndrome, a casualty of war. During the Civil War, they called it "soldier's heart" or "Da Costa's Syndrome," but there was no treatment available.

Franklin Dick liked a quiet life, and was bothered by his discontent. He was influenced by his experiences practicing law, serving on the assessment board in St. Louis during the Civil War, and the episode with the cartridge factory exploding. His life was shaped by serving as provost marshal general and living through the war for all those years, which had turned his thinking inward. When the war ended, Dick moved his family to Washington and practiced law with Montgomery Blair, as Francis P. Blair Sr. had proposed. They worked across from the White House in the Blair House, which was later bought as a guest house by the federal government. There is a plaque on the wall mentioning that the two practiced law in that building. At that time, Dick may have regained some of the courage and purpose he had before the war and felt himself to be planted as a tree.

Franklin Dick's legacy was a contrast; his three sons were opinionated and competitive. His eldest son, William Alexander Dick, was my great-grandfather. I remember him well at the age of ninety as a tiny old man with a huge temper. He used to bang his little cane on the floor for attention and terrify me. The bamboo cane had a smooth ivory handle with the end carved into a dog's head, which I loved to touch as a child.

When young, William had played with a marble and a baseball bat with the Blair children in front of the Blair House, and was hit in the left eye, losing sight. Franklin Dick writes of his concern on March 5, 1865, when young Wilmer Lewis lost his right eye in an accident, and how they spent the day helping the family. How must he have felt to have the same thing happen to his own son, caused by a child of his law partner? William went through the rest of his life blind in his left eye, a constant reminder to his sensitive father of how easily one can be injured. It still looked like a normal eye, but he squinted with that one and glared with the right one.

In 1881, William married Caroline Thompson Norris. Her uncle was Alexander J. P. Garesché, who Franklin Dick referred to as a "base man" and whose family he detested because of their Southern views. How William and Caroline managed to meet and spend any time together is a mystery, given the hatred between the families. In those days, engagement rings were not the fashion, yet I have a tiny one that Willie gave Carrie as a "promise ring." It is a little gold finger ring, fashioned like a small serpent wound around the finger several times, with a raised head, so that one can see its tiny diamond eyes.

I also have one of their engraved wedding invitations, addressed to Mrs. A. W. Meigs in a tiny ivory envelope with the Norris crest embossed on the back. The envelope was stamped as made by the company, "Dreka" at 1121 Chestnut St., Philadelphia. The invitation also has the crest at the top, and was issued by Caroline's grandmother, Mrs. Joseph Parker Norris, for the marriage ceremony on Thursday, April 21, 1881, at 1809 Pine Street, Philadelphia. Since her parents did not issue the invitation, one wonders if they attended, and also if Franklin Dick's family were there, since the two families hated each other. Willie and Carrie named their first and only child Franklin Archibald Dick II, for his father, which must have smoothed things somewhat with his family. The baby was born three years before Franklin Dick died. When Carrie died from kidney disease shortly after the birth of her son, her sister, Mai Garesché Norris took care of the baby. Her nephew called her "Tantie," a diminutive of the French word for aunt. When William later married Elizabeth Story Jenks, Mai was finally allowed to become a nun, which had always been her wish. She became Sister St. Anthony and lived in a convent in Philadelphia, where I remember visiting her. Both my mother and I were named for her. Elizabeth specified in her will that William, her husband, must be buried beside her in the Jenks family plot in Philadelphia, so William was separated from the Dick family in death.

I uncovered a family scandal when researching the descendants of the second eldest son, Frank Madison Dick, who had married Julia Biddle. She left him and they were divorced, which was very rare in that time, and Julia took one of their two sons with her. My mother later told me that the Dick family drew together in loyalty and never spoke of them again. I always thought that there was only one child from the marriage—my cousin Langhorne. My two cousins on that side had never heard that their grandfather had a brother until I discovered it and asked them. Franklin Dick had died the year before Frank Madison Dick's children were born, so he missed this part of the family history.

Evans Dick, the third son, is known mainly for building Dick's Castle on the Hudson River. It was a copy of the Alhambra, but he lost his money and never finished it. That branch of the family has drifted apart, so I have less information on it.

Franklin Dick's last child, Myra, was born only nine years before he died. The Dick brothers were always told by their parents to take care of their little sister. She married a French count, and her three brothers and their mother attended the wedding in Paris. I remember visiting her in the south of France and wish I had asked questions about her parents. Through the generations, her descendants in England and South Africa have stayed closely in touch with those of us in America, even now into the seventh generation.

When the three brothers had their investment company together, they must have bickered constantly, though each had his own branch—in Philadelphia, New York, and Boston. The Dick brothers were each difficult men, and constantly tried to outdo each other. My cousin Hebe later named three particularly aggressive geese after them. And my mother tells a hilarious story about William Dick driving one of the first cars in France, trying to best his brothers. And so it continues unto the present generation.

I am grateful to have had the excitement of deciphering and listening and feeling the daily words and thoughts of my great-great-grandfather as his life was indelibly altered by his divided country. His journals taught me that war is not about generals and battles, but real people and how they live during life-altering events. Franklin Dick ended his journal by asking "In what does happiness consist?" For him, it was avoiding St. Louis with its bad memories from the war, though it made him "a tree in a movable vessel." Within himself, he knew that happiness came from close ties to people, leading an honest, loyal, upright life dedicated to justice, providing financial and emotional support for his family, and trying to make a difference in the world. The most important quality for him was to live in peace, which he appears to have done for twenty more years. When I look around at the possessions my family has saved from Franklin Archibald Dick and other ancestors, I admire and respect them and their treasures. Each piece reminds me of listening to the gift of a story, and I continue to pass on these special tales to my grandchildren.

The important lesson is not about me and my family, but about every one of us. We all have a unique and universal perspective from a heritage of family stories, important to preserve. Learning from what we were in the past creates a better future for who we will be and where we are going in the next generation.

Appendix A

Biographical information is drawn from *The Dictionary of American Biography*, *Biographical Directory of the United States Congress*, *Generals in Blue*, and *Generals in Gray*. Additional sources used are noted after each entry.

George Alexander (1829–?) was Apolline Alexander Blair and Myra Alexander Dick's brother and Franklin Dick's brother-in-law. Alexander and Dick were involved in a cartridge making business at the beginning of the Civil War. He was convinced his cartridges could work when wet. Francis P. Blair Sr. and others did not agree with him. He married Mary Campbell, daughter of Judge James Campbell of Paducah. See Laas, *Wartime Washington*, 87–88, 95, 159, 213–14.

William Anderson (1840–64) was called "Bloody Bill" for his habit of riding into battle with Union scalps hanging on his saddle. He was raised in Missouri, and joined Confederate guerilla Colonel William C. Quantrill on the Kansas-Missouri border in 1862 as one of his lieutenants, along with Frank and Jesse James and the four Younger brothers. In 1863, Union soldiers arrested several women for sheltering guerilla bushwhackers, including three of Anderson's sisters and Jesse James' mother and sister, and imprisoned them in Kansas City. The building collapsed, killing several people, including one of Anderson's sisters. In revenge, in August 1863 Anderson rode with Quantrill to sack Lawrence, Kansas, where the orders were to "Kill every man and burn every house." Anderson disagreed with Quantrill in 1864 and joined Price's forces. In September 1864, Anderson and his bushwackers looted Centralia, Missouri, killing twenty-four unarmed Union soldiers on a train that arrived during his raid. When he was killed by the Union militia on October 26, 1864, in Richmond, Missouri, his head was cut off and mounted on a telegraph pole for all to see. See Monaghan, *Civil War on the Western Border*, 254, 274, 279–89, 316–19, 323.

D. Robert Barclay was a St. Louis attorney who lost two library cases of books in the first assessment by Henry Halleck. The assessment board set fines of

221

$16,340, collecting $10,913.45, most of which came from auctioning the seized property of disloyal persons who had refused to pay their fines. See Gerteis, *Civil War St. Louis,* 174–76.

Pierre Gustave Toutant Beauregard (1819–93), a French Creole from Louisiana, graduated from West Point, was wounded in the Mexican-American War, and became superintendent of the U.S. Military Academy. He resigned to join the Confederate army as a brigadier general. He commanded the attack on Fort Sumter, which made him popular, and was victorious at the First Battle of Bull Run, after which he was promoted to general. He later fell out of favor with Confederate president Jefferson Davis and General Lee, and was assigned command of Confederate forces in the West. After the war, he declined positions as commander of the armies in Romania and Egypt. He instead became involved in railroads, serving as company president. He also served in the Louisiana state government as adjutant general of the state militia and manager of the Louisiana lottery. See Faust, *Historical Times,* 51–52; and Denney, *Civil War Years,* 28.

Judah Philip Benjamin (1811–84), born in St. Croix to Jewish parents, entered Yale at age fourteen, and practiced law in New Orleans, where he owned a sugar plantation. He served in the Louisiana state legislature as a Whig (1842–44). In 1850, he sold his slaves and plantation, and was elected to the U.S. Senate (1853–61). Benjamin is best known in the senate for his brilliant answer to Benjamin Wade of Ohio, who called him "An Israelite in Egyptian clothing." Benjamin answered, "It is true that I am a Jew, and when my ancestors were receiving the Ten Commandments from the immediate Deity amidst the thundering and lightning of Mount Sinai, the ancestors of my opponent were herding swine in the forests of Great Britain." He was offered a seat on the Supreme Court in 1854, but declined. In 1861, after secession, he resigned his Senate seat and was named Attorney General of the Confederacy and then Secretary of War. When Roanoke Island was surrendered to the Union without a fight in February 1862, Benjamin took the blame, not revealing that the reason was the lack of soldiers. President Davis rewarded him in March 1862 by naming him secretary of state. Franklin Dick refers to Benjamin's proposal that any slave who served in the Confederate army would be emancipated. Benjamin hoped this would bring Great Britain to support the Confederacy, but it did not happen. At the end of the war, there was an anti-Semitic rumor that Benjamin had masterminded the assassination of Lincoln, so he left Jefferson Davis' fleeing Cabinet, burned his papers, and escaped, ending up in England, where he became a successful barrister in 1866. He published a treatise on law, and became Queen's counsel in 1872. See Faust, *Historical Times,* 54–55; Denney, *Civil War Years,* 21, 25, 97, 118, 143, 565; and Laas, *Wartime Washington,* 37–39.

Apolline Agatha Alexander Blair (1824–1908) was the wife of Frank Blair and sister of Myra Alexander Dick, wife of Franklin Dick. Apo and Frank had eight children. She was on the committee to plan the Grand Mississippi Valley Sanitary Fair, May 17, 1864, to raise money to alleviate the suffering of wounded soldiers, their families, and refugees. Apo and Myra's blind mother, Mira Madison Alexander, spent half the year with the Blairs in St. Louis and half at her place in Kentucky. See Smith, *Francis Preston Blair*, 189, 435-436, Gerteis, *Civil War St. Louis*, 100, 230–35; Laas, *Wartime Washington*, 42, 298, 306, 322; and Winter, *Civil War in St. Louis*, 91–93.

Francis Preston Blair Jr. (1821–75) grew up across from the White House, son of Franklin Preston Blair Sr., an influential founder of the Republican Party. After attending the University of North Carolina at Chapel Hill and Princeton College, he married Apolline Alexander, whose sister, Myra, married Franklin Dick. Blair practiced law in St. Louis with his brother Montgomery, served in the state House of Representatives (1852–56), and as a Republican in the U.S. Congress (1857–59). Blair's early political life was devoted to keeping Missouri in the Union and supporting President Lincoln. Blair served on the Committee of Safety, raised troops to help Lyon at Camp Jackson, and rose to be a major general in the Union army. He advised Lincoln on Missouri affairs in secret, feuded with Frémont, and was outspoken in his political opinions, in a speech calling Chase a traitor. Blair was praised by Grant and Sherman as an outstanding military officer and was an advocate for moderate reconstruction after the war. He was the unsuccessful Democratic candidate for vice president in 1868; he served in the state House of Representatives (1870–71), the U.S. Senate (1871–73), and as state insurance commissioner (1874–75). See Gerteis, *Civil War St. Louis*, 100–14; Goodwin, *Team of Rivals*, 23–24, 391–96, 569–71, 753; Winter, *Civil War in St. Louis*, 105–6; Smith, *Francis Preston Blair*, 188–90, 245–47, 290–309, 334–36, 420–21, 432–36; Faust, *Historical Times*, 64–65.

Francis Preston Blair Sr. (1791–1876) was a journalist and politician. As editor of the *Washington Globe* and trusted advisor to President Andrew Jackson, he was politically influential. In 1855, Blair was a founder of the Republican Party and presided at its first convention, supporting Frémont at the 1856 convention and Lincoln in 1860. When, at the beginning of the Civil War, Winfield Scott suggested to President Lincoln the appointment of Robert E. Lee as commander of the Union army, Blair was sent to offer Lee the command. After Lincoln's reelection in 1864, he sent Blair to meet unofficially with President Jefferson Davis to discuss peace negotiations. Blair proposed that the two sides join together peacefully to oust the French from Mexico, enforcing the Monroe Doctrine. Nothing came of the resulting Hampton Roads Conference of February 3, 1865, because Davis required negotiations "between two nations" and Lincoln's terms called for reunion of the nation. Blair saw his two sons successful in politics: Montgomery became Lincoln's postmaster general, and Francis Jr. was a congressman and major general in the Union army. See Goodwin, *Team of*

Rivals, 23–24, 349–50, 392–94, 690–91, 753; Faust, *Historical Times*, 65, 335–36; Laas, *Wartime Washington*, 1-10, 454–70; and Smith, *Francis Preston Blair*.

Montgomery Blair (1813–75) was the son of Francis P. Blair Sr. (founder of the Republican Party), and older brother of James, Francis P. Blair Jr., and Elizabeth Blair Lee. He argued the Dred Scott case before the Supreme Court and was Postmaster General in Lincoln's cabinet from 1861 to 1864. He feuded with other members of the cabinet, and supported his brother Frank in his quarrel with Frémont. During a Confederate invasion of Maryland, his country place, "Falklands," was burned. A private letter he wrote to Frank that criticized Lincoln was published in the newspapers, and Montgomery later lost his post due to political maneuvers. After the Civil War, he practiced law in Washington with Franklin Dick in the Blair House across from the White House. See Goodwin, *Team of Rivals*, 23–24, 188, 391–96, 429–30, 517–19, 526–27, 640–45, 659–61, 678–79, 753; Faust, *Historical Times*, 65; Smith, *Francis Preston Blair*, 92–93, 144, 155, 240–43, 310–35, 343–48, 351, 439; and McPherson, *Battle Cry of Freedom*, 776.

Henry T. Blow (1817–75), a Virginian, was the brother of Taylor Blow, who received the transfer of Dred Scott and his wife after the Supreme Court decision, and freed the family. Blow moved to Missouri in 1830, where he was successful in lead mining and the drug business. He served in the state senate and was appointed minister to Venezuela in 1861. As a Blair supporter during the war, Blow led a group to Washington to have General John M. Schofield removed for working too closely with Governor Gamble. The delegation wanted federal military protection for Missouri. Blow served in the U.S. Congress (1863–67), was minister to Brazil (1869–71), and was appointed a commissioner of the District of Columbia (1874–75). See Gerteis, *Civil War St. Louis*, 64, 81, 270, 281, 335; and Virtualology, "Henry T. Blow" (www.famousamericans.net/henrytblow/).

Henry Boernstein (1805–92) was born in Hamburg, Germany, and had a medical education. He served in the Austrian army, was a playwright in Vienna, and managed the German opera in Paris. Boernstein became the influential German editor of the *Anziger des Westens* in St. Louis, and led the Second Regiment of U.S. Volunteers under Lyon at Camp Jackson. He was a good friend and supporter of Frank Blair, and was loyal to the Republican party during the Civil War. He was named consul in Bremen, Germany, by Lincoln, but returned to help Frank Blair's election campaign in 1862. He wrote *Memoirs of a Nobody: The Missouri Years of an Austrian Radical, 1849-1866*, and other books. See Gerteis, *Civil War St. Louis*, 74, 100, 103, 108, 265; and Winter, *Civil War in St. Louis*, 43.

John Wilkes Booth (1838–65) was from a Maryland stage family; his father and brother were more famous than he. He served with Virginia's Richmond Grays at John Brown's Harpers Ferry Raid and was at the subsequent hanging.

Booth felt the South was an oppressed nation and became quite radical in his beliefs. He had planned to kidnap Lincoln before the 1864 inauguration, but failed. He plotted several times to capture the president and take him to Richmond for a prisoner exchange, but the fall of Richmond changed his plans. On April 14, 1865, at Ford's Theater, Booth shot Lincoln in the back of the head and slashed Lincoln's guest, Major Henry Rathbone, with a hunting knife. Despite breaking a leg as he jumped from the presidential box, he escaped with David Herold. That night, Dr. Samuel Mudd set his leg, and Booth fled to Virginia, but was trapped in a tobacco shed at the farm of Richard H. Garrett near Port Royal by detectives Everton J. Conger and Luther B. Baker. Herold surrendered, but Booth was shot as the shed burned. As part of the conspiracy, Lewis T. Powell attacked Secretary of State William H. Seward. A military tribunal tried the conspirators, hanging some and imprisoning the others. President Johnson pardoned the survivors in 1869. See Faust, *Historical Times*, 71, 440–41; and Denney, *Civil War Years*, 339, 559, 563.

Braxton Bragg (1817–76) was born in North Carolina and graduated from West Point. He served in the Mexican-American War, then became a Louisiana planter. A close friend of Jefferson Davis, Bragg was made a brigadier general in the Confederate army in March 1861 and given command of the area from Pensacola, Florida, to Mobile, Alabama. After being promoted to full general, he commanded the Army of Tennessee. Bragg lost at the battles of Perryville and Stones River, won at Chickamauga, and lost at Missionary Ridge. He then became President Jefferson Davis' chief of staff. After the war, Bragg served as chief engineer for the state of Alabama. See Faust, *Historical Times*, 75; and Denney, *Civil War Years*, 33.

John Cabell Breckenridge (1821–75) was born near Lexington, Kentucky, and practiced law in Iowa and Kentucky. He served as a major with the Third Kentucky Volunteers in the Mexican-American War, then returned to Lexington to practice law and enter politics. He was in the state legislature (1849) and the U.S. Congress (1851–55). In 1856 at age thirty-five, he was elected vice president under Buchanan, and in 1860, he unsuccessfully ran for president. He was again elected to the U.S. senate, but was expelled in December 1861 for supporting the rebellion. He entered the Confederate army, where he was brigadier general in charge of the Kentucky Orphan Brigade. He became secretary of war for the Confederate States (1864–65). Breckenridge scheduled the evacuation of Richmond and participated in surrender negotiations before escaping the country. In 1869, he returned to Kentucky and practiced law. See Faust, *Historical Times*, 78.

Benjamin Gratz Brown (1826–85) was a cousin of Frank and Montgomery Blair. He founded the *Missouri Democrat* with Frank Blair, mobilizing Unionists in St. Louis. Brown was wounded in the leg in a duel over politics with U.S. Attorney Thomas Reynolds. He served in the state legislature with Blair from

1852 to 1858, and they disagreed on issues of race and emancipation. That and criticism of Brown's financial management of the newspaper escalated to estrangement that lasted until both were Liberal-Republicans in the 1870s. Brown served in the Union army, then in the U.S. Senate (1863–67), where he favored women's suffrage and abolishing slavery, opposed voting tests, and promoted an eight-hour workday for government employees. Brown supported Frémont for president in 1864, was elected governor of Missouri in 1871, and ran for vice president with Horace Greely in 1872. See Gerteis, *Civil War St. Louis*, 60–71, 104; Parrish, *History of Missouri*, 103; and Winter, *Civil War in St. Louis*, 142.

Joseph Emerson Brown (1821–94) was born in South Carolina and graduated from Yale. He practiced law in Georgia and served in the state legislature (1849). He was elected governor (1855–65), and was known as intelligent and pro-Union, but strongly in favor of states' rights, especially the rights of his own state of Georgia. Before his state seceded, Brown had the Georgia militia seize Fort Pulaski and the Augusta Arsenal. He constantly fought with President Jefferson Davis during the war over protecting his state from the Confederate government. When Sherman invaded Georgia, Brown fled and was arrested, but was released at the end of the war. He angered many Georgians when he urged them to accept Reconstruction. Brown was later named chief justice of the state supreme court (1865–70). He served in the U.S. Senate (1880–91), dominating Georgia politics for ten years. See Faust, *Historical Times*, 83–84; and Denney, *Civil War Years*, 489.

Simon Bolivar Buckner (1823–1914) was born in Kentucky and graduated from West Point. He fought in the Mexican-American War with his friend Ulysses S. Grant. When Grant resigned from the army and was on his way home, Buckner loaned Grant money to pay his New York hotel bill. Buckner taught at West Point until entering active service during the Mexican-American War. He then taught until 1855, when he resigned to deal with real estate. In 1860, he organized the Kentucky State Guard and worked with Governor Magoffin to keep the state neutral. When this failed, he became a Confederate brigadier general. He led a division to reinforce Fort Donelson. His commanders there, Brigadier General Gideon J. Pillow and Brigadier General John B. Floyd, escaped across the Cumberland River, leaving Buckner the first Confederate to surrender a fort to Union General-in-Chief Ulysses S. Grant on February 16, 1862. Buckner was horrified at what he felt was Grant's ungentlemanly demand for unconditional surrender, considering their long friendship. This incident established his approach to the war; his initials were said to stand for "unconditional surrender." Grant provided his own funds to Buckner while he was a prisoner until his exchange on August 27, 1862. After his release, Buckner served in various posts and was promoted to major general and lieutenant general. Buckner was known as "Simon the Poet" for his poetry. He was a pallbearer at Grant's funeral, served as

governor of Kentucky (1887–91), and ran for the vice presidency in 1896 with
John Palmer on the gold Democratic ticket. See Denney, *Civil War Years,* 127–30;
and Faust, *Historical Times,* 88.

Don Carlos Buell (1818–98) was born in Ohio. He graduated from West
Point and served in the Mexican-American War. When the Civil War began, he
was an early organizer of the Army of the Potomac. He served as head of the
Department of the Ohio and helped Grant defeat the Confederates at the Battle
of Shiloh. Buell considered that his assistance was the only thing that prevented
Grant from losing the battle, which caused Grant to develop a dislike for Buell.
Because Buell owned slaves (inherited from his wife's family), many Northerners
were suspicious of him. In addition, he had a strict policy of not interfering with
Southern civilians while in Tennessee and Alabama, and severely punished a sub-
ordinate whose soldiers pillaged the town of Athens, Alabama. After halting
Confederate forces at the Battle of Perrysville, Buell failed to pursue the retreat-
ing troops; as a result, he was relieved of command. After the war he was president of the Green River Iron Company and served as a federal pension agent. See
Wikipedia, s.v. "Don Carlos Buell"; and Faust, *Historical Times,* 88.

Ambrose Everett Burnside (1824–1881) was born in Indiana. His father, a
South Carolina slave owner, had sold his slaves and moved to Liberty, Indiana,
where Ambrose grew up. Burnside graduated from West Point, served in the
Mexican-American War, and was later wounded by Apaches in the Indian wars.
He was known for his large side-whiskers, which the men called "sideburns" in a
play on his name. He resigned from the army in 1852 to manufacture firearms,
but went bankrupt after failing to get a government contract for a breech-loading
rifle he designed. Creditors took his patent, and later sold many "burnside car-
bines" during the war. Burnside next worked for the Illinois Central Railroad
under McClellan. He entered the Union army in the first wave of three-month
enlistments and served at the First Battle of Bull Run, then was made brigadier
general. Dick refers to an expedition Burnside took down the east coast to attack
Confederate seaports, where he captured Roanoke Island, New Berne, Beaufort,
and Fort Macon, and was made major general. After self-doubting and refusing
twice, Burnside, on November 5, 1862, reluctantly accepted Lincoln's offer to
replace McClellan. Ignoring Lincoln's warning not to attack, he lost the Battle of
Fredericksburg a few days later with 12,700 Union casualties, compared to only
5,000 Confederate casualties—the American Army's worst defeat in history. He
was plagued by bad weather, heavy rains, and his inept military decisions in "the
Mud March" across the Rappahannock River. Lincoln replaced him with General
Joseph Hooker on January 25, 1863. Later, Burnside, serving under General
Grant at the siege of Petersburg, approved a plan by Colonel Henry Pleasants,
leader of a Pennsylvania regiment of coal miners, to tunnel under the Confederate
lines and blow them up. On July 30, they blasted a section of the fortifications 170

feet long, burying an entire Confederate regiment. At the last minute, General George Meade changed the plan for trained black soldiers to attack, replacing them with James H. Ledlie's unprepared division, who were trapped in the hole and killed. The Battle of the Crater resulted in 4,000 Union casualties; Burnside was blamed and soon resigned. He later became governor of Rhode Island (1866–69) and served in the U.S. Senate (1875–81). See Faust, *Historical Times*, 96–98, 524; Laas, *Wartime Washington*, 102; Gerteis, *Civil War St. Louis*, 195; and Katcher, *Civil War Source Book*, 266.

Benjamin Franklin Butler (1818–93) was born in New Hampshire and moved to Massachusetts, where he practiced law and entered politics. He served in the state legislature (1853, 1859) and was delegate to the Democratic National Convention in 1860. He was an officer in the state militia and, in 1861, he entered the Union army when Lincoln appointed him major general of volunteers. Leading the Eighth Massachusetts Regiment, he was first assigned to occupy Baltimore and reopen vital railroad connections between Washington DC and the Union states. While commanding Fort Monroe in Virginia, Butler refused to return fugitive slaves to their owners, calling them "contrabands of war," which angered the South at the loss of property. Butler lost at the Battle of Big Bethel near Fort Monroe, but captured Forts Hatteras and Clark in North Carolina. After the capture of New Orleans in April 1862, Butler commanded the occupying forces; he was called "Beast" Butler for issuing an order that any Confederate woman who insulted his troops was to be treated as a woman of the streets, and "Spoons" for his supposed looting of homes. He had several failed assignments after that, and was relieved of command in January 1865. After the war, Butler served in the U.S. Congress (1867–75, 1877–79) and as Massachusetts governor (1882–84). See Katcher, *Civil War Source Book*, 266–67; Faust, *Historical Times*, 98–100, 273; Denney, *Civil War Years*, 36–37, 166–71, 193, 200, 511; and Barret, *Civil War in North Carolina*, 262–84.

Simon Cameron (1799–1889) was born in Pennsylvania. He was a printer and editor, involved in banking and construction through his political connections. He served as U.S. senator (1845–49, 1857–61, 1867–77), changing from a Democrat to a Republican in 1855. He was promised a cabinet post for Pennsylvania delegate votes at the 1860 presidential convention. Lincoln made him secretary of war, and Cameron filled his department with inept political and personal appointments and was charged with corruption, including being accused of buying guns that did not work and forcing General Winfield Scott's resignation. He named Dorothea Dix head of the nursing corps, and openly advocated the freeing and arming of slaves. Lincoln replaced him with Edwin Stanton and removed him from view by making him ambassador to Russia in January 1862. Cameron returned and ran for the U.S. Senate in 1863 and 1867, winning the second time. He dominated Pennsylvania politics for the next ten years, and his son replaced him as senator in 1877. See Winter, *Civil War in St. Louis*, 77; Faust, *Historical Times*, 107; and Gerteis, *Civil War St. Louis*, 93, 95–96, 117–18, 157–59, 263.

Given Campbell (1835–1906), graduated from the University of Virginia and practiced law in St. Louis. He served as captain under General Frost in the Missouri Volunteer Militia and was captured at Camp Jackson. After his release, he left St. Louis and joined the Confederate army, serving as a captain in the Second and Ninth Kentucky Cavalry. He commanded the escort that guarded Confederate President Jefferson Davis when he tried to escape at the end of the Civil War. They were captured at Irwinsville, Georgia, on May 10, 1865. After living in New Orleans, Campbell returned to St. Louis in 1878, where he practiced law and served on the city council. See Winter, *Civil War in Missouri*, 119n141.

John Archibald Campbell (1811–89) was born in Georgia and attended West Point, but left after three years due to the death of his father. He practiced law and served in the Alabama legislature. When President Franklin Pierce appointed him to the Supreme Court in 1853, Campbell immediately freed his own slaves. Known as conservative and able to compromise, he ruled on the Dred Scott case, which was argued by Montgomery Blair. Campbell tried to make peace during the Fort Sumter crisis, then resigned to practice law in New Orleans. Confederate President Jefferson Davis appointed him assistant secretary of war in 1862. He was one of the peace commissioners sent to meet with Lincoln and Seward in the unsuccessful 1865 Hampton Roads Peace Conference. At the end of the war, he was held at Fort Pulaski for six months, then returned to the practice of law in New Orleans. See Faust, *Historical Times*, 108; Denney, *Civil War Years*, 555; and Laas, *Wartime Washington*, 472.

Robert Campbell (1804–79) was born in Ireland and emigrated to join his brother, Hugh, in America. Campbell contracted lung infections, and Dr. Bernard Farrar in St. Louis (father of Franklin Dick's friends Bernard and Benjamin Farrar) suggested that his health would improve in the Rocky Mountains. He assisted on expeditions and became a fur trader, writing a series of letters to his brother describing his experiences. With a group of other wealthy St. Louisans, he supported Frémont's expedition to California in 1848, after which Frémont won election as senator. Campbell became a prominent businessman in the elite society of St. Louis and stood as a Conditional Unionist when secession began, supporting the Crittenden pro-slavery compromise, but not advocating secession. Campbell presided over a Conditional Unionist meeting held in front of the courthouse on January 12, 1861. The group endorsed either allowing slavery or having Missouri join with the South. After Lyon captured Camp Jackson, Campbell and others met with the mayor, Daniel Taylor, to find out how General Harney's conciliatory position could be supported and how Lyon could be removed from his post. Campbell changed his position to pro-Union as the war continued. See Gerteis, *Civil War St. Louis*, 73, 81, 115, 139, 215, 225.

Edward Richard Sprigg Canby (1817–73) was born in Kentucky and graduated from West Point. He served in the Mexican-American War and on the frontier, where he was placed in command of the Department of New Mexico in 1861, winning the battle of Glorieta Pass (called the Gettysburg of the West) and stopping the Confederate invasion of New Mexico. As the Civil War began, Canby was promoted to brigadier general and named Assistant Adjutant General in Washington. In July 1863, he was sent to control the New York draft riots. As major general and commander of the Military Division of West Mississippi after 1864, he captured Mobile and accepted the surrender of Confederate Generals Richard Taylor and Edmund Kirby Smith. After the war, as an army brigadier general and commander of the Department of the Columbia on a peace mission to the Modoc Indians in Siskiyou, California, he was killed on April 11, 1873. See Laas, *Wartime Washington,* 112–13, 441; Faust, *Historical Times,* 111; Katcher, *Civil War Source Book,* 267; Grant, *Personal Memoirs,* 646–47; and Denney, *Civil War Years,* 50, 551–52, 564, 567, 572.

The Rev. **Thomas Chalmers** (1780–1847) was a Scottish preacher and lecturer in mathematics and science. After the deaths of his brother and sister and ill himself, his interests shifted from mathematics to theology. He taught at the universities of St. Andrews and Edinburgh and lectured in London. He was one of the originators of the Free Church of Scotland. Franklin Dick was reading his sermons and early writings, *Sermons for Public Occasions.* See Wikipedia, s.v. "Thomas Chalmers."

Salmon P. Chase (1808–73) was born in New Hampshire, studied law in Washington DC, and practiced law in Cincinnati, Ohio. He frequently defended fugitive slaves at no cost and was a founder of the Liberty and Free Soil parties. He was elected to the U.S. Senate (1849–55, 1960–61) and was governor of Ohio (1855–59). He resigned from the Senate in 1861 when Lincoln named him secretary of the treasury, despite his having no financial background. To finance the war, Chase first used private loans, then war bonds marketed by Philadelphia banker Jay Cooke. As sources of capital disappeared and the government spent about $2.5 million a day for the war, Chase in 1862 printed federal paper money, called greenbacks, backed by Treasury gold under the Legal Tender Act in 1862. His picture was on the first bills as a subtle campaign for a possible future run for the presidency. Previously, individual states and banks had printed paper money. Chase expanded the treasury, and Congress passed the first Internal Revenue Act for a 3 percent income tax. He squabbled with Seward and was a contender for the presidential nomination against Lincoln in 1864. He resigned in 1864 due to conflicts with the president. Lincoln then made him chief justice of the Supreme Court (1864–73), where he presided over the impeachment trial of President Andrew Johnson in 1868. See Faust, *Historical Times,* 132; Laas, *Wartime Washington,* 130, 199, 217, 340, 399, 429.

William Mordecai Cooke (1823–63) was from a Virginia family who had been in America since 1650. He practiced law in St. Louis, where he married Eliza von Phul, moved to Hannibal, was elected judge of the Common Pleas Court, and was active in politics opposing Frank Blair. In 1861, Cooke was sent by Governor Jackson as a commissioner to Confederate President Davis, then returned to Missouri on Governor Jackson's military staff at Boonville, Carthage, and Wilson's Creek. Cooke was elected to the Confederate congress in 1861, serving until his death in 1863. His wife was detained by Franklin Dick when he served as provost marshal general. See Winter, *Civil War in St. Louis*, 138–39; and Gerteis, *Civil War St. Louis*, 181.

George B. Crittenden (1812–80) was born in Kentucky and graduated from West Point. He served in the Black Hawk War, and the Army of the Republic of Texas. He was captured in Mexico after the failure of the Mier Expedition and was released by the intervention of President Andrew Jackson. Crittenden's father, Senator John J. Crittenden, developed the Crittenden Compromise to avert secession and war. Both his father and his younger brother, Thomas L. Crittenden, stayed with the Union, creating a family rift when George Crittenden joined the Confederate army as a major general and was assigned to liberate Kentucky. After the defeat at Mill Springs and rumors of his drunkenness, he was transferred to Mississippi. Crittenden was found drunk at his post at Iuka and was arrested and court-martialed by Major General William J. Hardee. Crittenden resigned on October 23, 1862, and returned to Kentucky. He was a member of the Whig Party and later named State Librarian. See Faust, *Historical Times*, 191–93.

Jefferson Finis Davis (1808–89) was born in Kentucky, graduated from West Point, and served in the northwest. He resigned from the dragoons in 1835 when he eloped with Sarah Knox Taylor, the daughter of his commander and future president, Zachary Taylor. They both became ill, possibly from malaria, on their honeymoon on a Mississippi plantation. Sarah died, and Davis suffered from neuralgia and other maladies from the malaria the rest of his life. He served in the U.S. House of Representatives (1845–45) and married Varina Howell in 1845. He was wounded in the foot during the Mexican-American War and returned to serve as President Franklin Pierce's secretary of war (1853–57) and in the U.S. Senate (1857–61). Davis promoted the idea of importing camels for patrol use in the southwest. After secession, Davis resigned from the Senate and hoped for a military post in the Confederacy; instead, he was surprised to be elected president. As president, he personally supervised military affairs, squabbled with generals, and had six secretaries of war in four years. Stubborn and uncompromising, he was totally loyal to the South, and convinced he was right. He fled from Richmond after the surrender at Appomattox, was captured, and sent to prison at Fort Monroe. Never tried, he was released on $100,000 bail after 720 days. Living in Mississippi, he wrote *The Rise and Fall of the Confederate Government* in 1881. He never asked to have his citizenship restored, but President Jimmy Carter did it for him. See Katcher, *Civil War Source Book,* 268–69; Gerteis, *Civil War St. Louis,* 93; Faust, *Historical Times,* 63–64, 208–10; Cooper, *Jefferson Davis;* Denney, *Civil War Years,* 484, 540, 553–54, 557–59, 561–65, 568–70; and Grant, *Personal Memoirs of U. S. Grant,* 648n20.

Evans Rogers Dick was the third son of Franklin and Myra Dick, born in 1858. He married Elizabeth Tatam and had three children: Fairman, Isabelle Mildred, who married Stuyvesant Fish, and Evans Rogers Jr. He attended the University of Pennsylvania and the Towne Science School, but did not finish. Evans was involved in Dick Brothers, investing with his brothers, until the company failed. He is noted for building Dick's Castle, a copy of the Alhambra Palace, in 1903 in Garrison, New York. See *New York Times News Service – The Baltimore Sun,* August 7, 2005; and family information.

Frank Madison Dick was the fourth son of Franklin and Myra Dick, born in 1860. Frank had attended the University of Pennsylvania, but left during his junior year. He married Julia D. Bullitt and they had two sons, Langhorne and Julian. After Julia left with Julian, Frank raised Langhorne. Frank's second wife was Minette G. Mills; they had no children. He was involved in Dick Brothers for investments with his brothers, then successfully managed his own investments after the company failed. From family information.

Myra Madison Alexander Dick (1832–1918) was the wife of Franklin A. Dick. She was named for her mother, Mira Madison Alexander, the daughter of George Madison, governor of Kentucky. Myra and Franklin Dick had five children: William, Otis (who died at age seven), Evans, Frank, and Myra. See Gerteis, *Civil War St. Louis,* 100; Laas, *Wartime Washington,* 42, 295, 306, 323; and family information.

William Alexander Dick (1855–1945) was the oldest child of Myra and Franklin Dick. He married Caroline Thompson Norris of St. Louis, niece of one of his father's Garesché rivals. Caroline, who was called Carrie, died in 1882 after the birth of their only child, Franklin Archibald Dick II. Carrie's sister, Mai Garesché Norris, raised Franklin until Willie later married Elizabeth Story Jenks. He was involved in the Dick Brothers investment business with his brothers until it failed, and then managed his own investments in Philadelphia until his death in 1945. From family information.

Jubal Anderson Early (1816–94) was born in Virginia and graduated from West Point. He served in the Seminole War, practiced law, and served in the state legislature. He opposed secession, but when Virginia decided to secede, stayed loyal to his state and entered the Confederate army as a colonel, then he rose to the rank of lieutenant general. From Virginia, he raided into Maryland and Pennsylvania, burning Chambersburg, Pennsylvania in return for the devastation of the Shenandoah Valley by Union forces. He also burned Montgomery Blair's house and raided Francis P. Blair Sr.'s house in Silver Spring, Maryland. Early's goal was to invade Washington, but Grant sent reinforcements and Early retreated. After the war, Early escaped to Mexico and Canada, but returned to practice law in Lynchburg, and to write historical essays that were part of a literary movement that defended Southern leaders and the Southern way of life as noble and virtuous. He defended Robert E. Lee against James Longstreet in his writings and asserted that states' rights rather than slavery was the cause of the war. Early wrote his memoirs in 1867. See Faust, *Historical Times,* 233–34, 444–45; and Denney, *Civil War Years,* 296–97.

John Ericsson (1803–89), a Swedish immigrant inventor and engineer, designed a high-speed English locomotive, a screw propeller ship, and the ironclad USS *Monitor,* which was built at a Brooklyn shipyard for $275,000. It was a flat armored ship with a revolving turret and two eleven-inch guns; it sat eighteen inches above the water, and was 172 feet long and 41½ feet wide. The Confederates had raised the abandoned Union frigate *Merrimac* and covered its wooden sides with iron, renaming it the *Virginia* and placing it under the command of Confederate Commodore Franklin Buchanan, first superintendent of the U.S. Naval Academy. The CSS *Virginia,* looking like a huge half-submerged crocodile, entered Hampton Roads, sinking the USS *Cumberland,* and setting afire the USS *Congress.* Buchanan ordered the sailors rescued, one of whom was his brother, McKean Buchanan. The USS *Monitor,* under Lieutenant John L. Worden, arrived and fought with the *Virginia* on March 9, 1862. The battle was inconclusive, and the *Virginia* left for Norfolk. The long-term effect was that the blockade remained intact. Later that year, the *Monitor* sank in a storm. The *Virginia* was burned when the Confederates evacuated Norfolk. See Faust, *Historical Times,* 246, 335, 504, 787; and Denney, *Civil War Years,* 47–48.

Richard Stoddert Ewell (1817–72) was born in Georgetown and graduated from West Point. Nicknamed "Old Baldy," he served as a lieutenant colonel in the Mexican-American War. Ewell resigned from the U.S. Army to serve in the Confederate army, where he was quickly promoted to brigadier general in 1861 and major general in 1862. Ewell fought at the First Battle of Bull Run, Cedar Mountain, the Shenandoah Valley, Seven Days, and Groveton, where he lost a leg. When he returned to duty with a wooden leg, he was promoted to lieutenant general to replace Stonewall Jackson and won a victory at the battle of Winchester. Ewell lost at the battles of Gettysburg, the Wilderness, Spotsylvania, and North Anna, during which time he was wounded twice more. At the battle of Bloody Angle at Spotsylvania, he fell from his horse. Since he was unable to command in the field afterwards, he was transferred to Richmond for defense supervision. He was captured at the Battle of Saylor's Creek on April 6, 1865, during the retreat to Appomattox, and was imprisoned at Fort Warren, Massachusetts. After his release, Ewell retired to a Tennessee farm. See Denney, *Civil*

War Years, 173, 209, 289, 400, 410, 555; and Faust, *Historical Times,* 248–49.

Thomas Ewing Jr. (1829–96) was born in Ohio and raised with William Tecumseh Sherman, who Ewing's parents took in after the death of Sherman's father. Ewing left Brown University to be private secretary to President Zachary Taylor (1849–50), when his father served as secretary of the interior. He practiced law in Cincinnati, then moved to Kansas, where he was elected chief justice of the state supreme court (1861–62). Ewing tried to keep Kansas antislavery and was a delegate to the peace convention in Washington DC in 1861. He then recruited the Eleventh Kansas Volunteers, serving as their colonel. He fought in Fort Wayne, Cane Hill, and Prairie Grove. Ewing is best known for issuing General Order No. 11, which ordered the evacuation of rural areas in four Missouri counties to stop aid to the bushwhacker Colonel Charles Quantrill. All residents had to leave the counties, although those who could prove their loyalty were permitted to settle near a military post. After residents left, their land and houses were burned. The severity of this action caused both sides to hate Ewing. As brigadier general, he held Fort Davidson at Pilot Knob against General Sterling Price and successfully retreated to Rolla. After the Civil War, he practiced law in Washington DC, then Ohio, when he also served in the U.S. Congress (1877–81). See Faust, *Historical Times,* 249–50, 474–76, 602–3, 673; Denney, *Civil War Years,* 319, 463; Brownlee, *Grey Ghosts,* 3–10, 104–8; and Monaghan, *Civil War on the Western Border,* 310–15.

Benjamin Farrar (?–?) was a brother of Bernard Gaines Farrar and a good friend of Franklin Dick and Frank Blair. His father, Dr. Bernard Gaines Farrar Sr., a prominent St. Louis doctor, had five children: John O'Fallon, Benjamin, Bernard G. Jr., James, and Ellen. He and Franklin Dick had several joint real estate ventures over the years. Benjamin Farrar was a pallbearer for Frank Blair. See *Encyclopedia of the History of St. Louis.*

Bernard Gaines Farrar Jr. (1831–1916) was born in St. Louis, the son of a well-known doctor from Virginia. Major Farrar was an aide to General Nathaniel Lyon at Camp Jackson and served with Lyon at the Battle of Wilson's Creek. In October 1861, Farrar was made lieutenant colonel and aide de camp to General Henry Halleck, then provost marshal general for Missouri, serving until October 1862. As provost marshal, Farrar instituted censorship of the press, loyalty oaths, bond fees, and banishment for disloyal citizens. In one case, he ordered federal marshals to seize furniture for non-payment of assessments from William McPheeters' house as a child lay dying. He later dealt with issues of escaped slaves in St. Louis. He recruited and organized the Thirtieth Missouri Infantry, and led Frank Blair's brigade as a brigadier general in the siege of Vicksburg and at Natchez. Farrar also organized a black regiment (Sixth U.S. Colored Heavy Artillery) and was made brigadier general in 1865. He was Assistant U.S. Treasurer at St. Louis under President Harrison. See Brownlee, *Gray Ghosts,*

158–59, 175–76; Gerteis, *Civil War St. Louis*, 172–75, 178, 183, 356–57n5; Winter, *Civil War in St. Louis*, 119; and "Brevet Brigadier General Bernard Gaines Farrar Jr."

Giles Franklin Filley (1815–97), whose ancestors came to America on the *Mayflower*, founded the Excelsior Stove Works with his brother Oliver in September 1849 in St. Louis. By 1859, they were producing 23,000 stoves a year. Giles Filley was one of the 1848 organizers of the Free Soil Party in Missouri. He helped his friend Frank Blair obtain guns, which Filley hid in empty beer barrels for the Union Guards. In 1861, he made thirty cannons for the Union. In 1862, Schofield had Filley serve on his assessment board to fine disloyal people. Filley lobbied in Washington to support the banishment of the McPheeters family, who were Southern sympathizers. Filley published a "Card-to-the-Public" in the newspapers, explaining the Stove Company's position in the union strikes of 1864 and praising the men who continued to work in his shop. Filley was a key investor in the Kansas Pacific Railroad. See Gerteis, *Civil War St. Louis*, 41, 80, 185, 255–56; and "Marcus L. Filley (1807–1892) Papers, 1832–1915, Biographical Note."

Oliver Dwight Filley (1806–81) learned his father's trade as a tinner and went into partnership with his brother, Giles, in stove manufacturing in St. Louis. Filley became a leader in the Republican Party and was elected mayor of St. Louis in 1858. He was a member of the Committee of Safety with Blair and Dick. He instituted the Fire Alarm Telegraph System, the first paid Fire Department, and horse car railway lines. See Gerteis, *Civil War St. Louis*, 80; and "Marcus L. Filley (1807–1892) Papers, 1832–1915, Biographical Note."

Thomas C. Fletcher (1827–99) was born in Missouri and moved to St. Louis in 1856 as a land agent for the Pacific Railroad. Fletcher practiced law and became involved in politics; he was active in forming the Republican Party with Frank Blair and Gratz Brown, and attended the 1860 Republican National Convention. During the Civil War, he served as assistant provost marshal, and in 1862, recruited and commanded the Thirty-first Missouri Infantry in Frank Blair's brigade and fought in the Vicksburg Campaign. Fletcher was wounded and captured in December 1862 and spent five months in Richmond's Libby Prison before being exchanged. He then fought at Chattanooga, Lookout Mountain, and Atlanta before returning to St. Louis to recover from an illness. Rosecrans appointed Fletcher to command two volunteer regiments against Sterling Price's invasion. He fought successfully at Pilot Knob and was promoted to brigadier general. Fletcher also participated in Sherman's March to the Sea. In 1864, he was elected governor of Missouri in the first election since the state was placed under martial law at the beginning of the war. He issued an emancipation proclamation with a sixty-gun salute on January 14, 1865, and returned the state to civil law. The state's new constitution required a test oath of loyalty, which caused great controversy in Missouri. After serving as governor, Fletcher resumed his law practice in

St. Louis. See Winter, *Civil War in St. Louis,* 127; Gerteis, *Civil War St. Louis,* 292, 307–38; and Foner, *Reconstruction,* 42–43.

John Buchanan Floyd (1806–63) was born in Virginia. A lawyer and politician, he was governor of Virginia (1849–52) and secretary of war under President Buchanan (1857–60). He was accused of misusing Indian funds and sending federal arms to the South prior to the Civil War. As a Confederate brigadier general at Fort Donelson, he commandeered river steamers and fled across the Cumberland River with Brigadier General Gideon Pillow, a political appointee and inept soldier. They wanted to avoid the shame of being the first Confederate officers to surrender, and left Confederate Brigadier General Simon B. Buckner in command. Grant later told Buckner that the two were so incompetent that they "will do us more good commanding you fellows." Jefferson Davis suspended Pillow and Floyd for their desertion of Fort Donelson without a formal hearing, at a time when other deserters were shot. See Denney, *Civil War Years,* 127–28; and Faust, *Historical Times,* 265n29.

Andrew Hull Foote (1806–63) was born in Connecticut and entered the navy in 1822. He traveled to China, the South Pacific, and Africa, where he was active in capturing slavers and trying to break up the slave trade (1847–51). In August 1861, he was put in charge of naval defense on the Upper Mississippi River, building and refitting ships, manning and supplying them for service. Flag Officer Foote and his flotilla of seven gunboats, together with General Grant, captured Fort Henry, one of a string of small low-lying Confederate forts on the Tennessee River. Foote was wounded in his foot at the Battle of Fort Donelson on February 14, 1862, and had to remain on shore during the next battle for Island Number 10, another Union success. In June 1862, after failing health, he was named rear admiral and voted the Thanks of Congress, a citation that honored fifteen men in the navy and fifteen in the army between 1861 and 1866. In 1863, he was appointed commander of the South Atlantic Blockading Squadron, but died from his old wounds at Fort Donelson before arriving to take command. See Laas, *Wartime Washington,* 71; Faust, *Historical Times,* 265–66, 751–52; and Denney, *Civil War Years,* 296.

Nathan Bedford Forrest (1821–77) was born in Tennessee, the son of a blacksmith. He rose from poverty, supporting his family from the age of sixteen. Forrest, intimidatingly tall for the time, at six feet one and one-half inches, educated himself after only six months of school, becoming a successful planter and slave trader by the beginning of the war. Forrest enlisted with his eldest son, Willie, and rose quickly in the Confederate army to brigadier general in 1862, major general in 1863, and lieutenant general by 1865. A brilliant and feared cavalry leader, Forrest was known as the "Wizard of the Saddle," though he did not have a military background. He thought that most men looked at battle as horrifying, so he tried to attack before expected, and to shock and undermine the enemy as quickly and fiercely as possible. Disagreeing with the other Confederate commanders, Forrest escaped with every one of his men from Fort Donelson, captured Murfreesboro, and cut Union communications in West Tennessee. Forrest's controversial massacre of both black and white soldiers at Fort Pillow after the commander refused to surrender horrified both the North and South. Forrest also took Brice's Crossroads, and defended Tupelo, Mississippi. Known for his two Tennessee raids in 1862 and 1863, Forrest was finally captured at Selma, Alabama. Forrest's eloquent words at Meridian, Mississippi, were cherished by his troops: "Men, you have been good soldiers; a man who has been a good soldier can be a good citizen. I shall go back to my home upon the Mississippi River, there to begin life anew, and to you good old Confederates, I want to say that the latchstring of Bedford Forrest will always be on the outside of the door." He had lost all his wealth during the war, and returned home to attempt to keep his old world intact, instead of fleeing to serve Maximilian in Mexico, as did some other Confederate officers. Forrest tried various enterprises, all of which ended in bankruptcy. Forrest was the first Grand Wizard of the Invisible Empire of the Ku Klux Klan, and was questioned by a Congressional Investigating Committee on June 27, 1871, where he stated that he attempted to disband the Klan, though he was never a member. He spoke out repeatedly against racial discrimination in the last years of his life. When he died in 1877, his funeral procession was almost two miles long; Jefferson Davis was a pallbearer. See Katcher, *Civil War Source Book*, 271; Faust, *Historical Times*, 269–71; Denney, *Civil War Years*, 16, 97, 449, 459, 481–83, 505, 553–56; and Hurst, *Nathan Bedford Forrest*, passim, quote at 25.

Jessie Benton Frémont (1824–1902) was the vivacious and ambitious daughter of Thomas Hart Benton, leader of the anti-slavery Democrats in Missouri. She eloped with John Frémont, tried to make him assert himself, and turned him into "The Pathfinder" in California with her father's help. After Frémont, head of the Department of the West, took it on his own authority to issue an emancipation proclamation with which Lincoln disagreed, Jessie hurried to Washington to persuade Lincoln not to cancel it, but was unsuccessful. Lincoln was concerned that emancipation would antagonize the border states, and eventually removed Frémont from office. Jessie was a strong supporter of her husband through all his failures, even after his death, when she wrote magazine articles to exonerate him. See Goodwin, *Team of Rivals*, 392–93; Gerteis, *Civil War St. Louis*, 137–61; Winter, *Civil War in St. Louis*, 71–73; and Chaffin, *Pathfinder*.

John Charles Frémont (1813–90) was born in Georgia, was expelled from the College of Charleston, and was an instructor in the U.S. Navy (1833–35), then joined a U.S. Army team surveying and exploring the West. In 1841, Frémont eloped with Jessie Benton, daughter of Missouri senator Thomas Hart Benton, a longtime friend of the Blairs. In 1842, Frémont led his first expedition, mapping the Oregon Trail. His wife's ambition (and the assistance of his influential father-in-law) helped him get funding for his expeditions, and widespread circulation of his reports earned him the nickname "The Pathfinder." Frémont was elected a U.S. Senator in 1850. In 1856, he was the newly formed Republican Party's first candidate for president, losing to Buchanan. With the help of his political connections, Frémont was appointed major general in the U.S. Army and given command of the western military district, based in St. Louis. Frémont replaced General William Harney, who had negotiated the Price-Harney Truce with State Guard General Sterling Price to keep Missouri neutral. Lyon and other pro-Unionists were unhappy with the deal, and Frank Blair sent Franklin Dick to Washington to lobby for Lyon and ask for Harney's dismissal. Frémont was made commander on July 3, 1861; a month later, Lyon was killed at the Battle of Wilson's Creek and Frémont was blamed for his death, having failed to send troops Lyon had requested. Frank Blair tried to help Frémont deal with the mounting problems in Missouri, but the situation worsened. In August 1861, Frémont instituted martial law in Missouri, confiscated property of secessionists, and freed the slaves. A turmoil resulted, with Blair twice arrested and jailed by Frémont, eventually ending the long friendship of the two families. President Lincoln rescinded the orders and relieved Frémont of his command. Frémont served in West Virginia (1862–64), and was nominated for president in 1864 by the anti-Lincoln Radical Republicans, but withdrew on the condition that U.S. Postmaster General Montgomery Blair was removed from office. After the war, Frémont became involved in railroads, then was territorial governor of Arizona. He was accused of corruption, lost a fortune, and died penniless. See Smith, *Francis Preston Blair*, 293–306; Faust, *Historical Times*, 291–92; Goodwin, *Team of Rivals*, 186–87, 389–96, 391–93, 428–30, 658–59; Parrish, *History of Missouri*, 3:16–22; and Chaffin, *Pathfinder*.

Daniel Marsh Frost (1823–1900) graduated from West Point and served in the Mexican-American War and in Europe. After resigning from the army in 1853, he moved to St. Louis, where he entered the manufacturing business and served in the state legislature (1854–58). In 1858, Governor Jackson appointed him brigadier general in the state militia and placed him in command of the First Military District, which included St. Louis. Frost supported Governor Jackson's secessionist views and worked secretly with him to set up a militia training center at Camp Jackson. He was also part of the plot to capture the St. Louis arsenal. Frost surrendered and was arrested, along with other men, at Camp Jackson, but was paroled and exchanged. In 1861, Frost became a brigadier general in the Confederate army after being assessed by General Halleck. In 1863, Franklin Dick banished Frost's wife, Lily, from St. Louis; Frost left his post and moved his family to Mexico, Cuba, and Canada. He tried to re-enlist in the Confederate army, but was unable due to rumors of his desertion. After President Andrew Johnson pardoned him in 1865, he returned to St. Louis, where he took up farming and was active in Democratic politics. See Gerteis, *Civil War St. Louis*, 105–14, 180–81; Winter, *Civil War in St. Louis*, 140; and Faust, *Historical Times*, 293–94.

Hamilton Rowan Gamble (1798–1864), as presiding judge of the Supreme Court of Missouri, was the only dissenter in the Dred Scott case. A prominent St. Louis attorney and brother-in-law of politician Edward Bates, he was Missouri secretary of state, and a member of the Missouri House of Representatives. Gamble tried to keep peace between the Northern and Southern factions, and worked to keep Missouri in the Union. In 1861, he was elected to the state constitutional convention, which appointed him provisional governor of Missouri when Claiborne F. Jackson joined the secession party and was forced out of office. Gamble proposed a controversial plan of gradual emancipation. He served as governor until his death in Jefferson City, Missouri, on January 31, 1864. See Brownlee, *Gray Ghosts*, 20; Parrish, *History of Missouri*, 3:9; Gerteis, *Civil War St. Louis*, 81, 88–89, 142–43; and Faust, *Historical Times*, 297.

Alexander John Peter Garesché (1823–96) was a St. Louis attorney (sometimes called Alphabet Garesché in the newspaper), who participated in the state militia muster at Camp Jackson, and was arrested and paroled. His family was divided by the war; he sympathized with the South, as did another brother, Frederick Paul, a Jesuit priest whose sermons were so dangerously pro-Confederate that the Jesuits had to send him away from St. Louis during the war. Their youngest brother, Ferdinand Louis, was arrested with Alexander J. P. at the state militia muster at Camp Jackson, and was sent home in the custody of his parents. The oldest brother, Julius Peter, a West Pointer, served as a lieutenant colonel under Union General Rosecrans and was killed at Murfreesboro. Their cousin, Peter Bauduy Garesché, fled from St. Louis and became the inspector of the Confederate powder magazine in Columbia, South Carolina. Alexander J. P.'s and Peter Bauduy's wives were assessed as disloyal persons by General Henry Halleck in December 1861. After the war, Alexander J. P. refused to take the lawyer's oath of loyalty to the new "Drake" constitution, and his was the first test case heard by the state supreme court, State v. Garesché (1865). The state ruled against him, and he assisted with the next test case, Cummings v. Missouri (1866), for the Catholic archbishop who refused to take the clergy oath. That case went to the U.S. Supreme Court, assisted by Montgomery Blair, where the oath order was overturned. This forced the state supreme court to reverse the decision in the Garesché case. After that, Peter Bauduy Garesché returned to St. Louis to practice law. In his journals, Franklin Dick is quite frank about his dislike of all the Garesché family. It must have been difficult for his eldest son, William Alexander, when he married the daughter of Alexander J. P.'s sister. William's only child, born three years before Franklin Dick died, was named Franklin Archibald Dick for his grandfather. See Gerteis, *Civil War St. Louis*, 316–20; Holland, *Garesché, Du Bauduy and Des Chappelles Families*, 172–74; and family information.

Hugh Garland (1805–64) was a merchant in Petersburg, Virginia, who had financial problems in 1847 and moved to St. Louis, where he practiced law. He was married to Anne Powell Burwell, who had started a school in their house in Virginia to support the family during Garland's financial reverses. Captured at Camp Jackson, Garland rose to be a colonel in the Confederate army and was killed in battle at Franklin, Tennessee. See Winter, *Civil War in St. Louis*, 128; and Scott and Fitzpatrick, "American Women's History"; and Larimer, "Some Notes on the Burwell, Turnbull, Manlove, Farmer, Ferguson, and Gray Families."

Samuel T. Glover (1813–84) kept a rifle in plain sight in his law office at Fifth and Olive in St. Louis to remind clients that he was a Unionist. A friend of Franklin Dick's, Glover was a member of the original St Louis Committee of Safety. He strongly advised Lyon not to attack Camp Jackson and to deal with it legally with a writ of replevin to reclaim the stolen federal property, against the views of the others. He followed a conservative course on the political issue of emancipation and opposed assessments of disloyal persons. In 1865, he refused to take the new constitution's oath for lawyers and was fined $500. See Gerteis, *Civil War St. Louis*, 80–81, 96, 100–101, 319.

Ulysses Simpson Grant (1822–85) was born Hiram Ulysses Grant in Ohio; his name was accidentally changed when he entered West Point. He served in the Mexican-American War, then on the Pacific Coast, away from his beloved wife, Julia. He resigned in 1854 due to a conflict with his commander. He failed at several jobs, ending as a clerk in his father-in-law's tannery. At the start of the Civil War, he was named a colonel in the Illinois Infantry, then sent to Missouri, rising from colonel to brigadier general, with great success in battles at Fort Henry, Fort Donelson, Shiloh, Vicksburg, and Lookout Mountain. Rumors of his drinking followed his career, but he kept Lincoln informed of his plans and kept fighting. When he was given command of the Union armies as lieutenant general, he sent Sherman into Georgia, Butler to Richmond, and Sheridan into Virginia's Shenandoah Valley, while he went after Lee, finally forcing Lee's surrender at Appomattox, giving generous terms. Grant was commissioned the first full general since George Washington. He was elected president in 1868, serving two terms that were marred by corruption in his administration. After retiring, he and his wife, Julia, traveled around the world, arriving destitute in New York after being swindled by his business partners. Mark Twain suggested he write his memoirs, which he finished a week before his death. See Faust, *Historical Times*, 320; Winter, *Civil War in St. Louis*, 8–13; Gerteis, *Civil War St. Louis*, 242–46, 101–3; and Grant, *Personal Memoirs*.

Martin Green (1815–63), moved from Virginia to Missouri in the 1830s and ran a sawmill with his brothers. He became a Missouri guerilla fighter at the outbreak of the Civil War, serving with Confederate general Sterling Price at

Lexington, Pea Ridge, Corinth, and Iuka. Frémont was blamed for not stopping Green's marauding in northern Missouri. Eventually named brigadier general, Green was wounded and killed at the siege of Vicksburg. See Monaghan, *Civil War on the Western Border*, 199; and Faust, *Historical Times*, 323.

Willard Preble Hall (1820–82), a Yale attorney, served in Congress from 1846-1852 and practiced law in St. Joseph. Hall was lieutenant governor when Hamilton Gamble died in January, 1864. Hall completed Gamble's term of office, resisting Sterling Price's raids on the state. He had the state legislature authorize the voters to call a new constitutional convention to decide on emancipation and the electoral franchise oaths. Hall practiced law after the war. See Gerteis, *Civil War St. Louis*, 291, 307.

Henry Wagner Halleck (1815–72) was born in New York and graduated from West Point. He observed the French as a member of the Corps of Engineers, publishing several books and a translation of a book on Napoleon, for which he was called "Old Brains." He served as secretary of state for the military government in California and helped to frame the state constitution. He then became a San Francisco gold rush lawyer and writer. In 1861 he was commissioned a major general in the U.S. Army, succeeding Frémont as commander of the Department of Missouri. He declared martial law in St. Louis and assessed disloyal persons, creating a Board of Assessors in December 1861 that compiled a list of 300 names to contact to raise $10,000. If the people named did not make a contribution to the funds to support refugees in St. Louis, they were assessed an amount by the board, based on three degrees of disloyalty: joining the Confederate army, giving direct aid to the confederacy, and supporting the confederacy in print or speech. On December 20, 1861, sixty-four people received their "Christmas" notices of assessments based on tax records of property. If the assessment was not paid, a penalty was charged, then the property was seized and sold. By the summer of 1862, the funds from assessments were also covering payments to wounded Union soldiers, families of those killed, and other military expenses around the state. After complaints, President Lincoln suspended assessments in December 1862. Halleck was made general in chief in July 1862, and chief of staff in 1864. See Monaghan, *Civil War on the Western Border*, 208; Katcher, *Civil War Source Book*, 273, Faust, *Historical Times*, 332; Gerteis, *Civil War St. Louis*, 172–77; Parrish, *History of Missouri*, 3:68–69; Freehling, *Road to Disunion*, 150; and Winter, *Civil War in St. Louis*, 82–83.

William J. Hardee (1815–73) was born to a Georgia plantation family, graduated from West Point, and served in the Mexican-American and Seminole Wars. Hardee was famous for a book he published in 1855 that explained Napoleonic tactics of war and was used by both Union and Confederate troops. When the Civil War began, he resigned from the Union army and became a Confederate brigadier general. He had a brigade stationed at Pocahontas, Arkansas, which

President Jefferson Davis planned to use with Brigadier General Gideon Pillow's men from the Mississippi River and the forces under Price and McCulloch to defeat Nathaniel Lyon in Springfield, Missouri. Hardee successfully commanded at Shiloh, Antietam, Perryville, Stones River, Chattanooga, Atlanta, and commanded the Department of South Carolina, Georgia, and Florida, resisting Sherman at the end of the Civil War. When Sherman approached Savannah, Hardee escaped across the Savannah River using rice flats as pontoon boats. Hardee retreated from Charleston, Columbia, and then fought at Averasboro, losing to the Union forces. "Old Reliable" was captured April 25, 1865, at the Battle of Bentonville, where his only son was killed. Hardee spent the rest of his life on an Alabama plantation. See Faust, *Historical Times*, 338.

John Brooks Henderson (1826–1913) served two terms in the Missouri legislature (1848–50; 1856–58), and was a brigadier general in the State Militia in 1861. In 1862, he was appointed to fill the U.S. Senate seat vacated by Trusten Polk when he was expelled for supporting the rebellion. He was elected to the Senate in 1863 and served until 1869. On January 11, 1864, Henderson proposed the Thirteenth Amendment to the Constitution to abolish slavery. He was one of seven Republican senators whose votes defeated the impeachment of Andrew Johnson, which ruined Henderson's political aspirations. In 1875, he was appointed U.S. district attorney. See Gerteis, *Civil War St. Louis*, 329; Denney, *Civil War Years*, 359; Wikipedia, s.v. "John Brooks Henderson"; and Shoemaker, "John Brooks Henderson."

David E. Herold (1842–65) was born in Maryland; he had worked as a druggist's clerk, but was out of work. He was a companion of John Wilkes Booth and had been involved in the plot to kidnap Lincoln and exchange him for prisoners in Richmond. In the assassination plot, Herold was to help Lewis Paine escape through Maryland after killing Secretary of State William H. Seward. Instead, he fled, met with Booth, and helped him escape. Herold surrendered when the pair was surrounded in a burning tobacco shed at the Richard H. Garrett farm near Port Royal, Virginia. Herold was tried by a military court and hanged on July 7, 1865. See Faust, *Historical Times*, 440–41; Katcher, *Civil War Source Book*, 281–82; and Denney, *Civil War Years*, 559, 563.

Ambrose Powell Hill (1825–65) was born in Virginia. After graduating from West Point, he served in the Mexican-American War, the Third Seminole War, and other military posts. He resigned from the U.S. Army to become a Confederate colonel and was quickly promoted to brigadier general. He was known for his red battle shirt and his hard attacks in battle. Hill fought at Williamsburg, and was promoted to major general, commanding Hill's Light Division. They fought in the battles of Seven Days Campaign, Gaines Mill, and Frayser's Farm. Joining with Confederate Major General Stonewall Jackson, Hill fought at Cedar Mountain, Second Battle of Bull Run, Antietam, Fredericksburg, and Chancellorsville.

There he took command when Jackson was wounded, and was himself wounded as he carried Jackson to the rear. As lieutenant general, he did not perform well at the battles of Gettysburg, Bristoe Station, the Wilderness, North Ana, Cold Harbor, and Petersburg. Confederate General A. P. Hill was killed on April 2 as he returned from sick leave to rally his men. Both Stonewall Jackson and Robert E. Lee called for Hill and his Light Division to help as they were dying. See Katcher, *Civil War Source Book,* 274; Faust, *Historical Times,* 360–61; Denney, *Civil War Years,* 185, 213, 280, 282, 289, 296, 298, 333, 399, 429, 448, 553.

John Bell Hood (1831–79) was born in Kentucky and graduated from West Point. He served in the U.S. Army cavalry (1855–61), then transferred to the Confederate army (1861), rising to the rank of brigadier general. He commanded the Fourth Texas Infantry in Virginia, which was called "Hood's Texas Brigade." Hood rose to a division commander in the Army of Northern Virginia. Hood's success in battle was due to being in the right place at the right time; he was also popular with his men, who followed him when he seized the initiative. He was wounded in the left arm at Gettysburg and lost his right leg at Chickamauga, but returned to duty as a lieutenant general, leading the Army of the Tennessee. After the war he married and became a merchant in New Orleans; along with his wife and eldest child, he died in a yellow-fever epidemic of 1879, leaving ten children (three sets of twins) orphaned. His memoirs were published to support his children. See Faust, *Historical Times,* 368–69; Denney, *Civil War Years,* 437, 439, 445, 494–96, 505, 509.

David Hunter (1802–86) was born in Washington DC and graduated from West Point. He was a plain, calm soldier, who dressed in a regulation double-breasted military coat with an old-fashioned linen stock around his neck. While serving at Fort Dearborn, he married Maria Kinzie, the daughter of John Kinzie, the first Chicago settler. He resigned from the army in 1836 and moved to Illinois, where he worked in real estate. He rejoined the army in 1842. In 1860, Hunter began corresponding with Abraham Lincoln, discussing his strong anti-slavery views. Hunter (who had his mustache dyed to match his brown wig) accompanied Lincoln on his inaugural trip from Springfield, Illinois, to Washington DC. In Boston, Hunter's collarbone was broken by the mob of people crowding around Lincoln. He served in the Union army and was severely wounded in the First Battle of Bull Run. He took over command of the Western Department from Frémont and later controlled the Department of the South, where he started the First South Carolina, African Descent, the first Negro regiment to be used as guards on plantations and towns, giving him the nickname "Black David." In 1862, he issued General Order Number 11, which proclaimed the freedom of rebels' slaves in Georgia, Florida, and South Carolina; it was rescinded in ten days by Lincoln. The Confederates hated Hunter thereafter, and Jefferson Davis said he would be executed if caught. Hunter served in the

Shenandoah Valley Campaign and, while in Virginia, burned and looted the Virginia Military Institute, horrifying both North and South. Hunter served in the honor guard at Lincoln's funeral and headed the commission that tried the men who assassinated Lincoln. See Faust, *Historical Times*, 376; Denney, *Civil War Years*, 93, 168, 206, 422–23, 429, 567; and Katcher, *Civil War Source Book*, 158–60.

Robert Mercer Taliaferro Hunter (1809–87) was born in Virginia, where he practiced law and entered politics. A Democrat, he served in the state legislature and the U.S. House (1837–43, 1845–47) and Senate (1847–61) as a leading Southern conservative. He resigned in 1861 and was named Confederate secretary of state, then became a senator. He was sent to meet with Lincoln and Seward at the Hampton Roads Peace Conference in 1865. He was imprisoned at Fort Pulaski with Campbell after the war. He had heavy financial losses from his place being looted during and after the war. After being freed, Hunter served as Virginia's state treasurer and as port collector for Rappahannock, Virginia. See Faust, *Historical Times*, 376; and Laas, *Wartime Washington*, 472.

Claiborne Fox Jackson (1806–62) was born in Kentucky. In 1822, he moved to Missouri, where he practiced law and owned a business. After serving in the Black Hawk War, he served in the state legislature. He was elected governor of Missouri in 1860. He did not openly call for secession, but argued that Missouri should go with the south if the Union were dissolved. After Nathaniel Lyon disbanded Camp Jackson, Governor Jackson called out 5,000 militia to "drive out ignominiously the invaders." Jackson was deposed by the legislature in July 1861, but sustained his exiled rebel government of Missouri and served as brigadier general in the Confederate army. He resigned in failing health and died of cancer in Little Rock on December 6, 1862. Gerteis, *Civil War St. Louis*, 67–125; McPherson, *Battle Cry of Freedom*, 290–93; Monaghan, *Civil War on the Western Border*, 123–41; and Faust, *Historical Times*, 389.

Charles Rainford "Doc" Jennison (1834–84) was born in New York; he moved to Wisconsin, where he practiced medicine, then moved to the Kansas Territory in 1857. He was the leader of Jennison's Jayhawkers and a fanatical abolitionist hero of the Free-Soilers and the guerrilla war. Jennison was colonel of the Seventh Kansas Volunteer Cavalry. When Halleck complained about Jennison's military behavior, Jennison was transferred from Missouri to Humboldt, Kansas. He resigned and encouraged his men to desert; he was arrested April 17, 1862, and sent to the St. Louis Myrtle Street prison, where he was treated with deference and received frequent visits from his wife, daughter, and other supporters. He was released April 25, 1862, and opened a livestock business in Leavenworth, Kansas, where the horses were said to be "out of Missouri by Jennison." See Winter, *Civil War in St. Louis*, 83–85; and Monaghan, *Civil War on the Western Border*, 118–20.

Andrew Johnson (1808–75) was born in North Carolina and worked as a tailor in Tennessee. He served in the House of Representatives (1843–53), as governor of Tennessee (1853–57), and in the U.S. Senate (1857–62) as a pro-Union Democrat. After Tennessee seceded and was a divided battleground, Johnson remained in the Senate and Lincoln named him military governor of Tennessee. In 1864, he was nominated as vice president, becoming president after Lincoln's assassination. After the end of Civil War, he gave pardons to all who would take the oath of loyalty, requiring special presidential pardons for rebel leaders and the wealthy, which many Radical Republicans thought to be too lenient. During his administration, the Civil Rights Act of 1866, the original Reconstruction bill, and the Fourteenth Amendment were passed, with constant fighting between Johnson and Congress. The Radical Republicans imposed military rule on the Southern states and restrictions on the president, and tried to impeach him. He was cleared by one vote. After his term as president, he was elected to the Tennessee Senate in 1875, but died after only a few months in office. See Faust, *Historical Times*, 395–96; Laas, *Wartime Washington*, 480–84, 496; and Denney, *Civil War Years*, 133, 542.

Reverdy Johnson (1796–1876) was born in Maryland, practiced law in Baltimore, and was known for his outstanding memory. He was deputy attorney general of Maryland (1816–17) and chief commissioner of insolvent debtors in Maryland in 1817. He served in the state Senate (1821–29) and the U.S. Senate (1845–49). He represented the slave-owning defendant in the Dred Scott case and served as attorney general under President Zachary Taylor (1849–50). In 1861, sympathetic to the South, but devoted to the Union, he was a delegate to the Peace Convention and worked to keep Maryland in the Union. Johnson served in the Maryland House of Representatives (1860–61), the U.S. Senate (1863–68), and as minister to England (1868–69). He resumed the practice of law after his return, defending many Southerners. See Faust, *Historical Times*, 398; and Laas, *Wartime Washington*, 112–14.

Albert Sidney Johnston (1803–62) was born in Kentucky and graduated from West Point. He served in the Black Hawk and Mexican-American Wars. After resigning from the service to take care of his dying wife, he joined the forces in the Republic of Texas and served as secretary of war. He rejoined the regular army and was made brigadier general after the campaign against the Mormons in Utah. At the outbreak of the Civil War, he resigned, but did not leave his post in the west until his successor arrived, giving him the reputation of the finest soldier in the North or South. A friend of Jefferson Davis, he rode across the country to Richmond, where he was made the second-ranking Confederate general in charge of the western operations. He held the line of defense in Kentucky from the Appalachians to the Mississippi River until defeated at Mill Springs, Forts Henry and Donelson in 1862. At the Battle of Shiloh against Union General-in-Chief Ulysses S. Grant, he was wounded in the leg, and his boot filled with his blood. Continuing with his command, he hid his wound from his men, and bled to death. See Katcher, *Civil War Source Book*, 277–78; Faust, *Historical Times*, 399; and Denney, *Civil War Years*, 74, 150–53.

Joseph Eggleston Johnston (1807–91) was born in Virginia and graduated from West Point. He was wounded by Indians during John Wesley Powell's expedition to Florida, but led a successful retreat, and was then named a first lieutenant in the topographical engineers. Johnston served as a captain under Winfield Scott in the Mexican-American War and was promoted to brigadier general. An old friend of both the Blairs and the Lees, Johnston was named a Confederate brigadier general in 1861. He commanded at Harpers Ferry and the First Battle of Bull Run, but then had a disagreement with President Jefferson Davis over being promoted to full general later than Johnston felt he should have been, based on his previous rank in the U.S. Army. He fought against McClellan in the Peninsula Campaign and at Williamsburg, and was wounded at the Battle of Seven Pines. After recovering, Johnston was named commander of the Department of the West, then the Army of Tennessee, where he retreated to Atlanta pursued by Sherman's troops. President Davis replaced him with Lieutenant General John B. Hood, who then lost battles at Atlanta, Franklin, and Nashville. Johnston was reinstated at the end of the war to the command of the remnant of his troops for the Carolinas Campaign. He met Union Major General Sherman for the first time when they negotiated surrender terms. The first agreement was rejected by President Johnson and his cabinet. Sherman and Johnston had to use the same terms as Lee and Grant for the final surrender. From this beginning, Johnston and Sherman became good friends. Johnston was very popular with his men, but never rose in the ranks due to his bad relationship with Davis. After the war, he worked in the railroad and insurance businesses, served in the U.S. House of Representatives (1879–81), and was U.S. commissioner of railroads under President Cleveland. When Sherman died in 1891, Johnston was an honorary pallbearer. The funeral was on a bitterly cold day in New York, and Johnston marched bareheaded in the procession, saying that Sherman would have done the same thing. A month later Johnston was dead of pneumonia. See Denney, *Civil War Years*, 10, 38, 50–51, 505, 549–63; Faust, *Historical Times*, 400–401, 503, 736; Laas, *Wartime Washington*, 46, 155–56, 492, 496; and Flood, *Grant and Sherman*, 397–98.

William Darrah Kelley (1814–90) was born in Pennsylvania and trained as a jeweler, then studied law and practiced in Philadelphia. He was deputy prosecuting attorney for the city and county of Philadelphia (1845–46), judge of the court of common pleas in Philadelphia (1846–56), and delegate to the Republican Convention in 1860. Kelley was elected to the U.S. Congress fifteen times (1861–90) and served as the chairman of the Coinage, Weights and Measures Committee. Franklin Dick notes that Kelley was a critic of McClellan. See Laas, *Wartime Washington*, 45–46.

Admiral **Samuel Phillips Lee** (1812–87) was the husband of **Elizabeth Blair**

Lee (Lizzie) and brother-in-law of Frank Blair. He had served in the navy with Jim Blair, who introduced Lee to his sister. Lee was the son of Francis Lightfoot Lee, descended from Richard Henry Lee, and a cousin of Robert E. Lee. He served in the Union navy during the Civil War, while his wife Lizzie and their son, Blair Lee, lived with her parents at Silver Spring and in Washington at the Blair/Lee house. Originally Francis P. Blair bought a house across from the White House, then Phillips Blair built Lizzie an adjoining house. The two houses were joined together when the government bought them to be the guest house for the White House, calling them the Blair/Lee Mansion. Lee commanded the North Atlantic Blockading Squadron for two years, sinking or capturing over fifty ships and earning more prize money than anyone in the history of the navy. Franklin Dick represented Lee on several salvage cases. Smith, *Francis Preston Blair,* 92–96, 143, 181–83; Denney, *Civil War Years,* 170–72, 208–9, 265, 321, 338, 342, 375, 440, 464, 508, 562; Faust, *Historical Times,* 535; and Laas, *Wartime Washington.*

Nathaniel Lyon (1818–61), called "Daddy" by his troops for his discipline, graduated from the United States military academy in 1841. While serving in Kansas during the border conflict known as Bleeding Kansas, Lyon became a fervent abolitionist. In March 1861, he was sent to Jefferson Barracks in St. Louis, where he worked with Blair, Dick, and other Unionist leaders on the Committee of Safety. Lyon drilled and organized the Home Guards, who were mustered into federal service to protect the St. Louis Arsenal and its approaches. Governor Jackson refused Lincoln's call for troops in April 1861, and he and General Frost began to train militia, intending them for home defense only. Concerned that Jackson was planning to seize the arsenal, Lyon disguised himself in clothes borrowed from Mira Alexander, the blind mother-in-law of Franklin Dick and Frank Blair, and rode in her carriage to look over Camp Jackson during afternoon visiting hours to search for arms sent by Jefferson Davis. That night, Lyon told the Committee of Safety of his plan to use his troops to overtake the camp and arrest the men. Franklin Dick describes the Camp Jackson incident, which began the Civil War in Missouri. Lyon was promoted and given command of Union troops in Missouri. He led his troops to fight General Price in southwestern Missouri and was killed at the Battle of Wilson's Creek on August 10, 1861. Frank Blair accompanied Lyon's coffin to the burial in Connecticut. On December 24, 1861, Lyon was awarded the first Thanks of Congress for his gallantry and patriotism. This award honored men in the U.S. Army and Navy from 1861 to 1866. See Gerteis, *Civil War St. Louis,* 136; Monaghan, *Civil War on the Western Border,* 129–32; Faust, *Historical Times,* 66–67, 751–52, 454; and Parish, *History of Missouri,* 13–14, 27.

Beriah Magoffin (1815–85) was born in Kentucky. He practiced law, served as a state senator in 1850, and was governor of Kentucky from 1860 to 1862. He

248 Appendix A

tried to keep Kentucky nonpartisan, supporting the Crittenden Compromise, but also the Fugitive Slave Law. He issued a neutrality proclamation and attempted to call secession conventions twice in 1861, but was blocked by a pro-Union legislature. After Fort Sumter fell, Magoffin refused to furnish troops to either Lincoln or the Confederates. He was able to keep Kentucky uninvolved until September 1861, when the legislature declared allegiance to the Union, reacting to a Confederate invasion in violation of the state's neutrality. At odds with the legislature, Magoffin resigned in August 1862. After the war, he supported civil rights for blacks and urged approval of the Thirteenth Amendment. He later served in the state legislature (1867–69). Faust, *Historical Times*, 467–68; and National Governor's Association, "Kentucky Governor Beriah Magoffin."

James Murray Mason (1798–1871) was born in Virginia and practiced law. He served in the Virginia legislature (1826–32) and the U.S. Congress (1837–39) and Senate (1847–61). He was a staunch states-rights Democrat. In the Senate, he served on the Foreign Relations Committee, drafted the Fugitive Slave Act in 1850, and was president pro tempore during the Thirty-fourth and Thirty-fifty Congresses. He was expelled in 1861 for his support of the rebellion. As Virginia's delegate to the Confederate Congress, he was Commissioner to Great Britain in 1861. He and John Slidell were captured by the Union in the *Trent* incident. After his release, he stayed in England, where he tried unsuccessfully to convince the English government to support an independent Confederate state and to buy Southern cotton. Faust, *Historical Times*, 479, 692, 762–63.

George Brinton McClellan (1826–85) was born in Philadelphia and graduated from West Point in 1846. He served in the Mexican-American War, taught at West Point, designed a saddle used by the army, and was an observer in the Crimean War. He resigned from the army in 1857 to become vice president of the Illinois Central Railroad and then president of the Ohio & Mississippi Railroad. Known for discipline and care for his troops, who adored him, he was made a major general of Ohio volunteers at the beginning of the Civil War. In 1861, Lincoln made him general in chief of the Army of the Potomac. McClellan and Lincoln disagreed over strategies and plans. McClellan referred to Lincoln as a baboon, and was called the "Young McNapoleon" by his detractors. He constantly called for more troops, waiting to move until they arrived. He was removed November 7, 1862. It was said that he delayed action due to overestimating the Confederate forces and was too hesitant to engage the enemy. He ran unsuccessfully for president in 1864 against Lincoln, wrote his memoirs, and served as governor of New Jersey (1878–81). See Faust, *Historical Times*, 456, 606; Goodwin, *Team of Rivals*, 426–33; and Wagner, *Civil War*, April 1, 24.

Benjamin McCulloch (1811–62) was born in Tennessee and moved to Texas in the 1830s, where he was a Texas Ranger and neighbor of Davey Crockett. He was about fifty years old at the time of the Civil War. McCulloch sported long hair, black velvet clothes, Wellington boots, and a white Planter's hat. He looked magnificent on his horse and always carried a fancy rifle. He was a hero from the Mexican-American War and the Texas War of Independence, later serving in the state legislature. McCulloch was in the gold rush of 1849 and became sheriff of Sacramento during Charles Robinson's squatter's revolt. He joined the Confederate forces in Texas and fought Lyon at the Battle of Wilson's Creek. McCulloch had various commands in Arkansas, marauded into Missouri, and tried to enlist Indians to fight for the Confederacy. As a brigadier general, he was killed at the Battle of Pea Ridge in March 1862. See Gerteis, *Civil War St. Louis*, 144–45; Faust, *Historical Times*, 458; and Monaghan, *Civil War on the Western Border*, 156–57.

John H. McNeil (1813–91) was born in Nova Scotia and became a hatter in Boston at the age of sixteen. He moved to New York, then to St. Louis, where he expanded into wholesaling hats. Known to be modest and cheerful, McNeil served in the state legislature (1844–45) and was president of the Pacific Insurance Co. (1855–61). In 1861, he served as a colonel in the Missouri Volunteers at Camp Jackson. McNeil also captured Fulton, Missouri, and defeated General Harris. He was provost marshall of St. Louis until August 1861. He commanded the District of Northeast Missouri in Palmyra, where he campaigned against guerillas. The Confederates blamed him for killing some prisoners and said they would shoot him if he was captured. After the Civil War, McNeil served as clerk of the criminal court, sheriff of St. Louis County, and U.S. Indian inspector. See McPherson, Battle Cry of Freedom, 332; Monaghan, *Civil War on the Western Border*, 329–36; and Gerteis, *Civil War St. Louis*, 96, 103–4.

George Gordon Meade (1815–72) was born in Spain while his father served as a naval agent. A West Pointer, he served in the Seminole and Mexican-American wars, and then worked in engineering. Meade was made a Union brigadier general of volunteers in 1861. He was wounded in the hip and arm in the Peninsula Campaign, served at the battles of Second Bull Run, South Mountain, Antietam, Fredericksburg, and Chancellorsville. As commander of the Army of the Potomac in 1863, he fought Lee at Gettysburg and received the Thanks of Congress. Union General Ulysses S. Grant accompanied Meade and his troops until Appomatox, when Meade was promoted to major general. See Laas, *Wartime Washington*, 281–82; Denney, *Civil War Years*, 100; Katcher, *Civil War Sourcebook*, 284, and Faust, *Historical Times*, 482–83.

Montgomery Cunningham Meigs (1816–92) was Quartermaster General of the U.S. Army. He was born in Georgia, grew up in Philadelphia, and graduated from West Point, serving with the artillery and then the Corps of Engineers. In 1852, he constructed the Washington Aqueduct to provide a dependable water supply to the District of Columbia. He also designed and constructed the Capitol Dome, the National Museum, Post Office extensions, and the Pension Office

Building, all of which had plaques giving him credit, for which he was criticized. Secretary of War John Floyd clashed with him over political patronage versus good construction and sent Major General Meigs to the Dry Tortugas to work on military fortifications. When Floyd resigned in 1860, Meigs returned, was appointed Quartermaster General by Lincoln, and supervised the purchase of supplies for the army, using competitive bidding to end corruption. He began uniform sizing of clothing and shoes for the first time. Meigs designed strategy for campaigns, and wanted Union armies to forage in enemy territory in order to deny produce to the Confederates and speed the end of the war. The eldest of his seven children, John Rodgers Meigs, served under Sherman and was killed by Confederate cavalry in Virginia. Meigs was horrified; Sherman thought he had been shot in cold blood and ordered the area burned. After the war, Meigs served in the army as a major general and planned the remodeling of Washington based on Berlin and Paris. See Faust, *Historical Times,* 485.

Mosby Monroe Parsons (1822–65) was born in Virginia and moved to Missouri as a child. He commanded volunteers in the Mexican-American War. He served as attorney general in Missouri (1853–57) and was a state senator when the Civil War began. He supported Governor Jackson, serving in the Missouri State Guard, and became a brigadier general in the Confederate army, serving at Carthage and Wilson's Creek. He was commander of Price's van at Lexington and fought in the battle of Prairie Grove. After Kirby Smith's surrender, Parsons fled to Mexico, where he probably died in 1865 while fighting for the imperialist forces. See Faust, Historical Times, 560–61.

Gideon Pillow (1806–78), a Tennessee attorney and law partner of future president James Polk, was one of Jefferson Davis' worst political appointments. As brigadier general of volunteers in the U.S. Army, Pillow attempted to take credit for Winfield Scott's success in the Mexican-American War and was tried for insubordination. As a brigadier general in the Confederate army, Pillow is best remembered for his actions in the Battle of Fort Donelson, when he fled to avoid capture by U.S. troops, was suspended, returned to duty, and was later accused of hiding behind a tree during the Battle of Murfreesboro. At the end of the Civil War, he was in charge of Union prisoners. Bankrupted by the war, he returned to his law practice. See Faust, *Historical Times,* 585.

David Dixon Porter (1813–91) was the son of Union Commodore David Porter. His father had adopted David Glasgow Farragut (later an admiral) when he was young, and they grew up together with Porter's brother, William D. Porter (later a commodore), and their cousin Fitz John Porter, another navy man. David Porter first went to sea with his father when he was ten. He served with the Mexican Navy and the U.S. Navy. On April 1, 1861, he took command of the *Powhatan* to relieve Fort Pickens, Florida. Commander Porter had the brilliant idea of putting mortars on flatboats to attack river forts and was a major contributor to the Union's later naval successes. Porter relieved Admiral S. P. Lee from his command of the North Atlantic Blockading Squadron and captured Fort Fisher and Wilmington, North Carolina. He had a need for glory and took Lincoln on his boat for his entrance into Richmond at the end of the war. He was named Admiral and Superintendent of the U.S. Naval Academy after the war and received the Thanks of Congress. See Katcher, *Civil War Source Book*, 285–86; *Faust, Historical Times*, 594–95; and Laas, *Wartime Washington*, 141, 164, 449, 455–59.

William Preston (1816–87) was born in Kentucky, studied law at Harvard, and practiced law in Louisville, Kentucky. A lieutenant colonel in the Mexican-American War, he served in state legislature (1850–53), the U.S. Senate (1852–55), and was ambassador to Spain (1858–61). Preston's sister was married to Confederate General Albert Sidney Johnston, and Preston was Johnston's aide until Johnston was killed at the battle of Shiloh. As a brigadier general, Preston served at Corinth, Stone's River, Chickamauga, and the siege of Chattanooga. Preston was temporarily commander of the Department of East Tennessee after General Simon Buckner surrendered Fort Donelson to Grant. He was named minister to the court of Maximilian in Mexico in 1864, but could not reach Mexico City. He returned to Kentucky in 1866 and served another term in the state legislature (1868–69). See Faust, *Historical Times*, 601–2.

Edwin M. Price (1834–1908), a farmer, was the oldest child of Sterling Price, and was with his father at the Planter's House in St. Louis at the time Camp Jackson was surrounded, thereby avoiding capture. He served in the Missouri State Guard and as a Confederate brigadier general, and was returning from northern Missouri when he was captured near Stockton, Missouri. He was sent on to Rolla, then to St. Louis. Department Commander Halleck paroled him and exchanged him for a Union general, on the condition that he live in a Northern city. After his parole, he resigned his commission and obtained a pardon from President Lincoln so he could remain in Missouri. He publicly renounced the Confederacy, but reconciled with his father at the end of the war. Sterling Price passed his land to his son Edwin to avoid having it confiscated. See Winter, *Civil War in St. Louis*, 121–22; and Monaghan, *Civil War on the Western Border*, 230.

Sterling Price (1809–67), called "Old Pap" by his men, served in the Missouri House of Representatives from 1840 to 1844, and in Congress from March 1845 till August 1846, when he resigned to serve in the Mexican-American War, when he was military governor of New Mexico. He was governor of Missouri (1853–57), State Bank Commissioner (1857–61), and was selected presiding officer of the Missouri State Convention in February 1861. With the Harney-Price Agreement, he had opposed secession, but after Blair and Lyon seized Camp Jackson, Price was furious. Governor Jackson assigned him to command the Missouri State Guard in May 1861, and he led his troops in a campaign to secure southwestern Missouri for the Confederacy. Confederate Brigadier General Price joined with General Ben McCulloch and General Pearce, with Confederate troops and Arkansas militia, to defeat Union General Nathaniel Lyon at the Battle of Wilson's Creek on August 10, 1861. Price's raid into Missouri in 1864 ended in defeat. After the surrender of the Confederate armies, he founded an exile colony in Carlota, Mexico, which failed in 1866. Price returned to St. Louis impoverished and died there of cholera on September 29, 1867. Brownlee, *Gray Ghosts*, 14–19, 28–29; Gerteis, *Civil War St. Louis*, 145; Josephy, *Civil War in the American West*, 5; and Faust, *Historical Times*, 602–3.

James E. Rains (?–?) was a Missouri senator before the Civil War, then brigadier general in the Missouri State Guard fighting at Dug Springs, Wilson's Creek, Lexington, and Pea Ridge. Rains was then elected to the Confederate senate. See Monaghan, *Civil War on the Western Border*, 150–53, 190–93, 204.

Evans Rogers (?–?) was Franklin Dick's uncle and an iron merchant. Dick named his second son after Evans Rogers. Rogers married Caroline Augusta Fairman, daughter of Gideon Fairman, who had invented engine-turning banknote engraving and was a close friend of Washington Irving. Evans and Caroline had one child, Fairman Rogers. From family information.

Fairman Rogers (1833–1900) was a first cousin to Franklin Dick, related through Franklin's mother, Hannah Rogers. He was born in Philadelphia, the only son of Evans Rogers and Caroline Augusta Fairman. Rogers studied at the University of Pennsylvania and worked as an engineer measuring the baseline in the coastal survey in Florida in 1855. He married Rebecca Gilpin and they traveled in Europe. Rogers lectured at the Franklin Institute, the University of Pennsylvania, the Smithsonian Institute, and Harvard College. He served with the First Troop of Philadelphia City Cavalry at the beginning of the Civil War. Rogers then returned to lecturing as professor of civil engineering at the University of Pennsylvania, and served as a volunteer engineer officer during the rest of the war. Rogers wrote *A Manual of Coaching*, published in 1900. He served on many boards, was active in the arts, and died in Vienna on August 22, 1900. Thomas Eakins painted a portrait of Rogers driving his four-in-hand coach, with William Dick and his wife sitting behind Fairman and Rebecca. William Dick donated the painting to the Philadelphia Museum of Art. From family information and *Fairman Rogers*.

James S. Rollins (1812–88) was a friend of Frank Blair's from Kentucky, where he was born. Rollins practiced law in Columbia, Missouri, and was a slave owner. He was a major in the Black Hawk War, and served in the Missouri House of Representatives (1838–40, 1854, 1867) and Senate (1846–48). He was a delegate to the Whig National Convention in 1844. He ran unsuccessfully for governor in 1848 and 1856, the second time losing to Robert M. Stewart, a proslavery Democrat. In 1860, he was elected to the U.S. House of Representatives (1861–65). See Gerteis, *Civil War St. Louis*, 38, 345; and Wikipedia, s.v. "James S. Rollins."

William Starke Rosecrans (1819–98) was born in Ohio, the great-grandson of Stephen Hopkins, colonial governor of Rhode Island and signer of the Declaration of Independence. He graduated from West Point, but resigned from the army in 1854 and became an architect and civil engineer, supervising the direction of mining in what is now West Virginia. Rosecrans invented an odorless lamp oil, round lamp wicks, a shorter lamp chimney, and a new method of manufacturing soap. After recovering from burns from an overturned safety lamp, he enlisted in the Union army and became drillmaster of the Marion Rifles. He was made brigadier general after the Union victory at Rich Mountain, Virginia (West Virginia) against Confederate General Robert E. Lee. McClellan took credit for the victory, although Rosecrans had devised and carried out the battle plans. When Rosecrans served in the west, he and Grant did not get along, hampering his career. He was in battles at Iuka, Corinth, Stones River, and Chickamauga, and besieged the Confederates at Chattanooga. Next, Rosecrans commanded the Department of Missouri. He was loved by his enlisted men, but noted for his harsh dealing with officers. When under stress in battle, he stuttered, making his commands hard to understand. He resigned from the army in 1867; he later served as minister to Mexico (1868–69) and congressman from California in the U.S. Congress (1881–85). See Katcher, *Civil War Source Book,* 286; and Faust, *Historical Times,* 642–43.

William (Billy) Howard Russell (1820–1907) was an Irish reporter for The Times (London) who gained popularity through his coverage of the Crimean War. His dispatches covering the Civil War were published in Union and Confederate papers. Due to his scorn of Americans, he became an unpopular correspondent in both North and South. He also covered the Indian Mutiny, the Austro-Prussian War, and the Zulu War. He was knighted in 1895. See Faust, *Historical Times,* 649.

John McAllister Schofield (1831–1906) was born in New York and graduated from West Point. While teaching physics at Washington University, he rode with Brigadier General Nathaniel Lyon to disband Camp Jackson. Schofield was Lyon's adjutant at the battle of Wilson's Creek. He found Lyon dead and carried his body to the rear. As a brigadier general, he was appointed, removed, and then reinstated as head of the Department of Missouri. In 1862, Schofield and Governor Gamble restored the system of assessments and banishment of disloyal persons in St. Louis and the state, using the funds to pay for the uniforms and arms of the new Missouri Militia and other expenses. The provost marshal general, Thomas T. Gantt, supervised the system. In 1863, all assessments in Missouri were ended by the War Department. Schofield put control of recruitment under provost marshals. Since Schofield's critics felt he was unable to protect the state from bushwackers, Shelby's raids, and the Cherokee, Lincoln replaced him with General Rosecrans in 1864. Later Schofield commanded the Union XXIII Corps, serving with Major

General Sherman in Atlanta, through Georgia, at the battles of Franklin and Nashville, and in the final maneuvers against Confederate Joseph E. Johnston. After the war, he was superintendent of West Point, Andrew Johnson's Secretary of War, and Commanding General of the Army in 1888. Schofield is known for recommending that the U.S. make Pearl Harbor, Hawaii, into a military base. See Faust, *Historical Times*, 661; Gerteis, *Civil War St. Louis*, 143–44, 177–78, 195, 270–71, 276–84; and Winter, *Civil War in St. Louis*, 43.

Winfield Scott (1786–1866) was born in Virginia and served as a brigadier general in the War of 1812 and as general in chief in the Mexican-American War. As the Civil War began, he was elderly, ill, overweight, and unable to mount or ride a horse, but was the highest ranking military officer. He developed a strategy to blockade ports in the South, hold the Mississippi River, and take Richmond. The press ridiculed him and called it the "Anaconda Plan," named for the snake, as it would strangle the South. After the defeats at the First Battle of Bull Run and Balls Bluff, he was replaced by McClellan and retired November 1, 1861. Grant eventually used his plan to win the war. Scott was called "Old Fuss and Feathers" for his love of elaborate uniforms and protocol. See Faust, *Historical Times*, 662–63; and Wagner, *Civil War*, s.v., January 31 and map.

William H. Seward (1801–72) was born in New York and practiced law. He was governor of New York (1838–42) and a U.S. senator (1848–61). In 1860, he was an ambitious contender for president against Lincoln, who named him secretary of state. Seward felt he was a "prime minister" to govern for the inexperienced new president. He thought Fort Sumter should be evacuated to cool things off and let the states revoke the secession. Against Lincoln's specific instructions, he secretly met with Confederates to promise that the fort would be abandoned. Lincoln notified South Carolina Governor Francis Pickens that he would resupply the fort, showing his independence from Seward, thus beginning the Civil War. Seward wanted war with England over the Mason and Slidell incident, but Lincoln said, "One war at a time," and sought peace so he could get the saltpeter he had secretly bought from England to make gunpowder. Part of the plot to kill President Lincoln was to also assassinate Seward. At the time John Wilkes Booth was shooting Lincoln, Lewis Powell went to Seward's house, where Seward was bedridden from a carriage accident. Powell stabbed Seward in the head and neck, and wounded his sons and a secretary. Seward was wearing a heavy neck brace for his injuries and survived the attack. Powell escaped and was later arrested at Mary Surratt's boardinghouse in 1865. He was found guilty and hanged on July 7, 1865. Seward served out his cabinet post under President Johnson and is known for "Seward's Folly," when he bought Alaska from Russia in 1867 for $7.2 million. See Faust, *Historical Times*, 668–69; and Laas, *Wartime Washington*, 494–95.

Joseph Orville Shelby (1830–97) was born in Kentucky to a wealthy family and was a planter and rope manufacturer. During the Bleeding Kansas conflict on the Kansas/Missouri border, Shelby (who then lived in Missouri) led a company of pro-slavery forces. When the Civil War broke out, he enlisted in the Confederate army, where he was known as an effective cavalry leader and for always wearing a black plume in his hat. His men were known and feared as Shelby's Iron Brigade of the West. Shelby was in the battles of Carthage, Wilson's Creek, Pea Ridge, Prairie Grove, Helena, and Jenkins' Ferry. He led a cavalry division for Price's invasion of Missouri in 1864. He refused to surrender at the end of the war, leading his brigade to Mexico, where their services were not accepted by Emperor Maximilian. Shelby stayed in Mexico, on land given him by the emperor, until the fall of the empire. He returned to farming in Missouri in 1867. See Faust, *Historical Times*, 673–74; and Denney, *Civil War Years*, 476, 478, 569, 572.

Philip Henry Sheridan (1831–88) was born in New York and attended West Point. He was suspended for attacking another cadet with a bayonet, but later returned and graduated. When the Civil War began, he was a captain in the Thirteenth Infantry in southwest Missouri, but rose to the rank of major general and commander, and was known for his aggressive cavalry raids and victories in the Shenandoah Valley. After pursuing and skirmishing with General Robert E. Lee in his flight from Richmond and Petersburg, Virginia, Sheridan was at Appomattox when Lee surrendered to Grant. After the war, Sheridan was commander of the Fifth District during Reconstruction in Texas and Louisiana. He was known for his harsh treatment of Confederates and was charged with "absolute tyranny" and transferred after six months. In 1868, he was assigned to subdue the Indians in northwest Oklahoma. In 1869, Sheridan was promoted to lieutenant general and succeeded Sherman as commander of the Division of Missouri, which covered the Rocky Mountains to the Mississippi River. From 1884, he again followed Sherman as commander of the U.S. Army, then was promoted to full general. He also wrote his memoirs. See Katcher, *Civil War Source Book*, 288–89; Faust, *Historical Times*, 121, 233, 679–80; Denney, *Civil War Years*, 189; and Grant, *Personal Memoirs*, 599–608, 623–34.

William Tecumseh Sherman (1820–91) was born in Ohio, the son of an Ohio Supreme Court justice. He was orphaned and raised by U.S. Senator Thomas Ewing, whose daughter he later married. Nicknamed "Cump," he graduated from West Point and served in the Mexican-American War, then went into banking in San Francisco. He took command of the Thirteenth U.S. Infantry Regiment at the start of the Civil War, and served at the First Battle of Bull Run. He then was in Kentucky, at the battles of Shiloh, Vicksburg, and Chattanooga, taking command of the western theatre after Grant went east. He invaded Atlanta, laid waste across Georgia to Savannah in his March to the Sea, and then fought his way north to join Grant. Sherman moved toward Raleigh, North Carolina, and received news that Lee had surrendered on April 10, 1865. Three days later, General Joseph Johnston sent a flag of truce. As Sherman was leaving

Price to invade Missouri, and concentrated on guerilla raids until surrendering on May 26, 1865, to Union Brigadier General Canby. After the war, Smith served as the president of the University of Nashville and taught at the University of the South. He was the last full Confederate general to die. See Faust, *Historical Times*, 695, 736; and Denney, *Civil War Years*, 203, 208–14, 561, 569, 575.

Thomas Lowndes Snead (1828–90) was born in Virginia. He was a lawyer and editor of the *St. Louis Bulletin*, a secession newspaper, before the Civil War. He joined with the Confederates, becoming Major General Sterling Price's right-hand man and rising to acting assistant general. After 1865, he practiced law in New York City. He wrote *The Fight for Missouri* in 1866 about his war experiences. See Winter, *Civil War in St. Louis*, 68, 128.

Edwin McMasters Stanton (1814–69) was born in Ohio, where he became a successful attorney. He moved to Pittsburgh, Pennsylvania, then to Washington DC, where he continued to practice law. He was an antislavery Democrat and a no-nonsense lawyer. He was the first to use temporary insanity as a murder defense, when he successfully defended General Daniel Sickles, who had killed his wife's lover, Philip Barton Key (son of Francis Scott Key). In 1860, Stanton was named Attorney General by President Buchanan. He was a critic of president-elect Lincoln, calling him "an imbecile, the original gorilla," and "a well-meaning baboon," remarks that were picked up and used by McClellan with racial inferences. Despite this, he served as legal advisor to Secretary of War Simon Cameron and wrote the section in the annual report about freed slaves being armed to fight against the Confederacy, which caused Cameron to be fired and Stanton named war secretary. Stanton managed the telegraph lines, censored the press, and doubled the size of the War Department. He closed recruitment offices in the spring of 1862, thinking the war would soon end. Over time, Stanton changed his opinion of Lincoln, calling him, "the most perfect ruler of men the world has ever seen." After the Emancipation Proclamation, Stanton authorized formation of regiments including "persons of African descent." Rumors blamed Stanton for the assassination of Lincoln, though he had his National Detective Police find and capture John Wilkes Booth and the other conspirators. When President Johnson tried to remove Stanton from the Cabinet, radical senators claimed Johnson was violating the Tenure of Office Act and initiated impeachment proceedings. Stanton resigned and returned to private practice. President Grant appointed Stanton to the Supreme Court, but he died only four days after being confirmed. See Faust, *Historical Times*, 712–13; and Gerteis, *Civil War St. Louis*, 261, 280, 284–85.

Alexander Hamilton Stephens (1812–83), called "Little Aleck" since he weighed ninety pounds, was born in Georgia. He practiced law and entered politics, serving in the state legislature and the U.S. House of Representatives (1843–59) as a Whig and a Democrat. A longtime friend of Abraham Lincoln, he was opposed to secession, but remained loyal to his state when it voted to secede. As

Confederate vice president, he constantly disagreed with President Jefferson Davis. He used his office to improve conditions for the wounded and to speed up the exchange of prisoners, visiting hospitals and prisons. He was sent as a commissioner to discuss peace with Lincoln and Seward on the *River Queen* in Hampton Roads. After the war, Stephens was imprisoned at Fort Warren in Boston for five months. He was elected to the U.S. Senate the following year, but denied the right to take office, so returned to his law practice. He was also editor of an Atlanta newspaper, and published a book on the Civil War. He later served in the U.S. House of Representatives (1873–82) and as Georgia governor (1883). See Faust, *Historical Times,* 335–36, 716–17; Laas, *Wartime Washington,* 33–35, 285–86, 472; and Denney, *Civil War Years,* 25, 294, 302, 309, 524–27.

John D. Stevenson (1821–1912) was born in Virginia and practiced law in Missouri. He served with the First Missouri Mounted Volunteers in General Stephen W. Kearny's invasion of New Mexico. After his return, he served several terms in the legislature, serving one term as president of the state senate. He was made colonel of the Seventh Missouri Regiment in June 1861, commanded a brigade at the Battle of Corinth, and was made brigadier general in 1863. He left the army in 1870 and returned to St. Louis to practice law. See Winter, *Civil War in St. Louis,* 117.

Samuel D. Sturgis (1822–76) was born in Pennsylvania and graduated from West Point. He was captured in the Mexican-American War. After the war, he served in the West, fighting Indians. When the Civil War began, Sturgis was ordered by Lyon to bring his battalion of trained, Indian-fighting cavalry to reinforce him in southwest Missouri. He fought at Wilson's Creek and commanded the Union retreat to Rolla. He was breveted brigadier general, and evacuated Missouri frontier posts due to Indian threats, and was sent after Confederate General Forrest in Mississippi. Forrest defeated him at Brice's Crossroads in June 1864, and Sturgis retreated to Memphis, where he remained for the rest of the war. After the Civil War, Sturgis fought in the Indian wars as a lieutenant colonel. His son, James G. Sturgis, served under Custer and was killed at Little Big Horn. See Faust, *Historical Times,* 729–30.

Richard Taylor (1826–79) was born in Kentucky, the son of Zachary Taylor and brother-in-law of Jefferson Davis. He was educated in Europe and at Harvard and Yale, serving as his father's military secretary during the Mexican-American War. He owned a plantation in Louisiana and was active in state politics. Taylor entered the Civil War as a Confederate colonel of the Ninth Louisiana Infantry, then became a brigadier general in 1861, major general in 1862, and lieutenant general in 1864. He served in the battles of the Shenandoah Valley Campaign, Seven Days, and Mansfield, Louisiana, where he had an important victory over Union Major General Nathaniel P. Banks. Taylor was given command of the Department of East Louisiana, Mississippi, and Alabama, despite criticizing his superior, General E. Kirby Smith. After Lee and Johnston surrendered, Taylor delivered the last large force east of the Mississippi to Union Major General Canby on May 4, 1865. After the war, he worked to relieve the effects of Reconstruction in the South and for leniency for former President Jefferson Davis. His memoirs were published a week before he died. See Faust, *Historical Times*, 743–44; Denney, *Civil War Years*, 390–91, 397, 448, 516, 521, 564–67; and Katcher, *Civil War Source Book*, 290–91.

George Henry Thomas (1816–70) was born in Virginia, graduated from West Point, and served in the Mexican-American War and the Indian wars. When the Civil War began, he stayed in the Union army as a colonel, alienating his family, rising to major general. He commanded troops at Shiloh, Perryville, Chickamauga (where he was known as the "Rock of Chickamauga" for keeping a line until night), Chattanooga, Lookout Mountain, and Nashville. After the war, he commanded the Division of Tennessee and the Departments of the Cumberland and Tennessee. He received the Thanks of Congress in 1865. He was urged to run for president, but he refused to challenge his superior, General Grant. He died at his command as major general at the Military Division of the Pacific in 1870. He insisted on detail and rules, and once said, "The fate of an army may depend on a buckle," as a reprimand to an officer not in correct uniform. See Faust, *Historical Times*, 754.

Lloyd Tilghman (1816–63) was born in Maryland and graduated from West Point. He served in the Mexican-American War and then worked as a railroad construction engineer. In Kentucky when the Civil War began, he joined the Confederate Army and rose to the rank of brigadier general, serving at various posts. When he inspected the forts on the Tennessee and Cumberland rivers, he reported that Fort Henry and Fort Donelson were badly maintained, but received no help from Major General Leonidas Polk, the district commander. When General Grant approached Fort Henry, Tilghman sent most of his men to Fort Donelson and defended Fort Henry with eighty soldiers against Flag Officer Foote and his gunboats, until forced to surrender on February 6, 1862. On August 27, 1862, he was exchanged for John R. Reynolds, and commanded a brigade in the Army of the West at Corinth, Holly Springs, and Vicksburg. He was killed by a shell as he supervised his artillery on May 16, 1863, at the battle of Champion's Hill. See Faust, *Historical Times*, 756; Katcher, *Civil War Source Book*, 26; and Denney, *Civil War Years*, 121.

James Totten (1818–71), "Old Bottle Nose," had a large red nose and kept brandy in a wooden canteen. He had been a classmate of Nathaniel Lyon at West Point. He was chief of artillery at Camp Jackson, Booneville, and Wilson's Creek, serving in the First Missouri Volunteers under Lyon and Frémont. He became a brigadier general in the Missouri State Militia, commanding the central district of the state. He was made inspector general of the Department of the Missouri in

May 1863, and chief of artillery and chief of ordinance in 1864. On March 13, 1865, he was brevetted colonel in the U.S. Army "for gallant and meritorious conduct during the siege of Mobile, Alabama," and brigadier general in the U.S. Army "for gallant and meritorious service in the field" during the Civil War. In 1870, President Grant dismissed him for drinking; Totten wrote to him that Grant, of all people, should overlook it. See Winter, *Civil War in St. Louis*, 39; Gerteis, *Civil War St. Louis*, 86, 95; and Monaghan, *Civil War on the Western Frontier*, 144, 171, 174–75, 350.

John Ellis Wool (1784–1869) was orphaned at age four on the upstate New York frontier. In 1812, he joined the U.S. Army and was known as a severe disciplinarian during his fifty years of service. He served in the War of 1812 and the Mexican-American War. Wool directed the Cherokee relocation in 1836 known as the Trail of Tears, and was head of the Department of the Pacific (1854–57), where he put down Indian uprisings, and the Department of the East (1857–61). The statement "The only good Indian is a dead Indian" was attributed to him, but he denied having said it. As senior brigadier general in 1861, Wool secured Fort Monroe (an important supply depot) for the Union and for Norfolk. George B. McClellan was promoted over Wool when General Winfield Scott retired as commander of the Union army. Wool was given command of the Department of Virginia, promoted to major general, then transferred to command the Middle Department. In 1863, he again commanded the Department of the East and quelled the New York draft riots; he retired shortly afterwards. See Faust, *Historical Times*, 842; and Denney, *Civil War Years*, 68, 168.

James E. Yeatman (1818–1901) moved from his native Tennessee to St. Louis to open a branch of a Nashville iron manufacturing facility in 1842. He was one of the founders of the Merchant's Bank in 1850 and its president in 1860. After Robert Campbell's Conditional Unionist meeting in 1861, Yeatman went with Hamilton Gamble to discuss conciliatory policies in St. Louis with Lincoln, who followed the opposing advice of Frank Blair. Yeatman was a slaveholder, but a Unionist, an important force in St. Louis with civic posts such as president of the library. In September 1861, Jessie Benton Frémont persuaded her husband, John C. Frémont, to approve the Western Sanitary Commission. On September 5, 1861, Yeatman became its president, serving with Carlos S. Greeley, Dr. J. B. Johnson, George Partridge, and the Reverend Dr. William Eliot. The commission worked with the St. Louis Ladies' Union Aid Society to help sick and wounded soldiers, families, and refugees; establish soldier's homes and hospital steamers; and provide relief for freedmen and former slaves. The Grand Mississippi Valley Sanitary Fair on May 14, 1864, was a major fundraiser on which Yeatman worked. See Winter, *Civil War in St. Louis*, 91–93, 130–31; and Gerteis, *Civil War St. Louis*, 44, 115, 190, 206–8, 226–27, 292.

Felix K. Zollicoffer (1812–62) was born in Tennessee and became a printer and newspaper editor. He was a veteran of the Second Seminole War, then served in the state senate (1849–52) and the U.S. Congress (1853–59). He was a member of the peace convention held in 1861, which tried, but failed, to prevent war. He joined the state troops, then the Confederate army. In late November 1861, Brigadier General Zollicoffer advanced into neutral Kentucky. On January 19, 1862, as he was backed up to the rain-swollen Cumberland River, Zollikoffer was ordered by Major General George B. Crittenden to attack Union Major General George H. Thomas at Mill Springs. Zollicoffer, who was very nearsighted, rode in the advance; he was killed and the attack failed. The Confederates, losing 533 men and officers, retreated from Kentucky and fled to Knoxville. The Union troops lost 261 men, and moved to occupy Bowling Green on February 14, 1862. See Faust, *Historical Times*, 495, 850.

Appendix B

GENERATION I
Archibald Dick (1715–1782)
  m. – Mary Barnard Hughes

GENERATION II
Children of Archibald Dick and Mary Barnard Hughes
1. Elisha Cullen (1762–1825)
  m. – Hannah Harman
2. Thomas Barnard (1766–1811)
  m. – Phebe (Brinton) Hart (1766–1840)

GENERATION III
Children of Thomas Barnard Dick and Phebe (Brinton) Hart
1. Archibald Thomas Dick (1794–1837)
  m. – Hannah Rogers (1796–1856)
2. Mary Brinton
  m. – Zedekiah Flower
3. Brinton
4. Phebe

GENERATION IV
Children of Archibald Thomas Dick and Hannah Rogers
1.   Franklin Archibald (1823–1885)
    m. – Myra Madison Alexander (1832–1918)
2.   Mary E.
    m. – Peter Hill Engle
3.   Phebe Ann
    m. – James H. Castle
4.   Emma L.
    m. Prof. E. Otis Kendall

GENERATION V

Children of Franklin Archibald Dick and Myra Madison Alexander

1. William Alexander (7/8/1855–1945)
   m. (1) – Caroline Thompson Norris
   m. (2) – Elizabeth Story Jenks
2. Otis (3/1857–5/27/1863)
3. Evans Rogers (8/13/1858–?)
   m. – Elizabeth Tatham
4. Frank Madison (5/23/1860–1936)
   m./d. (1) – Julia D. Biddle
   m. (2) – Minnette G. Mills
5. Myra (1876–1968)
   m. – Conte de Breviare d'Alaincourt

GENERATION VI

Children of William Alexander Dick and Caroline Thompson Norris

1. Franklin Archibald II (4/27/1882–1/23/1918).
   m. – Jean Boyd Leonard

Children of Evans Rogers Dick and Elizabeth Tatham

1. Fairman R. (8/7/1885–2/19/1976)
2. Isabelle Mildred (2/17/1884–1972)
   m. – Stuyvesant Fish
3. Evans Rogers Jr. (2/17/1888–8/1967)

Children of Frank Madison Dick and Julia D. Biddle

1. John Julian (1/22/1886–?)
2. Langhorne Bullitt (2/6/1889–3/20/1956)
   m. – Hebe Wright

Children of Myra Dick and Conte de Breviare d'Alaincourt

1. Alix (?–?)
   m. (1) – Conte Bernard de Richard d'Ivry
   m. (2) – Captain Belleville
   m. (3) – Langley, Lord Russell of Liverpool

GENERATION VII

Children of Franklin Archibald Dick II and Jean Boyd Leonard

1. Franklin Archibald III (12/10/1913–3/10/2003)
   m. – Marjorie MacQueen Wise
2. Mai Garesché Norris (1/29/1915–)
   m./d. (1) – Tilghman Goldsborough Pitts Jr.
   m. (2) – George Gordon Saulsbury
   m. (3) – Harry Flickwer West

Children of Langhorne Bullitt Dick and Hebe Wright

1. Hebe Mary (7/23/1912–6/24/1985)
   m./d. (1) – Thomas Evans Dunn Jr.
   m./d. (2) – Alfred Chapin Rogers
   m./d. (3) – Barton Baldwin
2. Charles Wright (1915–1/11/1957)
   m. – Anne Child

Children of Alix d'Alaincourt and Conte Bernard de Richard d'Ivry

1. Ghislan de Richard d'Ivry (?–)
   m. – Miriam
2. Roland d'Ivry Russell (10/17/1932–)
   m. – Ursula Garrett Paver

GENERATION VIII

Children of Franklin Archibald Dick III and Marjorie MacQueen Wise

1. Marjorie MacQueen (5/8/1944–)
   m./d. (1) – George Cooper V
   m./d. (2) – Michael Van Meter
   m. (3) – Sheldon Anderson
2. Elizabeth Story (10/27/1946–)

Children of Mai Garesché Norris Dick and Tilghman Goldsborough Pitts Jr.

1. Mai Garesché (3/29/1940–)
   m./d. – Henry Lee Carter

Children of Hebe Mary Dick and Thomas Evans Dunn Jr.

1. Thomas Langhorne (1/17/1942–)
   m./d. (1) – Lucy Day Kramer
   m. (2) – Mary Louise Fowler

Children of Charles Dick and Anne Child

1. Anne Caroline (4/5/1940–)
   m./d. (1) – George Oliver Jackson Jr.
   m./d. (2) – Frederick Waters
   m./d. (3) – Larry Neighbors

Children of Ghislan de Richard d'Ivry and Miriam

1. Ian (8/29/1954–)
   m./d. – Susan

GENERATION IX

Children of Marjorie MacQueen Dick and George Cooper V

1. George VI (11/24/1969–)
   m. – Caroline Carter Noel
2. Franklin Cullen (6/14/1971–)
3. William Wise (6/5/1974–)
   m. – Amanda Cecily Smith

Children of Mai Garesché Pitts and Henry Lee Carter

1. Caroline Norris Garesché (11/7/1967–)
    m. – John Bateman McClure, III
2. Llewellyn Henry Sullivan (8/21/1970–)
    m. – Laura Lee Yager

Children of Thomas Langhorne Dunn and Lucy Day Kramer

1. Thomas Langhorne Jr. (10/14/1964–)
    m. – Diane Lynn Shivers
2. Jonathan Wright (10/2/1967–)
    m./d. (1) – Donna Pepe
    m. (2) – Theresa Ann Mohn

Children of Anne Caroline Dick and George Oliver Jackson Jr.

1. Gretchen (7/21/1962–)
    m./d. – Preston Randall Martin
2. George Oliver III (12/28/1963–7/8/1990)
    m. – Cynthia Leigh Funk

Children of Ian d'Ivry and Susan

1. Stuart (7/9/1982–)
2. Matthew (11/30/1985–)
3. Natalie (4/25/1988–)

GENERATION IX

Children of George Cooper VI and Caroline Carter Noe

1. Eleanor Carter (5/20/2006–)

Children of Llewellyn Henry Sullivan Carter and Laura Lee Yager

1. Alden Gray (12/18/1999–)
2. Aaron Tilghman (2/22/2002–)

Children of Thomas Langhorne Dunn Jr. and Diane Lyn Shivers

1. Cooper Jung Ho (12/29/2002–)
2. Chloe Son Hee (12//13/2005–)

Children of Jonathan Wright Dunn and Theresa Ann Mohn

1. Rachel Lenore (4/1/2000–)
2. Kelly Elizabeth (1/25/2006–)

Children of Gretchen Jackson and Preston Randall Martin

1. Trey Charles Henry (11/15/1990–)
2. Meghan Samantha (12/18/1994–)

Bibliography

There are many books on the Civil War which I consulted in researching. The following are the ones that were most pertinent to Franklin Dick's journals.

Barrett, John G. *The Civil War in North Carolina.* Chapel Hill: University of North Carolina Press, 1963.

Bierce, Ambrose. *Civil War Stories.* New York: Dover Publications. 1994.

Biographical Directory of the United States Senate. Available online at http://bioguide.congress.gov.

Black, Robert C., III. *The Railroads of the Confederacy.* Chapel Hill: University of North Carolina Press, 1998.

Boernstein, Henry. *Memoirs of a Nobody: The Missouri Years of an Austrian Radical, 1849–1866.* Translated and edited by Steven Rowan. St. Louis: Missouri Historical Society Press, 1997.

"Brevet Brigadier General Bernard Gaines Farrar Jr." Online at http://home.usmo.com/~mollus/CiCmtg/Farrar.htm.

Brownlee, Richard S. *Gray Ghosts of the Confederacy: Guerilla Warfare in the West, 1861–1865.* Baton Rouge: Louisiana State University Press, 1958.

Chaffin, Tom. *Pathfinder: John Charles Fremont and the Course of American Empire.* New York: Hill & Wang, 2002.

Cooper, William J., Jr. *Jefferson Davis, American.* New York: Alfred A. Knopf, 2000.

Cunliffe, Marcus. *The Age of Expansion, 1848–1917.* Springfield, MA: G. & C. Merriam, 1974.

Davis, William C. *Brothers in Arms.* Edison, NJ: Chartwell Books, 2000.

———, and Bell I. Wiley, eds. *The Civil War, the Compact Edition.* New York: Black Dog & Leventhal, 1998.

Denney, Robert E. *Civil War Prisons and Escapes.* New York: Sterling, 1993.

———. *The Civil War Years.* New York: Sterling, 1992.

Dictionary of American Biography, edited by John A. Garraty. 10 vols. New York: Scribner, 1964–95.

Dictionary of American History, 3rd ed. New York: Charles Scribner's Sons, 2003.

Donald, David, and J. G. Randall. *The Civil War and Reconstruction,* 2nd ed. Lexington, MA: D. C. Heath, 1969.

Dressel, Gene. *A Self-Guided Tour of Confederate Graves at Bellefontaine Cemetery.* St. Louis, MO: Sterling Price Camp, Sons of Confederate Veterans, 1992. Available online at http://www.missouridivision-scv.org/camp1846.htm.

Encyclopedia of the History of St. Louis: A Compendium of History and Biography for Ready Reference. New York: Southern History Co., 1899.

Fagan, Brian. *The Little Ice Age: How Climate Made History 1300–1850.* New York: Basic Books, 2000.

Fairman Rogers. Philadephia: Privately printed, 1900.

Faust, Patricia L., ed. *Historical Times: Illustrated Encyclopedia of the Civil War.* New York: Harper Perennial, 1991.

Flood, Charles Bracelen. *Grant and Sherman: The Friendship That Won the Civil War.* New York: Farrar, Straus, and Giroux, 2005.

Foner, Eric. *Reconstruction: America's Unfinished Revolution, 1863–1877.* New York: Perennial Classics, 1988.

Frazier, Charles. *Cold Mountain.* New York: Atlantic Monthly Press, 1997.

Freehling, William W. *The Road to Disunion,* Vol. I, *Secessionists at Bay, 1776–1854.* New York: Oxford University Press, 1990.

Gerteis, Louis S. *Civil War St. Louis.* Lawrence: University Press of Kansas, 2001.

Goodwin, Doris Kearns. *Team of Rivals: The Political Genius of Abraham Lincoln.* New York: Simon & Schuster, 2005.

Grant, Ulysses Simpson. *Personal Memoirs of U. S. Grant.* Old Saybrook, CT: Konecky & Konecky, 1992.

Grun, Bernard. *The Timetables of History: A Horizontal Linkage of People and Events.* New York: Simon & Schuster, 1991.

Hattaway, Herman, and Archer Jones. *How the North Won: A Military History of the Civil War.* Chicago: University of Illinois Press, 1983.

Hayes, Carlton J. H. *A Political and Cultural History of Modern Europe,* Vol. 2, *A Century of Predominantly Industrial Society Since 1830.* New York: Macmillan, 1939.

Hirshson, Stanley P. *The White Tecumseh: A Biography of General William T. Sherman.* New York: John Wiley & Sons, 1997.

Holland, Dorothy Garesché. *The Garesché, De Bauduy and Des Chapelles Families: History and Genealogy.* St. Louis: Privately printed by Schneider Printing, 1963.

Hurst, Jack. *Nathan Bedford Forrest: A Biography.* New York: Alfred A. Knopf, 1993.

Josephy, Alvin M., Jr. *The Civil War in the American West.* New York: Alfred A. Knopf, 1991.

Katcher, Phillip. *The Civil War Source Book.* New York: Facts on File, 1982.

Laas, Virginia Jeans, ed. *Wartime Washington: The Civil War Letters of Elizabeth Blair Lee.* Urbana: University of Illinois Press, 1991.

Larimer, Mary B. "Some Notes on the Burwell, Turnbull, Manlove, Farmer, Ferguson, and Gray Families." *William and Mary Quarterly,* 2nd ser., 15, no. 3 (July 1935): 304–10.

Linderman, Gerald F. *Embattled Courage.* New York: Free Press, 1987.

"Marcus L. Filley (1807–1892) Papers, 1832–1915, Biographical Note." Rensselaer Polytechnic Institute, Institute Archives and Special Collections. Online at http://www.lib.rpi.edu/archives/access/inventories/manuscripts/MC12.

McPherson, James M. *Battle Cry of Freedom.* New York: Oxford University Press, 1988.

———. *For Cause and Comrades: Why Men Fought in the Civil War.* New York: Oxford University Press, 1997.

Mearns, David C. *The Lincoln Papers.* Garden City: Doubleday & Company, 1948.

Monaghan, Jay. *Civil War on the Western Border, 1854–1865.* Lincoln: University of Nebraska Press, 1955.

Morris, Richard, ed. *The Encyclopedia of American History, Bicentennial Edition.* New York: Harper & Row, 1976.

Parrish, William E. *Frank Blair: Lincoln's Conservative.* Columbia: University of Missouri Press, 1998.

———. *A History of Missouri*, Vol. 3, *1860–1875*. St. Louis: University of Missouri Press, 1973.

Ritter, Charles F., ed. *Leaders of the American Civil War: A Biographical And Historiographical Dictionary*. Westport, CT: Greenwood Press 1998.

Scott, Anne Firor, and Ellen F. Fitzpatrick, eds. "American Women's History." Available online at http://www.lexisnexis.com/academic/guides/womens_studies/southern_women/swmncasp

Shoemaker, Floyd C. "John Brooks Henderson: Author of The Thirteenth Amendment Abolishing Slavery in the United States." In *Missouri's Hall of Fame: Lives of Eminent Missourians*. Columbia: Missouri Book, 1918. Available online (introduced and transcribed by Kirby Ross) at www.civilwarstlouis.com/history2/henderson.htm.

Smith, Elbert B. *Francis Preston Blair*. New York: Free Press, 1980.

Sneden, Private Robert Knox. *The Eye of the Storm*. New York: Free Press, 2000.

Sutherland, Daniel E., ed. *A Very Violent Rebel: The Civil War Diary of Ellen Renshaw House*. Knoxville: University of Tennessee Press, 1996.

Wagner, Margaret E. *The Civil War: 365 Days*. New York: Harry N. Abrams, Inc. in association with the Library of Congress, 2006.

The War of the Rebellion: A Compilation of the Official Records of the Union and Confederate Armies. Published under the direction of the Secretary of War. Washington DC: Government Printing Office, 1880–1901. Available online at http://moa.cit.cornell.edu/moa/moa_adv.html.

Warner, Ezra J. *Generals in Blue: Lives of the Union Commanders*. Baton Rouge: Louisiana University Press, 1964.

———. *Generals in Gray: Lives of the Confederate Commanders*. Baton Rouge: Louisiana University Press, 1959.

Weigley, Russell F. *A Great Civil War: A Military and Political History, 1861–1865*. Bloomington: Indiana University Press, 2000.

Winter, William C. *The Civil War in St. Louis, a Guided Tour*. St. Louis: Missouri Historical Society Press, 1994.

Woodward, C. Vann, ed. *Mary Chesnut's Civil War*. New York: Quality Paperback Book Club, 1981/1995.

About the Author

Gari Carter was given her great-great-grandfather's journals from the Civil War era and spent years deciphering his handwriting and researching his life. These writings of Franklin Archibald Dick awakened Carter's deep respect and appreciation for the adversity he dealt with and the wisdom it offered her in dealing with her own journey. Her first book, *Healing Myself,* was written after her life-changing auto accident. She is a dynamic public speaker and lives in North Carolina.

Carter can be reached through her website at http://garicarter.com.